THE REPLACEMENTS

All over but the shouting

an oral history

Jim Walsh

Voyageur Press

First published in 2007 by Voyageur Press, an imprint of MBI Publishing Company LLC, Galtier Plaza, Suite 200, 380 Jackson Street, St. Paul, MN 55101 USA

The information in this book is true and complete to the best of our knowledge. All recommendations are made without any guarantee on the part of the author or Publisher, who also disclaim any liability incurred in connection with the use of this data or specific details.

The publisher has made every attempt to identify and secure permission to reproduce copyrighted material. No permission is hereby granted by the publisher to in any way further reproduce any previously copyrighted material. Any errors or omissions should be brought to the attention of the author and publisher.

We recognize, further, that some words, model names, and designations mentioned herein are the property of the trademark holder. We use them for identification purposes only. This is not an official publication.

"The Replacements" appears courtesy of Tommy Womack, © 2002 Tommy Womack Tunes (BMI)/Administered by Bug Music. "We're the Replacements," words and music by John Flansburgh and John Linnell, © 1987 TMBG Music/Administered by Warner-Tamerlane Publishing Corp. All rights reserved. Used by Permission of Alfred Publishing Co., Inc. "Story Untold" appears courtesy of Slim Dunlap, © 1996 Hinky Music (ASCAP). "Bobby Stinson's Guitar" appears courtesy of Jim Ruiz, © 1998 Mij Amsterdam Music (ASCAP)/Minty Fresh.

MBI Publishing Company titles are also available at discounts in bulk quantity for industrial or sales-promotional use. For details write to Special Sales Manager at MBI Publishing Company, Galtier Plaza, Suite 200, 380 Jackson Street, St. Paul, MN 55101 USA

Library of Congress Cataloging-in-Publication Data

Walsh, Jim, 1959–
  The Replacements : all over but the shouting : an oral history / by Jim Walsh.
    p. cm.
  Includes bibliographical references and index.
  ISBN: 978-0-7603-3062-3 (hardbound w/ jacket) 1. Replacements (Musical group) 2. Rock musicians—United States—Biography. I. Title.
  ML421.R47W35 2007
  782.42166092'2—dc22

2007022576

Designer: James Kegley

Title page photograph © Daniel Corrigan

Printed in the United States of America

For The Falls (from South Minneapolis) and all the other new garage bands whose parents gave them roots and wings and rock and roll.

CONTENTS

PREFACE

The first time I saw the Replacements was at their first bar gig on the night of July 2, 1980. They opened for Minneapolis rockers the Dads, at the old Longhorn Bar in downtown Minneapolis, and they were tremendous, even then: a burst of song-to-song energy with a singer/guitarist whose heart positively pushed against his chest cavity; a teenage bass player with flailing, splaying legs and a Sir Lancelot haircut who would drop to his knees and yell "Fuck you!" to the bar; and his older brother, a Young Frankenstein with a wicked falsetto and an even more wicked wrist on guitar. They did covers by 999 and Johnny Thunders, and originals like "Off Your Pants" and "Toe Needs a Shoe (Problem)." By the end of the set, I ended up on the small dance floor with my friend Cecelia and a half dozen other kids, pogo-ing to what everyone in the dank, air-conditioned room agreed was an exciting new find.

The only reason I'd ended up at the Longhorn that night was because I knew the drummer, Chris Mars, from DeLaSalle, the hippie-Catholic high school in downtown Minneapolis where his older brother, Jim, and I had become friends. So that night after my band finished practice, we all went down to the Longhorn, which was the launching pad for Minneapolis' original music scene of the day. We snuck our guitarist, Kevin, and our drummer, Rick—who were fifteen and sixteen at the time and who smuggled a tape deck in to record the show—through the club's backdoor near the alley, which was always left wide open in those days.

Before the 'Mats took the stage, I remember watching Paul, whom I'd never met, going to the stage and fussing with something on his guitar, and nervously drinking out of a plastic cup. Water, I think. I remember liking him immediately—he wore a raggedy green-and-white baseball/football shirt and tennis shoes, no safety pins or leather, and he pretty much looked not like a rock star or an anti-rock star or a punk, but like a dozen guys I'd grown up with in South Minneapolis. After the show, Chris introduced me to Paul, who looked at me suspiciously. Already, he didn't trust people gushing over his music, which is what I did briefly that night. But I think he also recognized in me someone who knew what he was talking about.

A couple months later, after we'd gotten to know each other a little bit, I called him at his folks' house. He came to the phone and I said, "What are you doing?" He said, "Listening to (Joni Mitchell's) *Blue*," as if this was a code between us—an acknowledgement of the fact that we both knew we'd gleaned strength and self-understanding from our older brothers' and sisters' sensitive singer/songwriters as much as the ferocious punk rock that was blowing up all around us.

We were the same age. Like me, he was nervous to go on stage that first night at the Longhorn, but he couldn't help himself. My band, REMs (later Laughing Stock), was just starting up, we were a month or two away from playing out for the first time, and these bastards had beaten us to the punch and won Twin/Tone Records co-founder Peter Jesperson's affection and devotion, and, yes, that is how it was in those days: healthy competition between young men who wanted to change the world and/or get laid. "We wanted them to fail," Paul would tell *Magnet* magazine years later about their chief Twin Cities rivals, Hüsker Dü. "We wanted them to be the second-best band in town." My band wasn't even in the running, or so it seemed, probably because I liked to watch. And listen.

The 'Mats pissed me off, too, because I was trying to figure out how to be in a band, something that came to them so naturally (Soul Asylum's Danny Murphy describes them as "four guys in four different bands," another way of saying the sum is greater than the parts). One night when Paul and Mars and I were hanging out at Jesperson's apartment, I bitched at Paul for playing like they were satisfied. It was during the *Hootenanny* days when most of the time they were just being funny or boring, and I needed so much more. It rankled Paul, and he stood in the doorway of Peter's place, ticked off at me and saying to Mars, "I'm not satisfied. Are you satisfied? Are you satisfied?" The song "Unsatisfied" came soon after; I don't recount that here to seek muse credit, only to show how songs sometimes happen and to head up the long, cosmic line of people who feel like they had a hand in writing Paul's (our) songs.

The truth is, there was very little camaraderie in those days. We didn't hang out much (then or now), other than during sound checks or in the dressing room before or after shows. Whenever we played with the 'Mats, we tried our best to trump them. We'd get up there, at Regina High School, or Duffy's, or the Longhorn, or the 7th St. Entry, or the Sons of Norway ("We are the sons of no one . . .") for a high school dance, and we'd play what was for us a great set, and then they'd come on, challenged like prizefighters, and they'd be the best band on the planet, which is to say they'd simultaneously crush you and charm the life out of you. "They were more than a band. They were a gang," was how Marc Perlman, later of the Jayhawks, reacted to seeing them the first time, around *Stink*. "Everybody wanted to be the fifth Replacement," reminisced *The New York Times'* David Carr in June 2006.

That much has been said about a great many great bands, but after hearing so many stories for so many years, I've come to the conclusion that, in fact, we all were/are the fifth Replacement. Peter Jesperson and Slim Dunlap and Steve Foley could have been you or me (the founder of the long-gone 'Mats 'zine *Willpower* once signed his editor's note with "Bill Callahan, editor and 6789th Replacement"), and maybe that is the 'Mats' ultimate legacy: It was a shared experience that eschewed the normally exclusionary nature of rock stardom in favor of the larger extended adoptive family. How else do you explain the fact that kids who were born long after the 'Mats broke up feel a kinship with them, feel like they're part of something, a lifelong member of Our Gang?

My brother and I figured it out one night: We saw the Replacements 150 times over the course of their twelve years. They changed my life, saved my life, made my life richer, and at the moment, I feel not necessarily nostalgic (punk was and is decidedly anti-nostalgia, and if ever a band kicked against the pricks of preservation societies like books and halls of fame it was these guys), but I admit that I feel a need to know if any of it mattered, or if it even happened. I also fear that if some of this doesn't get written down, it will all be forgotten. And it's important not to forget, because, for a good while there, they were the best band in the world. Here's why:

Because they weren't for everybody, and they didn't try to be. Because they made it look like it was fun to be alive, to be in a band. Because they were so powerfully awful, and so awfully powerful. Because whenever you saw them play, you savored every moment because you knew the clock was ticking. Because Steve Perry's cover story for the October 1989 issue of *Musician* magazine called them "The Last, Best Band of the 80s," and the next month, Jon

Bon Jovi wrote a letter to the editor that asked, "How can the Replacements be the best band of the '80s when I've never even heard of them?"

Because when Steve Albini ripped *Tim* in *Matter* magazine, Paul responded in *Rolling Stone*'s year-end issue, naming Albini's band, Big Black, as best of the year, followed by wusses-of-the-day like Julio Iglesias, etc. Ninety percent of *Rolling Stone*'s readers didn't get it, but those of us who did never forgot it.

Because when I was writing for *The Minnesota Daily*, the University of Minnesota's college newspaper, I did an article on *avante* rock, which included stuff like Big Black, led by Albini, who'd light firecrackers on stage and put a microphone up to the Black Cat chaos and blow the hell out of everyone's ears. One night when Paul and I and our wives were having dinner at his house, he looked at the piece, tossed it down, cut to the chase and said, "I wish they'd just flush all that shit down the toilet."

Because—shhh—not everyone in Minneapolis is proud of Prince, but everyone worth a shit loved, and still loves, the 'Mats. Because of what Jakob Dylan told writer Mark Brown a few years ago:

> "I do find (Westerberg) to be one of the better songwriters America has ever offered. I listen to all his stuff. I've always been a huge fan of Paul Westerberg. I really admired and was interested in the fact that he seemed to be this reckless character in this somewhat punk-pop group. He had this attitude, then somewhere, these songs started creeping through, songs like 'Sixteen Blue,' 'Androgynous,' 'Unsatisfied,' and 'Answering Machine.' You started to realize he had this undeniable gift for writing that the average guy in these kinds of groups could never touch on. He seemed to resist it for a long time, also, but he obviously was into something he couldn't deny.
>
> "To me, Paul Westerberg sounded like he never wanted to be a songwriter. He just wanted to be engulfed in this rock and roll outfit and make a lot of noise, play songs by the MC5 or something. Then one day it just dawned on him that he had this way of writing things that maybe he did or didn't want to do.
>
> "People have taken advantage of him. I'm sure it must be very painful for him to watch these groups that are far inferior to him being very successful doing a very watered-down, B-version of what he started. But there's always guys like that. America particularly seems to need those people, whether it's him or Alex Chilton. The

14

point is you hope they persevere and keep making good records for the people who do want to hear them. A lot of us *need* those good writers."[1]

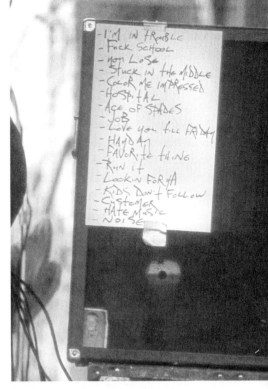

Set list and a Bob school photo, Harriet Island, St. Paul, 1983.
© Joan E. Bechtold

Because you could go see the 'Mats to see Paul's soft heart, or you could go to see Bob's outfits—tutus, dresses, evening gowns, or garbage bags. Because there has never been a cooler *Saturday Night Live* host–musical guest combination than Harry Dean Stanton and the Replacements, and in some circles, there are people who can tell you exactly where they were when they saw it, the way their big brothers and sisters can about the Beatles on *The Ed Sullivan Show*.

Because of the Turf Club in St. Paul, which for a long time was run by some guys who weren't around in the 'Mats' heyday, but who moved there because they loved the 'Mats so much, and who worked to get a park bench in Bob Stinson's name after he died, and adorned their bar with huge posters of the band members—all of which is the kind of shit that would embarrass the hell out of Paul and the others, but which feels absolutely right, like an absolutely perfect homage, to anyone who grew up listening to Bob play guitar and Paul opening his veins.

Because like so many of us, Jesperson, their manager/mentor/fan/friend, loved them so much, he couldn't contain himself. Because on "Take Me Down to the Hospital," when twenty-one-year-old Paul is screaming, "Pete, Pete, Pete," he was doing so because he was in physical pain, but he was also crying out for someone to help him make sense of all that loneliness at the bottom.

Because of what Courtney Love said about them in *Vanity Fair*. "Commercial success in the alternative world ruins your credibility," the article's author,

Lynn Hirschberg, wrote in her notorious piece, "Strange Love," "and Kurt (Cobain) is deeply concerned with staying true to his vision."[2]

Hirschberg went on to quote Love: "I'm neurotic about credibility. And Kurt is neurotic about it, too. . . . But there are all kinds of fame. Like the Replacements had Respect Fame. Big Respect Fame. And that kind of fame can really mess with your head."

Because of what Stewart Cunningham, singer/guitarist for a band called Brother Brick, wrote in the liner notes to *I'm in Love . . . With That Song*, a Replacements tribute compilation by twenty-three Australian bands: "The first time I ever met a girl at a gig in Sydney and went home with her was because I was wearing a Replacements shirt. . . . I was about 19, we were watching the band and she was standing in front of me and she just turned round and started passionately/drunkenly kissing me. When I asked her why she did this out of the blue, she later told me it was cos I was wearing a Replacements shirt and she was a huge fan of theirs."

Because there were a lot of cool bands in the '80s, but there were also a lot of eat-your-vegetables bands, and the 'Mats were all meat and potatoes and slaw with maple syrup dressing. Because they were a mass of contradictions. Because they were kings of irony before irony was everywhere; because they were an ongoing critique of absolutely everything, including themselves; and because they hated rock stars, but loved rock. Because their name was one of the greatest rock band names ever, fraught with the duality of pushing the dinosaurs out of the way, and the suggestion that they were merely warm bodies filling a slot. Because their longtime roadie/tour manager, Bill Sullivan, was right one night at the 7th St. Entry in Minneapolis, when, during an awards ceremony, he mocked the common critical saw of the day, saying, "Every Replacements show is like a snowflake—no two are alike."

Because one night at First Avenue, the video for "The Ledge" came on, and when Paul's face filled the screen, the whole place cheered. Because when *Pleased to Meet Me* came out in 1987, Warner Bros. did a six-minute video interview tape, and there has never been a cooler, more uncomfortable-looking rock band. All four (including newly installed guitarist Slim Dunlap) are sitting next to each other in white T-shirts and clownish pants. Paul is chain-smoking and drinking a beer. This is the first thing he says: "We write about what we want to write about, and we act the way we are, we don't pretend, and it's like people won't accept that because they're used to a packaged kind of thing where you have to put on to be accepted. You know, you have to look good on TV, you have to look like you're into it, and sometimes we're not into it, and we don't pretend that we are."

Because one night in 1989, the 'Mats were booked on something called *The International Rock Awards* on ABC with the likes of the Bangles (cute but terrible, no matter what Robbie Fulks says), Living Colour (doing an unwatchable cover of "Johnny B. Goode"), David Bowie (looking very Michael Douglas), and Lou Reed (looking purposeful, epic-y, New York-y), and it was all very '80s. I taped it.

Halfway through the show, the Traveling Wilburys are awarded "Album of the Year" for *The Traveling Wilburys, Vol. 1*, and the clip of them that follows is actually pretty good. Then a canned female voice that has been creaming over the likes of Hall & Oates, Lita Ford, and Grace Slick in her introductions, says, "We apologize. Here they are—the Replacements."

The camera floats in over the top of the room, over all the tables stuffed with suits, gowns, silverware, folded napkins, candles, money. Women fan themselves with their programs. As Slim plays the irresistible first chords of "Talent Show," Paul says into the mic, "What the hell are we doing here?"

The first verse kicks in, and Paul stares straight into the camera as he sings. Then he loses it, and laughs. He sticks his tongue out at the camera and gives the same disdainful look he did at the 7th St. Entry ten years prior when, during "Shutup," he looked into a camera and said, "Don't tell me about your cameraman." He sings, "Well we got our guitars and we got our thumb picks/We go on after some lip-synch chicks." The network bleeps out the next line, "We're feeling good from the pills we took," and Paul rolls his eyes, finishes the lyric, plows ahead.

The song is great, a true rock 'n' roll moment, and the camera continues to pan the crowd, which for the most part sits in nervous bemusement. The 'Mats are bulls in a china shop, the third-class passengers on the *Titanic* coming up from the céili below to crash the ballroom dance. It is an awesome four minutes, by far and away the highlight of the show, to the point where you can imagine Lou Reed shrinking off to be by himself somewhere. At the end, the camera catches Matt Dillon in the audience, whistling and clapping furiously, which has always made me like his films, though if you put a gun in my ear I could only name two: *The Outsiders* and *Crash*, fittingly. The song ends, and the canned woman's voice comes up: "Please welcome the trend-setting leader of the Cars, an artist to whom the '80s matter most, Ric Ocasek."

Not long after the *International Rock Awards*, I sang with the 'Mats in a club in Gainesville, Florida. I was touring with them for a few nights during the Tom Petty tour. We did "California Sun," and for a moment it felt like the old days, when my band would play with the 'Mats and Paul would ask me to

17

come sing on "Love You Till Friday" or something (one summer afternoon in 1984 he also recruited Mars and me to run over to Blackberry Way and sing backup vocals on "I Will Dare," which were wisely edited out by Peter Buck and Jesperson). This night, the song was sloppy fun, and even though I remember it as being one of the last great shows I saw from them, it was easy to see the end was near.

"Anything different," said Mars afterward, happy that we'd taken a flyer together. "Sounded like shit," said Paul.

They broke up soon after, and at the moment of this writing there are, yet again, rumors flying about a Replacements reunion. Check that. They aren't rumors. They're wishes. And they're being cast out there by a bunch of newbies and grownups who don't necessarily want to go out and drink and get stupid with the 'Mats, but who want to know that those songs, all those great songs, are alive, being played across the land somewhere, gleaning new meaning and perspectives.

Since that may not happen in this lifetime, after watching the "Talent Show" tape the other night, I popped in a video that Twin/Tone Records made in 1980. It's a live set from Hüsker Dü and the Replacements. The Hüskers look almost new wave, arty, with Bob Mould wearing a head band and whipping up a hardcore frenzy. People slam dance politely, and smile. Then the 'Mats come on, and the first thing we see is Tommy, in a red and black cowboy shirt, giving the finger to the camera. He's fourteen years old, and—talk about your *Outsiders*—he looks like something out of a S. E. Hinton novel.

They blast through a ferocious "Takin' a Ride" and Paul says, "Thank you." They do "Staples in Her Stomach," a sweet tribute to masturbation, which at the time was actually somewhat racy. They do "Stuck in the Middle," and Paul sing-laughs, pointedly, "You're taking it all too seriously, you're taking it all too seriously," as the adulation-storm around him grows. Everybody in the room knows they're in the presence of budding greatness, the kind that doesn't happen to everyone, and it feels electric.

At one point, he laughs, like he's nervous with the attention, like he wants to be a normal guy, but he's got this thing in him, like the thing in *Alien*—the movie that came out in 1980, the same year the 'Mats recorded their first record—that's pressing through his chest to get out. Mars is ripping his kit apart, eating the cymbals, and with that engine, they look to be on a mission that they can't articulate through any mode other than bursts of racket. Bob drags the microphone stand on his guitar—not chaotically, but just once to create a specific noise. People are dancing as Paul sings a worried song about his hero, Johnny Thunders.

I remember the night it was filmed. My brother Jay's band, the Neglecters, opened for them, and even though they were horribly out of tune, all I know is that on that night, like on so many nights, the Replacements made me feel like I was on fire. They made me want to write better songs and practice harder, they fueled my competitive juices as a musician, and mostly they made me want to write, capture life and lightning in a bottle, and put stuff like this down for posterity: Plenty of bands have been described as "raw," but the 'Mats were an open wound/heart/book that has yet to scab over.

Another video I've got is one someone gave me years ago that I never watched until recently. It's an outdoor show from a St. Louis–area speedway, and the quality isn't great. They're on their way out, Steve Foley is on drums. "They're Blind" is more poignant than ever, and by the end, they're sleepwalking through the shit. But those songs still soar on their own power, even as their makers are doing the Wicked Witch of the West meltdown. One of Paul's most soulful vocals comes on "Bastards of Young," which he sings with real conviction to a crowd of kindred souls. At the end, he says, "I love you" or "Fuck you." Hard to tell which.

In researching this book, the word I came across more than any other in interviews with those guys was "scared"—scared to write vulnerable songs, scared to perform live, scared to be part of what "some blowhards call the Greatest Rock and Roll Band in the World."[3] Pretty sure you and I would be scared, too, if you knew something was passing through you, some holy spirit, and you had no idea what it was or why you'd been tapped for tin-can-to-tin-can shaman-conduit-to-God when all you ever wanted to do was rock.

"It's almost like it happened to somebody else," no-shits Paul somewhere in these pages, speaking for all of us who were and weren't there, including him. Beyond the fact that we crack each other up and we're both still moved by writing, music, girls, and family, I suppose it's part of the reason he and I have been close over the years, and why he has enjoyed good rapports with writers such as Mark Brown, David Ayers, Bill Holdship, and Bill Flanagan: They ask questions—good questions—about what it all means and how it all happened, and by doing so helped explain it to the very guys who were responsible for making it happen.

The first night I spent any time with Paul was in the summer of 1980. I had met him a few months earlier, and, like so many would come to, I recognized something of myself in him. This night, though, we may have never been more alike—both singers in bands, both in love with rock 'n' roll, girls, and our hometown of Minneapolis. We found ourselves in Peter Jesperson's

19

apartment, the Modesto, which sat up the street from Oarfolkjokeopus, the record store Peter managed.

Plenty of musicians, writers, and other creatures of the night spent similarly long nights/early mornings there, curled up on that apartment floor, listening to the Beatles, Big Star, Prince, Captain Beefheart, Bowie, the Only Ones, B. B. King, or whatever Peter's passion of the moment was, with Jesperson—bombed on Scotch and more, sometimes incoherent, always zealous—manning the turntable, shaping our tastes, broadening our horizons, teaching us. About music and how to listen. How to live.

After a couple hours of this, Paul and I split. Peter ushered us out the apartment door and into the hallway with a grin, like a big brother unleashing his two young bucks out into the world to romp. We went to a party a couple blocks away, where a band was playing. There was a keg, and we grabbed beers, but the party was a dud. The band was ordinary, a generic sort of leather-pantsed new wave thing that happened a lot in those days, and as we stood watching them play an original that could have been a Cars song, I could feel Paul getting antsy.

When they got done with their first set, a couple of the guys from the band came up to us and chatted. It was weird: The 'Mats' first record wasn't even out, yet their legend was already budding in Minneapolis' nascent indie-rock scene, and these guys seemed star struck and/or jealous. When they went to the keg, Paul leaned in to me and said, "Let's jam." I said, "I dunno, man. This is their gig."

It was like he didn't even hear me. He got on the phone that was nailed to a cement pole in the basement, called Mars, and said, "Walsh is here. You come, play drums, I'll play guitar, and he'll sing." It was midnight. I was hoping Mars would say no, that he was in for the night, which is what he said. I was relieved, Paul was disappointed, and in that moment, I knew we were headed down different paths: I was happy to be there, he couldn't stand watching. He needed to be playing, making noise, connecting the best way he could with the world. We left the party and I drove him home to his folks' house, which was next door to my cousins.

Paul, like me and Mars, grew up in the Catholic ghetto of South Minneapolis, and it's only very recently that I've come to know what that means. Some of us read the Bible every day, and others of us did the rosary every night after dinner while the other kids in the neighborhood were outside playing. Some of our parents were alcoholics; some of our parents treated booze and sex like it was one and the same and the road to hell.

Every year on Ash Wednesday since we were in first grade, we had a priest rub our foreheads with ashes and say, "Remember man that you are dust and to dust you shall return." Have that done enough times, and not only will it provide a soul with freedom, inspiration, humility, and beautiful, mysterious ritualistic imagery, but it'll fuck with a boy, and a man.

On Good Friday, we did those scary-cool Stations of the Cross, went to confession, and were infused with all those mind-bending parables of sin, death, blood, and resurrection. We grew to see great hypocrisy in flawed adults who told us how to feel, what to repress, what to believe in. We started bands to help make sense of it all, to get girls, to not have to get jobs, and to make our mark.

These days, whenever I think about what makes a great rock band, I think about the 'Mats, and their chemistry on and off stage. I think about how much they loved each other for a brief, shining moment, and what happened one night near the end.

During the Petty tour in the summer of 1989, Paul had gotten me a hotel room with the band somewhere in Georgia ("This is the guy who's gonna write our book," he insisted to their asshole tour manager), and when I woke up the next morning, I went down to the lobby restaurant. The whole band was there, except Paul. Tommy asked the waiter to pour a cup of coffee for his buddy, so that when Paul came down, it would be cool enough for him to belt it down and they could be on their way. Call me a "pussy" (as they often would about their softer sides/sets), but there was real caring in that moment, and I've never forgotten the tenderness of it or the looks that they would exchange between each other on stage, a quadruple-play combo for the ages: Westerberg-to-Mars-to-Stinson-to-Stinson-to-Neptune.

Paul and I don't talk much these days. We're both healthy and fucked up but plugging along, just like everyone who came up on the 'Mats, I suppose. We've been through weddings, funerals, births, divorces, and rock shows together. We both have kids and we're still trying to get our voices out there. More than anything, I think, we're looking for peace and quiet.

A few years ago, I called him up to read him something I wrote for the *St. Paul Pioneer Press*. I knew he'd never actually buy the paper, but I wanted him to hear what I had to say. I had recently met one of our mutual boyhood heroes, Jackson Browne, and my column about the experience was about to go to press.

I left four consecutive messages on his answering machine. I read it slowly—a private reading for a private person. He called back almost immediately and left a message on my machine. He said something disparaging about

Tom Petty tour stop, Gainesville, Florida, August 1989 *Author photo*

Browne's personal life, and what he said next somehow gets to the heart of why I still love him, why I still listen to him:

"Yeah, you can write, you can feel, you can think. Whaddaya want, a medal?"

A few years ago, my friend Craig and I were driving home from a music festival I was covering for the *St. Paul Pioneer Press*. It was okay, but we had a 'Mats compilation tape that saved the night. As we drove, we started talking about them, and I finally articulated why they meant so much to me: When they were on, they were *everything*. They were anger, joy, possibility, fear, romance, goofiness, passion. They embodied every emotion, feeling, thought. They taught me the meaning of the word pretentious, but above all, the message of that time, that band, was: Go Forth. Have fun. Question authority. And look at what we're all doing now. We're doctors and bums and lawyers and divorcees and parents and songwriters and screenwriters and artists and copywriters and musicheads and out-of-touch-but-fighting-it teens and twentysomething, thirtysomething, fortysomething, fiftysomething couples.

But enough about now, and me. Back then was an incredible era in American music: a time when college radio, indie labels, fanzines, and independent record stores supported bands in a pre-Internet underground, and everyone felt some ownership in these insanely great bands. We put them all up on our shoulders, pushed them up as far as we could so that they could pop through the ceiling of the glossy music and entertainment of the day, like in *Horton Hears a Who* when the little people say, "We are here, we are here, we are heeeere!"

And some of them broke through. Some of them were heard. Some had careers and continue to have careers. The Replacements did not. The Replacements came like a comet, flamed out, and left the rest of us breathless, elbowing each other with "did you just see what I saw?" and vowing to tell anyone within earshot why they were special.

INTRODUCTION
Gimme Noise

The Replacements played rock 'n' roll
They were the last of a dying breed
Damn-the-torpedoes types
They could really let it bleed
They weren't afraid of anything
Or anybody
Like skinny little dogs in a cage
They'd get drunker than you've ever
Gotten in your entire life
And have another drink
On top of that one
And walk right out
Onto the stage

I first went to see 'em
'Cause Jeff Sweeney said I should
It was Cantrell's in January
They weren't any good
The lead guitarist was nekked
They'd all had too much beer
They had Marshalls turned up to ten
Which ordinarily wouldn't be such a bad thing
But they were trying to tune up
By ear

The Replacements

So I gave 'em another chance
At the shed, openin' for Petty
What could go wrong?
Well, this time they were wearing dresses
Drinking whiskey
And never finished a song
So now I'm angry
'Cause money don't grow on trees
Standin' out in the parking lot
With tickets for the next night
Already in my hands thinkin' to myself
Geez, what am I gonna do with these?

So I went
Largely to say I was there
Drove home white-knuckle straight-jacket dumb-ass blind
They were the greatest rock and roll band
I ever did hear
Had to look twice
To make sure it was the same guys
An astonishing transformation
From pupa to butterfly
Saul to Paul
Cougar to Mellencamp
Like crawlin' inside of Exile on Main Street
And pullin' Never Mind the Bollocks
Up to your chin like a sonic quilt

They were nice guys
And they were dicks
You wouldn't know
What they'd do
One show might run 25 songs
And alter your perspective
And the next might fall apart
Before it got to
Number two

But folks come out to see 'em
If only to say they saw 'em before
They were dead
And others to see
If they could be
Anywhere near as good or as bad
As everybody else said

They snorted lines and lost their minds
And notched their guns
All over the sphere
Got to where they couldn't tell you
What day it was, what month it was
They couldn't even zone in on a year

They puked in their hands and tossed it on the ceilings
Of dressing rooms on tour
And college rock and roll journalists wrote it all down
Truth, lies, they weren't sure
They burned every bridge they didn't blow sky high
Then started pissin' off each other, too
It was brother against brother then
And not enough drugs to do

It all came crashin' down
'Cause it couldn't do much else
That way life is a flaming star
That grows real big
And red and giant
And then it falls in on top of itself

Chris, he's a painter now
Solo artist, he's cool
Slim Dunlap is the proof of the existence of God
A guitar genius, a role model, a credit to the gene pool
Tommy moved to California
To work for Axl Rose

27

I think he should team up with Slash
And form Slash 'n' Pop
They'd rock the house
They'd sell tickets
It'd be the most
Paul is in the basement
Writin' ballads
Drinkin' O'Doul's
Bob is up in heaven
Shootin' speed and smokin' Kools

The Replacements played rock and roll
They were the last of a dying breed
Pernicious damn-the-torpedoes types
They could make you holler, make you sweat
They'd do "Only Women Bleed"
They were Charles Bukowski
With watts and vomit
You paid and you took your chance
'Cause when they were good
When they were good
When they were good
God got up to dance

—Tommy Womack, "The Replacements"

Billie Joe Armstrong: First time was when I was fifteen years old, at the Fillmore in San Francisco. My sister made me go. They all came out in really bad plaid suits; it was right when *Pleased to Meet Me* came out. It was amazing. It changed my whole life. If it wasn't for that, I might've spent my time playing in bad speed-metal bands.[1]

Cecelia Deuhs: When I was sixteen or seventeen, I was a sort-of regular at Jay's Longhorn Bar in Minneapolis, the only "punk rock" club in town. The woman who cut my hair, Margaret, was Jay's [of Jay's Longhorn] girlfriend. Margaret worked at the Longhorn most evenings, checking—or not—IDs and collecting the cover charge. In the mid- to late '70s, the drinking age wasn't really an issue; if there was a show I wanted to see, I'd stop by the salon in my

Catholic school uniform to ask Margaret if she'd let me in the club that night.

Her rules were as follows: a two-beer limit and no hanging out with the bands. During my shift at the Y, between handing out towels and making racquetball court reservations, my friend Jim called. The conversation was something like this: "Hey, there's a new band playing at the Longhorn tonight. [Paul] Kaiser—another pal—played baseball with one of the guys in grade school. You want to meet us?"

After work I hopped the 16A bus to downtown Minneapolis to see this new band, which turned out to be the Replacements. One of the first things I noticed was how young Tommy was and how funny it was when he'd come to the microphone between songs to say "Thank you." The microphone he used was taller than he was, and his bass sure seemed that way. Paul sang out of the side of his mouth.

Bill Tuomala: I was eighteen years old and finishing up my freshman year at the University of North Dakota in Grand Forks. There was a UND-sponsored end-of-the-school-year dance held on a Saturday night in a ballroom at a motel across the river in East Grand Forks. It was May of 1984.

That afternoon was the first time I had heard of the Replacements. Someone in my dorm said they were a punk band from the Twin Cities. Some of us decided to go check the show out. We were all small-town kids who were into classic rock and had no use for punk, but figured we'd go for some kicks. Anticipation in the dorm increased when we were told that punkers from the Cities followed the band around from town to town.

Later, somebody claimed that punkers had been spotted at Taco John's. We were looking forward to the people-watching. After the opening band's set, we watched some punks near our table. One of them was drunk out of his skull and was laughing and talking with the others. He proceeded to spit up a red liquid down the front of his shirt, yet never quite stopped talking. Minutes later the Replacements hit the stage. The guy who had spit up was fronting the band, still wearing the stained shirt. The lead guitarist was wearing some sort of pants that were loose, flimsy, and sheer—you could say he was letting it all hang out.

They played loud, mostly beyond recognition and the sound often burst into feedback. More than once we ran out to the hallway to escape the noise. They absolutely butchered cover tunes such as "Substitute," "Folsom Prison Blues," and "I'm Eighteen." Lord, were they horrible. Drunk, sloppy, and inept. We hated them.

Jay Walsh: My brother Jim told me about them, about this band with a four-teen-year-old kid playing bass. They were playing at the Longhorn one night. I remember walking around that corner of the bar and seeing them onstage. They were all in white T-shirts. Tommy was wearing a baseball cap over his eyes and they were playing "Slow Down." They were so fucking good I was plastered up against a wall watching them. Within ten seconds, I knew they were the best band in town. And that was saying something back then.

Marc Perlman: My bandmate Jay [Walsh] cajoled me into checking out this band he was into. I'd heard of the Replacements but less about the music and more about how "punk" they were and that they had this nine-year-old bass player. We got to the Entry late. The club was near empty. We missed a good chunk of the set. For all practical musical purposes, the show was long over. Jay was looking around, offering a disclaimer about the lack of a crowd. The band was long on the other side of the liquor light switch by then.

We only heard two songs that night. A few verses of "Hitchin' a Ride." Then "Hello, Dolly." Then another "Hello, Dolly." And another. By the eighth "Hello, Dolly" Tommy had a huge shit-eating grin. By the ninth, Chris and Bob had the same shit-eating grin and so did Jay and I, and you realized these guys were more than a band. They were a gang.

Jodi Chromey: We were at the Camaraderie, "the Cam" to us regulars, in Eau Claire [Wisconsin], and drunk. I started whining for some change so I could play the jukebox. After much begging, Kelly dropped four quarters into my upturned palm. He had one condition, "You have to play the Replacements."

I wrinkled my nose and curled my lip. "Who the fuck are the Replacements?" I spent most of my college career trying really hard to love grunge, and doing quite an admirable job of faking it. This was 1994. I was the arts editor for the school newspaper at the University of Wisconsin–Eau Claire. It was practically my job to love grunge. I had never heard of these Replacements.

"You don't know the 'Mats?" he asked.

I shook my head to dismiss his inane questions and found *All Shook Down* on the jukebox and picked the first song on the disc, without even looking at the song titles.

Hush was the first word you were taught . . .

The song started up and Kelly sidled up to me, throwing an arm around my shoulders, "Come on Chromes, you know the words."

I stared at him open-mouthed, as he sung along. I couldn't sing. I was too busy listening to the words. I didn't know who was singing, but he was singing about me. I was sure of it. The hushing and the writing down of dreams, it just fit.

It wasn't until then that I realized how good that could feel. A six-five girl with too-long arms and too many scratchy opinions, I was born not fit. Nothing ever fit. Not dresses or jeans or depressing songs without a hint of humor. But this song it fit me, from the moment I heard the word "hush."

Terri Sutton: Okay. Fall 1984. Jill Fonaas and I living in the Haight-Ashbury in a roach-infested walkup. I'd just started working for *BAM* magazine, dinosaur-rock free monthly. Jill's commuting down to Stanford, working at a library, which is hell after staying up until 3 a.m. as we do show nights. A college friend from Minneapolis played us *Let It Be*, and we were instantly smitten—probably something to do with commonalities between Scando-influenced backwaters of Pacific Northwest where Jill and I grew up and Scando-influenced backwaters of Upper Midwest that spawned the 'Mats . . . we knew the '70s-rock references.

All 'Mats records have been on constant play leading up to Berkeley Square show. I take BART over early because I'm interviewing them. Day-lit bar of Berkeley Square, talking nervously to Sully [Bill Sullivan] having my first beer to take the edge off. Interview a blur of nerves: are they mocking me? Probably. Was that a stupid question? Definitely. Then drinking and waiting, as Jill is late, and I don't yet know all the people I will know—mostly due to the Replacements.

Turns out Jill is having a Replacements-worthy adventure: gets a ride from a notoriously inattentive driver who plows into another car and ends up in the hospital—but later shows up at the 'Mats! Jill plucked off the side of the road by friends of the driver, who carry her off to unknown house where she inadvertently locks herself in the bathroom. When she finally arrives at the club, half-concussed and bandaged, I am drunk with relief—interview over—and more than a few beers.

Show is nonstop—little fartsing around. Spring-strung Tommy nearly colliding with ceiling, Chris all dazed good nature, Bob the zigzag warrior, and Paul not sick of the songs yet, wrenching up out of himself, out of me, an insistence that we were all worth more than we had grown used to believing. Highlight: DiFranco Family's "Heartbeat" played like they meant it, but of course they did *and* didn't. I sang along: "Heartbeat, it's a LOVE beat"—

and it was: a pulse familiar and frizzing with newness, like at long last I'd found my people.

Dan Wilson: It was at 7th St. Entry. I was in my early twenties, I think. Because of all the talk around town, and the fashions of the time, I figured the Replacements would be another angular punk or new wave band, stylish and ironic. I'd started playing in bands but wasn't serious about it, at least my memory tells me I couldn't have been. Because my memory is of witnessing something more dead-serious than I'd ever thought a band could be.

I walked into the club as they started "Johnny's Gonna Die." I am forever thankful for my timing. What a song. I had no idea. The bass player was sixteen, everyone said. A new band. But new wave? This song was more like Bad Company than Elvis Costello. It was rock, pure and giant. But it also seemed to ratchet the stakes up about ten notches. I will never forget how blown away I was by this song and the performance, and I have to admit it made me feel like a hobbyist. I was afraid I'd never be this scary, this passionate, this ruthless, this cruel and pleasing at the same time.

And yet, here it was, in a local dive with about 150 people watching, and the band playing it was a bunch of Minneapolis kids, locals like me. I knew I wouldn't ever sound like this, but "Johnny's Gonna Die" gave me license to try my own thing, and to imagine I could raise the stakes too.

Bill Schneck: Bob [Stinson] was at a tryout for the first band I was ever in, Andy Jam and the Duponts. It was about 1979. They were a rich kids' band, and I was their token "poor kid in a leather jacket." Anyway, before I got into the band I had to try out and Bob was at the tryout place jamming before me. He was awesome. It was at a YMCA building by Ramsey High School [in Minneapolis]. Bob didn't get the spot probably because he was too wild and Andy, the leader, wanted to be the showman. I was just learning to play and we were mutually satisfied that I could just hang back and play rhythm guitar. But I distinctly remember Bob. I thought he kicked ass.

First time I saw the Replacements was at sound check when I was with the Neglecters, and we opened for them. I was working at Art Song's Chicken Wings and Slip's Soda Fountain that used to be on the corner of Hennepin and Lake. I worked with this long-haired hippie cook who said he was in a band called Dog's Breath and used to brag that they had a twelve-year-old bass player who was the brother of the guitar player. I put two and two together when we were at the sound check and there was this little brat-

ty kid playing bass along with the crazy ass-kicking guitarist I had met at the tryout.

Years later while playing at a party over Northeast with another band of mine, I was hanging out before we went on and here comes walking up this same long-haired cook. I said, "Hey man, remember me? We used to work together at Art Song's." I told him I learned to play guitar and that I was in the band playing there that night. He said, "Yeah, I used to be in the Replacements." I had to correct him and say, "You were in Dog's Breath before they became the Replacements."

The story I always heard was Westerberg was walking by the house where they practiced, heard them playing, and stole the whole fucking band from this guy. I don't think he liked that I corrected him, but since I was in the band playing that night, and one of my bandmembers was tight with the biggest, baddest dudes at the party, including the bouncer, he didn't fuck with me.

David Menconi: I believe it was late January/early February 1985 in Austin, Texas. They played this open-air joint called Liberty Lunch, which management tried to turn into a year-round venue by creating a temporary "ceiling" out of plywood. That did nothing to keep the cold out; it was frigid enough that even people from Minnesota were going to feel it. There wasn't anything like security at Liberty Lunch, so we just walked on into the backstage area—where we found Westerberg and Tommy Stinson huddled around a fire they'd started in a trash barrel. They were throwing everything that would burn in there and passing around a bottle of something strong. After some awkward small talk, I went to leave. Westerberg grabbed my sleeve and mock-whined, "No, don't go." I believe he wanted my coat for kindling.

The show itself was one of those amazing *Shit Hits the Fans*-style debacles. I remember they started a lot more songs than they finished, that everybody went just nuts during "I Will Dare," and that Bob Stinson came out for the encore in the raw, with his guitar strategically placed to keep it PG-13. Like I said, it was cold as hell. But by then, wasn't nobody feeling a thing.

Missy Roback: It was 1986, which means *Tim* was out, but the DJ at WFCS in New Britain, Connecticut, was pretty much stuck on *Let It Be*. I think I heard another cut off the album first, but it was the voice in "Unsatisfied" and "Answering Machine" that made me go, "Who *is* this guy?" He sounded raw and fragile and desperate and pissed. He sounded like how I felt.

I was twenty-three, two years out of college, slowly suffocating in a conservative New England town, not sure what to do with my life, but sure that I needed to get out of Hartford. I went to work at my soul-sucking insurance company job in my purple hair and black clothes. I was confused and angry and sad and not really sure why. At the time, I couldn't even describe these feelings—I just knew that everything felt wrong. "Unsatisfied" made me feel like someone else got it. *This is how it feels.* This is how *I* feel.

It took me a few more years to escape the suffocating town and quite a few more to start putting a name on my feelings. Songs like "Unsatisfied" and "Answering Machine," and later, "Achin' to Be," didn't give me all the answers, but they helped me feel less alone in the world.

Kevin Bowe: The '70s didn't exactly go out with a bang for me. A charming little stint in rehab right at the end of high school ruined my plans for a bong-fueled summer spent playing Who and Stones covers with my equally wasted peers. Apparently rehab wasn't quite enough fun because it was strongly recommended to me by the powers that be to go live in a halfway house, leaving my spoiled suburban life behind to room with a bunch of other lost causes. On weekends they would herd us like shell-shocked sheep out to "sober teen dances." Usually the bands were playing the kind of music that had driven me to try to numb myself with angel dust in the first place.

So there I was trying to disappear into the crowd when four odd-looking, self-conscious, skinny white kids tottered onto the stage. The Replacements. Odd-looking only because they looked just like us, not like the members of Journey. They had the same cheap guitars that kids like me had in our garages—but when they turned up and started rocking, it was like nothing I'd ever heard. Their set was cut short because they got busted drinking in their green room.

But in their forty or so minutes of glory they changed my life. All they had was a few Johnny Thunders covers, maybe a couple of originals, that's about it. Tommy had a stupid pot leaf decal on his bass, which was about as big as he was. Chris had that drop-jawed caveman thing going on while he pounded the drums. Bob was . . . Bob. And Paul—obviously nervous and obviously the leader of the best rock 'n' roll band I'd ever seen.

The word "roll" is important here because these guys were not just "rock" like so many other '80s bands. Not technically gifted enough for mainstream music, too distrustful of the in-crowd for punk, too young to be Baby Boom hippies, but too old to be whatever came after that—they were stuck in the

middle just like us. And that's what Paul's songs were about, written and played by outsiders for other outsiders. Who knew there were so many of us?

Craig Wright: I was in college at Moorhead State University. There was this guy I'd heard a lot about who was notorious for his writing ability, and when we finally met at Ralph's Bar one night, we had the kind of immediate antipathy I've since come to recognize as the annoyingly indecipherable, heat-muddled mirage of an approaching lifelong friendship. That first night we met, we walked out of Ralph's Bar to his car to get high, and while we did, he played me "I Will Dare." After three years of nothing but Bruce Springsteen—I wore only jeans and white T-shirts at the time . . . amazing—my whole world changed. All my deep, long-forgotten love for plain old pop came bursting up through the dirty, jumpy bass line of that song; Springsteen suddenly seemed massively beside the point.

Jim Peterson: I graduated from the University [of Minnesota] in May of 1980, and wasn't really sure what I was going to do next. I thought about grad school, but didn't really know what I wanted to do with a degree, so that didn't seem like a good idea. Plus, although I loved going to school, I needed a break after eighteen years.

I had been hanging out at Oarfolkjokeopus Records pretty religiously for the last couple of years, and was good friends with [store managers] Peter [Jesperson] and Terry [Katzman]. Sometime that spring the idea of me working at Oarfolk came up, and it sounded perfect to me. It was the coolest record store I had ever seen, and those guys had a lot of fun there every day.

After I graduated in May, I started working at the store, and I remember that Peter used to listen to band tapes in the office at the back of the store, catching up on paperwork. It was around the same time that I started working at the store that Peter got the original Replacements tape from Paul.

Peter was totally knocked out by it, and played it for everyone, and you could tell the band really rocked and had some great songs. I actually remember the excitement leading up to the first show more than I remember that specific show itself. Seeing them live blew the tape away. I was really impressed that they did a Heartbreakers cover or two, as *L.A.M.F.* was a total favorite record for both Terry and I at that point. And a few of their originals really sounded like the Heartbreakers, too.

Mark Anderson: The first time I really heard "Unsatisfied" I was alone at

The Cabooze and Sheila was at a Tiger's barbecue. This was in April of '84, back when I was temping for a Richfield landscaping company.

Earlier in the week Sheila said that she'd for sure go to the Replacements show at The Cabooze with me on Saturday night—she wouldn't poop out on me like last time. Last time: The Replacements were at Duffy's, we'd planned on going, we'd been talking about it all week, but when we got to the door they were carding everyone, and Sheila discovered that she'd forgotten her ID.

We drove back to her tiny apartment, and just as we were ready to head back to Duffy's, Sheila said that she felt tired and didn't really feel like going anymore. That night I didn't want to be alone, I really wanted to be with Sheila, so we put on Van Morrison *Astral Weeks*, and then I held her as she slept. Around midnight, I walked home alone.

Sheila and I hung out nearly every day back then. She said she just wanted to be friends, but we did hold hands, kiss, and snuggle now and then. The night before the Replacements' Cabooze show, though, the night after I'd spent the day laying sod at some big rich-fuck house by Lake of the Isles, we both got drunk at a party, spent the night at her apartment, and made mad love for the first and last time.

When we woke up naked in her bed the next day, we tried to pretend that this was cool and casual and no big deal, but I sensed that she was freaking out about it. I wanted to go out for breakfast and prolong our night for the rest of the day, but she said she had some things she needed to get done: water her plants, do her laundry, feed her cats.

I wondered, of course, if Tiger had anything to do with what Sheila needed to get done. She met Tiger sometime around April, and she thought he was one of the coolest people she'd ever known. Tiger was an older hippy guy—32 years old!—who rented a house with overgrown grass and weeds that he refused to cut. Tiger didn't use deodorant, and Sheila thought it cute and funny when he said, "I stink real good today!"

She said they were just friends, but I sensed that there was something more animal going on between Sheila and Tiger.

I called Sheila up in the late afternoon to see when she wanted to head to The Cabooze and she said she was tired and still a little bit hung over and really confused about things between us and she was really not in a mood to see the Replacements. Plus, Tiger called and said he and his friends were having a barbecue at his place—and that was more where she was at mood-wise.

The night Sheila canceled on me, I went to The Cabooze alone, depressed and feeling like a girlfriendless loser who didn't know what to do with my life.

How good could a guy feel about himself when his toughest competition was a hippy named Tiger whose signature line was "I stink real good!"?

I'd heard "Unsatisfied" before that night, but I remember hearing the song first and best on that night: "Look me in the eye/And tell me that I'm satisfied." I wished so much that Sheila was there with me hearing Paul Westerberg rip out those words: "I'm so, I'm so unsatisfied/I'm so dissatisfied."

Then again, if Sheila was with me that night, I wouldn't have felt so unsatisfied and I wouldn't have heard the song so right.

Laurie Lindeen: I was with my friend—and future bandmate—Coleen at Headliner's in Madison, to see X. We went to the University of Wisconsin and had a lot of college friends who hailed from South Minneapolis who were way into the 'Mats and knew them well. Co and I were those vintage dress–wearing types and we were way into X, particularly Mr. John Doe. We were just starting to warm up to the 'Mats' *Hootenanny*. Oddly—I was a party girl—I don't remember the 'Mats' set so well except that they did an early version of "Can't Hardly Wait" with different lyrics about heaven; I've always been sort of song-centered and that song stood out.

I remember standing on the side of the stage watching X while our college friends shuffled back and forth from backstage where they were helping themselves to the 'Mats' free beer. Billy Zoom was making googly eyes at Co and I, and Paul, who I did not know, whispered in my ear, "Want to meet the biggest asshole in the world?"—referring, I presume, to Zoom. Paul's gravely voice pretty much did me in for life. So that was the first time; things evolved—revolved, devolved, dissolved, resolved, revolved—from there.

Joe Henry: In the spring of 1984 I was living in Ann Arbor, working as the book acquisitions clerk for the University of Michigan's medical library. I was writing the songs that would make up my first record a year later, and doing so mostly on the library's clock; but I had a very understanding boss who knew my heart wasn't in my work, and she kindly turned a blind eye to my extracurricular activity. She would even call me on the phone from across the room before approaching my desk, thus giving me time to tear out whatever verse I was laboring over and spool another order form into the typewriter.

As a matter of research—like some people look for graduate schools—I was buying records like a fiend from Schoolkids', the great local record store, trying to get a handle on the new wave of indie labels that were springing up across the country like angry dandelions. It's worth mentioning that the girl working

the register most afternoons at Schoolkids' was none other than Lori Bizer, who would years later become the first Mrs. Paul Westerberg. She was a doll, and on at least one occasion I know I purchased some great record I already owned—Mingus? Muddy Waters?—just so she could see what kind of serious young man I really was, in case she was wondering.

At some point, in amongst albums by bands like the dBs, Love Tractor, Game Theory, and R.E.M., I wound up with *Let It Be* by the Replacements. I must've read something about them somewhere, and their label Twin/Tone, but I have no memory of expecting anything, much less what I heard. The sound was raw and unmannered, yet folksy, all at the same time. It was funny and pissy and arrogant and mopey, without being too self-conscious about any of it. And I heard it long before I knew anything much about how records technically got made; so when the iron lung of the piano wheezed and squeezed me into the grainy picture of "Androgynous," for instance, I wasn't distracted by what compressor or EQ it might've taken to achieve the effect; I only heard the creepy sound of someone grappling with confusion from the far end of a sewer pipe, trying to glue pieces together that probably wouldn't still be stuck in the morning. Choices were clearly being made, sonically speaking; but words, music, and production came together as a seamless amalgam, and the record stands as a milestone for a moment that was fragile and headed for a big crash.

I saw the Replacements a short time later, when they swung through town as the opening act for X. The old Michigan Theatre on Liberty Street was in flames with angst and excitement, but the 'Mats weren't. Bob Stinson didn't show up to play until at least halfway into their set, and even then he seemed a few songs behind the rest of the band. They irritated me that night the same way they would every time I saw them over the next five years or so, and I saw them quite a few times—always hoping to see them pull the cork out of one of the really good bottles they were clearly hoarding and let those great songs unfurl.

But unlike many of my peers, I never saw a great Replacements show. My theory was—and still is—that in the raucous post-punk days of the early and mid-'80s, it was bad form to care too much. You weren't supposed to give a fuck about a good couplet, even if you wrote one; and because the recordings revealed Paul's emotional investment in his songs, it seemed to me he felt obliged to piss on them once he got out in front of people. And that offended me. Offended me as a struggling songwriter and as a fan, which I was. I *knew* they were a great band, but knew as well they'd never assume that as a public posture. Better to fall off the face of the earth with your Chuck Taylors on than have to live up to the responsibility of being *good*, for God's sake. Then you might have to somehow *keep* being good, and who needs the trouble?

Funny that I still managed to care enough about them as a band to feel hurt when they wouldn't honor their potential. I suppose I wanted the opportunity I saw them squandering, and knew I would never have it. True enough. But beyond that, I just hated to see their songs scattered, smothered, and covered, because I really loved a lot of them.

But enough of that. The first time I heard the Replacements? It was a spring day in 1984 in Ann Arbor, Michigan. I'd just gotten home from the medical library where I was being paid to waste my time, and I pulled a new record called *Let It Be* out of its sleeve and set it spinning. Even before the vocals came in on "I Will Dare," I was sold. It swung; and the Replacements sounded funny and pissy and arrogant and mopey all at once. I had felt for a long time like a forgotten soldier, but on an afternoon that was unseasonably warm after a hard Midwestern winter, they sounded to me like the goddamn cavalry coming through.

CHAPTER 1

Raised in the City

Pray for us,
Paul

—Paul Westerberg's parting salutation
in his liner notes for *The Shit Hits the Fans*

Curtiss A: Rock music is egomaniacal music. Everything you do that's creative comes from the ego, but rock is super-ego. Everyone goes out there to prove that they're better than everybody else. And the biggest thing about rock, it doesn't always have to be perfect music. It's more about exuberance. And the cool thing about Minneapolis is the total exuberance.

Lori Barbero: I personally know at least twenty people off the top of my head who have told me they moved to Minneapolis—from Pittsburgh, New York, California, Texas, Nashville—because of the Replacements.

Martin Devaney: It's a Midwestern thing—but especially a Minnesota thing—to embrace our underachievers. It even stretches to our sports teams: The Twins that won two [World Series] had the worst regular-season record for a champion [1987] and [in 1991] had to go worst-to-first from their previous year. The Replacements are the perfect band for us. Whether they fell flat or knocked it out of the park, they were out there hollering about their lives and, in turn, ours.

Craig Finn: They're my favorite band, and I think about them more than I should. Them and the [Minnesota] Twins occupy an unhealthy amount of my brain.

Bob Mould: The thing I always tell people is, and it's not the most flattering thing, if you see ten Replacements shows, one of them you're going to think they're the greatest band that ever walked the face of the earth, and the other nine might degenerate into drunken covers. And if it's your first exposure to the Replacements, you hope that you get the great show. Because if you get the other ones, you're gonna walk away scratching your head.

Martin Devaney: That's why the 'Mats have always felt special to me: They sang about the places and people that are us. We drink where they drank, our bands play where they played. They were off-the-charts influential by just walking out of our lives and into their songs. I've always felt close to those songs not only because they spoke to me, but *for* me. And hell, I never even saw them live.

Danny Murphy: Those guys were a really pivotal thing for me in figuring out I wanted to do music. I saw 'em probably a hundred times over the years.

Phil Davis: The Replacements' subject—Midwestern angst—hasn't been better rendered by any punk band. The endless car rides to nowhere, Stop-N-Go snacks, familial pressures, drug-induced escapism—they all have psychic consequences.[1]

Steve McClellan: They were just another [Minneapolis] band at the time, like the Outpatience or the Panic or the REMs. I remember hearing that Paul [Westerberg] was pissed because I paid them $25 to open for somebody. But that's what I paid everyone.

Curtiss A: People say, "The Minneapolis Sound." To somebody that means Prince, to somebody that means Hüsker Dü, to somebody that means Soul Asylum. It's hard to put your finger on it, but most of it is exuberance. I don't know what it is, if it's the magical lakes or what, but we've got a lot of smart people here.

www.minneapolis.org: Central Connecticut State University named Minneapolis number 2 in a 2005 study of "America's Most Literate Cities."[2]

www.Forbes.com: Coming in second [behind Milwaukee] on our list [of "America's Drunkest Cities"] is another chilly metro: Minneapolis—St. Paul. The Twin Cities ranked No. 2 for adults who reported having had a drink in the last month, No. 3 for binge drinkers and No. 12 for heavy drinkers.[3]

Don Holzschuh: Everybody who moved from New York to Minneapolis in the early '80s was coming to go into treatment [at Hazelden].

Grant Hart: A month after Soul Asylum did well with their single ["Runaway Train," in 1994], which was a month totally separate from any other month of that band, all of a sudden you had cartoons in the *City Pages* of [Dave] Pirner freaking out if there's enough rips in their jeans.

It's not like you get it on the way up and on the way down here; you get both at the same time. You get the "Oh, they've worked so hard" at the same time as "They shouldn't let it get to their head." Everybody is constantly chewing from both sides of their mouth.

It's almost like the more good somebody says about a project, the more pressure there is somewhere else, building to humiliate. We're always looking out for everybody else's humility in this town. Flamboyant doesn't play here. Maybe with the colder climate, it's, "Don't stray too far from the barn. I'm not gonna go out there and find ya."

Craig Finn: I've never met any of those guys [in the Replacements]. I don't know what I'd say to Paul. I'm a little scared. He's my favorite songwriter. I look up to him so much, I don't know how I'd have a normal conversation.

Paul Westerberg: For every one person who loves you, there's five lined up to just hate you.[4]

Lizz Winstead: Whenever Minnesotans think something is even mildly weird or outside the lines, they say, "Well, that's . . . *different*." I remember being at my ten-year class reunion [at Minneapolis Southwest High School] in the bathroom talking and one of my former classmates said, "So Lizz, I hear you moved to New York and live in an old factory. Well, that's . . . *different*." To which I replied, "It's actually a loft." A few minutes later she leaned over and whispered, "Do you need some money?"

Bob Mould: I never really felt the "Keep 'em down on the farm" thing, because I guess I always thought I was a world-beater right off the bat. Definitely [with

Hüsker Dü] I had a "We are going to be the best thing in the world" kind of thing. But because of the climate, you really are forced to be indoors for a lot of the year. And you have to find ways to keep yourself occupied.

Bob Dylan: Northerners think abstract. When it's cold, you don't fret because you know it's going to be warm again . . . and when it's warm, you don't worry about that either because you know it'll be cold eventually.[5]

Jessica Lange: I was born and raised in Minnesota. I know that Minnesotans are stubborn and independent and I know that's where I get those qualities.[6]

Curtiss A: In later years, after [Bob Stinson] got kicked out of the Replacements, he started hanging around me, which was kind of annoying. But the reason he wanted to hang around me was because he wanted to talk to me about this guitar player, who was my friend in junior high and high school. His name was David Lloyd Forsberg, and he was the guitar player in Cain.

Cain was the first serious metal band in Minneapolis. [Forsberg] was a guitar player like Eddie Van Halen, or whatever. There weren't any heavy bands then. We had the Litter, and they weren't heavy, and we had Lightning, and they were trying to be Cream. Cain based themselves on Led Zeppelin, and [Stinson] liked Steve Howe from Yes, and Forsberg wasn't that far away from that.

Matthew Tomich: Last night, I got into Minneapolis—the city of Westerberg, [Dave] Pirner, Mould, Hart, [Gary] Louris, [Billy] Dankert, and too many et al's [*sic*]. It's hard to believe that this cosmopolitan jewel just rises out of the stoic agricultural wastes of Middle America. The whole feel of the city is much farther east than a due north of Iowa. The look of the populace runs the gamut from the original flannel and jeans (Minneapolis knew snow before Seattle knew Sub Pop) to a European-tinged dark professional somberness of the very-very-well-to-do young professionals that fill the downtown skyways and always newly-paved blacktop with their Saturns and reserved demeanor. The Twin Cities is America's Toronto thrown into the middle of a farmer's field.[7]

Grant Hart: I would say that between the two cities, Minneapolis is more paranoiac about its image in the nation, or in the world. I've heard it put this way: Minneapolis would do anything necessary to not be compared to

other cities of its own size. St. Paul is a capital city; it doesn't need to [blow its own horn].

Bob Mould: There are parallels between Minneapolis in the early and mid-'80s and Detroit in the late '60s, where you had two different cultures—a black culture and a white culture that both produced great music and occasionally shared the pulpit. Whether it was the MC5 and Stooges and the history of Motown and the Black Panthers and all that going on in Detroit, and then you look at First Avenue, which was really the pulpit for both North and South Minneapolis. They're both cold-weather cities that have that commonality: Detroit's a lot of Greeks and more of the Catholic side, whereas Minneapolis is more Lutheran.

Bob Stinson: Well, Motown, Tamala, [Berry] Gordy—all those records back when, was a different direction. I don't know how the black people feel now, but I'm just wondering if hip hop is the same answer to that. Leave it to them: They made rock n roll, they made soul, they made rap. All three things. Without them, there wouldn't be any of us white assholes.[8]

Curtiss A: [Bob Stinson] used to come up to me and ask for a drink or a joint or a five-dollar bill, but when he found out I knew [the guitarist] Forsberg, he changed. He got really quiet and just asked questions. His dream had crashed and burned, that band had been everything to him, and he just wanted to talk about this guitar player he liked as a kid. I thought that was really poignant. He died a little while after that.

Mary Lou Philipp Westerberg: My brother [Bob Philipp, Paul's maternal uncle] earned his livelihood all his life playing musical instruments. He had a band way back. After that he played piano and organ at Murray's [steak house in downtown Minneapolis] and the Normandy and the Leamington [hotels in downtown Minneapolis]. It was his whole life. My brother Paul also played in a band, so I guess they kind of come by it from my side of the family. I had always listened to music. I knew every word to every song that ever came out in my day, and I played piano a little. I absolutely loved their [the Replacements] music.

Paul Westerberg: It would never be confused or misconstrued that he [Westerberg's father, Harold "Hal" Westerberg] likes me because of what I do or what I've done. You know, he likes me because I'm his son. I have to go long

45

A GREAT TEACHER

He is an exciting hard working man at Incarnation. He has done a great deal concerning sports, and he also teaches math. It is none other than Mr. Tim Gagliardi.

Mr. Gagliardi was born on the East side of St. Paul on December 9, 1948. He attended Blessed Sacrament school, Hill High School, and St. Thomas College for his education.

Mr. Gagliardi has put in a lot of time, work and money to make the sports program of this school an enjoyable and profitable one. He suggested the Intramural activities that are played at lunch time, and designed the awards for the games himself. He started the program to give the kids a sense of responsibility and sportsmanship.

Mr. Gagliardi became a teacher because he enjoys being with young people – especially the kids at Incarnation.

Mr. Gagliardi works very hard. He coaches our boys' football, basketball and baseball teams. He also takes slides and pictures of the games for our enjoyment to show afterwards.

So as you can see he is very involved in this parish, and he has contributed everything he has for our benefit.

By: Jimmy Reddin, Tim Coryell, Paul Westerberg, Thomas Kotz

* * * * * * * * * *

An early writing credit from the Incarnation School newspaper, *Word Incarnate*, February 1973. *Courtesy Jean Heyer*

and far to find someone who knows me just as me, rather than me the songwriter or whatever.[9]

Jim Mars: There's seven of us [in the Mars family]. My dad would always be singing, in the background. He was always in a good mood. And my mom was always singing; she was in a choir. We didn't play a lot, but we all were always humming. My mom and dad didn't have a stereo, but they'd be singing these old tunes from the '30s. Everywhere [Jim's younger brother] Chris walked, he was humming. I remember my brother-in-law once said, "God, he's always got a song in his head, don't he?"

Paul Westerberg, eighth grade, Incarnation School yearbook, 1973. *Courtesy Jean Heyer*

Paul Westerberg: It was quite ordinary, middle-class Middle America. Maybe that's where the frustration came into play. My mom was always encouraging me to go out and play, but I tended to want to be alone. It's the way I've always been. I'm comfortable with it, I guess. . . . No [I don't go on vacations]. I never did as a kid, so it probably holds over until now. The first time I ever went out of the state was on tour.[10]

Anita Stinson: Bobby got a guitar for Christmas when he was 12. He taught Tommy. Once, Tommy got distracted and Bobby threw pizza at him.[11]

Westerberg (first row, far left), Incarnation School yearbook, 1973. *Courtesy Jean Heyer*

Grant Hart: The best relationship I had with anybody in that band, and it was just because he was too simple to go to that [ego] place, was Bob Stinson. You could be friendly with the guy without it being a rock-star event. You didn't have to have a drink ticket to get a drink with him.

Kevin Martinson: Bob came up to me once when I had this Music Man 212 [amp]. He said, "Man, you gotta get some encased speakers. You're not getting any compression pushing the noise out. You gotta get some Celestions or some Marshalls." That was a good piece of advice. He was kind of a technical wizard; everybody wrote him off as this dumb, off-center druggie guy, but he was a pretty smart cookie.

Paul Westerberg: [My dad is] old, he's gonna retire. He's easy going. He sells Cadillacs. He never owned one, just leased one. It's kind of sad. They should just give him one for all the years he's worked there. We're closer than we used to be. He asks me the same thing every time I see him, which is, "When are you gonna play? You making any money? Oh, that's nice." . . . [He doesn't like any of my songs but] my mom does. She's weird—her favorite song is "Take Me Down To The Hospital." She likes Bo Diddley, Creedence, bluesy songs with a wild beat. She's hip.[12]

Mary Lou Philipp Westerberg: Harold [Paul's father] and I met at a dance. It was at the [Minnesota] State Fair, and my brother's band was playing in the beer garden. I had wanted to go to a baseball game, but my mother said, "For once in your life, you're going with your family." And I went over there, and by golly that's where I met Harold. He asked me to dance.

Jim Mars: I just remember Chris tapping on everything. Then my mom gave him a bunch of kettles to bang on with some spoons and sticks. Then they got him a drum set when he was about seven, a Sears drum set, and he broke through it because it was basically paper. For a long time after that, he didn't have [a kit], so he finally went out and bought one.

Tracie Will (*née* Holzinger): We were next-door neighbors with the Westerbergs for thirty-two years. Paul was two years younger than me, and I was kind of in love with his older brother, Phil. He was so cute. I didn't really pay much attention to Paul, because he was younger. And Mary [Lucia, Paul's sister] was just a little kid, so she wasn't really included in anything.

His parents were awesome. His dad was totally gregarious. He sold Cadillacs, he was a big golfer. They were big drinkers. He was like Bob Hope—a little more handsome—with the natty golf sweaters and plaid pants, and always driving a Cadillac. And his mom was always made-up to the T.

Mary Lucia: I got a fake ID when I was 13 and started going to clubs. This is why I'm not impressed now, at this age. It's like, "Show me something I haven't seen." It just seems like we came from that Catholic, everyone's-in-a-band, alcoholic-father neighborhood. I just think it was in the blood, in the genes.[13]

Paul Westerberg: I started playing guitar in 1974. I was 14, [inspired by] seeing the Raspberries on "Rock Concert." I remember I just got my guitar, and learned my first three chords—G, C, D—and there's Eric Carmen playing the same chords, "Go All the Way." I don't know if it sounds right to say the Beatles, but I got an older sister. . . . She

Chris Mars, ninth grade, DeLaSalle High School yearbook, 1976.
Author collection

was like 14 when the Beatles hit in 1964 and stuff. So I grew up with all the Beatles and Stones, and Motown stuff. I remember a lot of that, like "Mickey's Monkey" and shit. The Miracles, the Temptations, Rod Stewart, watching like "Help" on TV. My cousins were over, I can remember seeing it. That might've planted the seed, although it sounds dumb . . . the screaming girls, probably. Creedence Clearwater. . . .[14]

Jim Mars: [Chris] learned guitar after he learned the drums; he just loved music so much that he pursued it more than anyone in the family. He liked windsurfing, he did it for six months and loved it, and then he quit. Then he did music. But the art, the drawing, is what he stayed with. He would do things in steps—get interested in something and go full bore, and that's all you'd hear

49

about for a while. That's what set him apart from the rest of the family. He was a participator, not just a spectator.

Bob Stinson: In '73/74, everything was on the same station. Actually, I could fall asleep to it. It was beautiful: "Stairway to Heaven" next to "Rocky Mountain High," you can't go wrong with that.[15]

Tracie Will: The neighborhood was really tight. We all played together: kick-the-can, Red Rover. Each family had four to six kids. We all hung together, played bike tag, stubbed our toes. Nobody tattled or narced on anybody else; if somebody was in trouble, you all covered it. We used to do the goofy things like lighting the sewers on fire, throwing snowballs at cars, and go down to 38th and Grand [in South Minneapolis] in the winter and grab onto the back bumpers of cars and go for a ride.

Mary Lou Philipp Westerberg: There were fifty kids on our block when we moved into that house in 1954.

Paul Kaiser: Chris and Paul and I went to Incarnation [grade school] together. Paul and I played baseball together, and we both rode the bench and talked about how "We're gonna prove the coach wrong" and all that. I played second base and a little outfield, and he was outfield. He was pretty quiet, and so was I. We got in [the games] once in a while, but we never started. He used to live close to [future NBA player] Chris Engler, and we used to go over there and play basketball once in a while.

Kurse Stockhaus: The thing I remember most about Paul Westerberg is that he wouldn't say "boo" to anyone in school, and that after lunch, he and Paul Kaiser would go to the corner store and buy candy and come back and give it to the girls.

Paul Westerberg: I never had a girlfriend until the day I joined the band. When we started, it was like being let loose in a candy store. Gimme, gimme, gimme. Then you realize, "Gee, I'm making an asshole of myself, this is no way to live."

. . . I haven't gone [to church] for a while. I'd feel out of place, a sore thumb. But I think about it. Somebody once said that all Catholics come out of the system either knowing their place in life and feeling totally happy, or they

want to take over the world. There is some definite truth in that; I'm lost in the cracks somewhere in between.[16]

Jay Walljasper: Paul Westerberg's childhood home is on the next block from my house. I show it to my son now [in 2007], an aspiring songwriter, and tell him, "Yes, it's possible to make it." It's funny because it is actually a pretty grand house for a band that fancied itself a bunch of working-class fuck-ups from South Minneapolis. It's big and brick with an iron fence around it, and looks like some family mansion from the 1910s. The people living there now say that in the basement young Paul painted the walls with a tribute to his favorite band: "I love the Suburbs."

Paul Westerberg: I went to the [Faces] show with my buddy, Bob Waterman. We were in 10th grade. And I remember on the way to the show, the radio had just announced a new artist, and it was Bruce Springsteen. So we heard "Born to Run" for the first time on the way to the gig. November. It was cold; a day like today. I was in front of Woody [Ron Wood], about three deep. I had a girl on my shoulders. I was this geeky 15-year-old boy, never been kissed, and in three minutes I had this chick on my shoulders—probably in a halter top! I was like, "Yeah! This is great!"[17]

Marc Perlman: Paul went to the same Faces concert I did. I was pretty young and I'm fairly sure Paul was, too. If you've ever seen the way the Faces make an auditorium seem like a pub, you'd understand why I bring this up.

Lori Barbero: Whenever I saw the Replacements play—and I remember this vividly—I would go into the ladies room and ring the sweat out of my tank-top. It was like somebody dumped a pitcher of water over me. Sopping wet. I used to go crazy. I loved them so much.

Chris Mundy: Did the Replacements have an "us against the world" feeling as a band because each of the members felt it individually?
Paul Westerberg: I would say that's fair. I think that's why we became friends. I don't think a well-adjusted class president could have made it to play lead guitar for us. There was not a high-school diploma on that stage. We all had something in common.
CM: But you actually finished school.
PW: I went twelve years but never got the diploma. They wanted me to come back to get it. But I didn't want one.[18]

Tommy Stinson, eighth grade, Anwatin Middle School yearbook, 1981.

John Beggs: I went to Southwest High School [in Minneapolis], and Tommy was a freshman and I was a senior. I don't think he was too into it. I took driver's ed with him, and there was a lot of looking out the window and drumming pencil erasers on the desk.

Kim Walsh: Apparently [Westerberg] went to [Minneapolis] Central [High School for a year but didn't graduate with the class of 1977], but I never saw him. I was in Prince's class [of 1976]. Prince hung out with the cute athletic black guys and I hung out with the hippie chicks, so we didn't really cross paths. I remember him sitting in the window well by the music class playing his guitar. Prince was always a decent guy. Not a bully. Pretty popular, I think. Always cute.

I liked Central. It was a nice mix of kids and you could pretty much be who you wanted to be. It was a neighborhood school. Plus there was a segment of rich hippie kids who went to Central that fascinated me; I couldn't believe someone would choose to go there. But money wasn't an issue there. Most kids were poor or working class.

Paul Westerberg: Yeah, I went to Catholic school all the way—all the way and nowhere. I was constantly drunk and stoned, just messed up with drugs and stuff. I did that all through high school, that's why I think I have a real bitter attitude toward it now. It was the worst four years of my life.

It was also bad because they would send kids from [alcohol and drug] treatment there, supposedly getting a good atmosphere. So you would have like half these goody-goody rich kids and the other half were these fucking loads from the inner city. I mean, being drunk every day in typing class and by the time you get your paper out the drill's over.[19]

Bea Hasselman: I was the music teacher at Central, and in my opinion that '71–'81 Central was the most peacefully integrated school in the history of the state. People chose to come here because of its curriculum. Science. Math. Language. The arts. People thought of it as an "inner-city school," but it could compete with any school in the state. And we did.[20]

Paul Westerberg: [Prince has] always been a great musician: If he's a pop star or he's in vogue is irrelevant. Like Coltrane or Sly Stone, he's creative, he's great. He's the shit. He's a great, great musician. And in a way, I think that I am—you know, not as great—but maybe more of a songwriter. I am a musician and a writer, and I'll always be. And if I'm hip or if I'm an old man, that shouldn't really matter. I'm gonna do this forever, and I think we have that in common.[21]

Dave Ayers: Tommy's brother, guitar player Bob, is seven years older and the only Replacement with a job, the only one living away from home. He's been a cook for the last six years, has no plans to quit. Bob was "pulled out" of school in ninth grade; "incorrigible" he says they called him. Small-time arson, vandalism, that kind of stuff. He's quieter now, almost reserved aside from the odd bender and his stage gear. "If they hate it, I'll wear it," is how he describes his stage appearance. He collects dresses, polyester jackets, fur vests. Beats settin' fires.[22]

Slim Dunlap: I was driving the cab one night, and I saw Bob [Stinson] walking down Lake Street, and I asked him if he needed a ride. He said, "No." And about two hours later, I was way in East St. Paul, and there he was, walking. So I gave him a ride back to his house. We talked a little bit about music and he said he had that little band going with his brother and a drummer.

Curtiss A: I lived in that milk store on 26th and Lyndale [in South Minneapolis], right by the record store [Oarfolkjokeopus]. When Tommy was nine, he had a little purple bike with a banana seat. He didn't look much different than he ended up looking, with the hair. He would ask me all kinds of questions about stuff. He was getting very interested in the rock music. He would come and talk to me about what I liked, and that's how come he ended up liking the Raspberries and Terry Reid. No kid liked that shit.

Casey MacPherson: I was working for the Suburbs when the Replacements started. Tommy lived right up the street from me in those days and would come down to visit all the time. He was thirteen or fourteen, and I sometimes had to walk him home as there was a fella from his school that was always waiting on the corner to terrorize him in one way or another. I remember an interesting conversation we had on one of those walks. This was at a point when the wheels were starting to come off a bit for the Suburbs. I remember

Tommy saying to me, "We'll never make the mistakes that the Suburbs are making." I said, "No, you'll make your own."

Jim Peterson: The Stinson brothers spent a lot more time hanging out at Oarfolk than the other guys did, and Bob spent by far the most amount of time there. I can only remember seeing Chris there a few times, and Paul just a little more often. He might come by after practice to talk to Peter for a bit—more in the early days, pre- or just post-*Sorry Ma* [*Forgot to Take Out the Trash*, the band's first album]. Tommy would come by after school just to hang around and listen to music. He was a lot more interested in what records we were playing in the store, asking questions and getting turned on to new or older music. Tommy definitely got a crash-course in music history there.

Eric Tretbar: Ultimately, my memory of the Replacements is a still-imagined show at the Uptown [Bar], years before I arrived in Minneapolis—when Tommy was fourteen and the Minneapolis scene was still caught between bikers, hippies, punks, and disco. I was still in Kansas then, probably in junior high somewhere, waiting for something—anything!—to save me from the horrible AM radio blather of Journey, Styx, Toto, and Blue Öyster Cult.

Lori Barbero: I went to high school in New York, and I went to tons of shows at CBGB's in the day. And that was really fun. It was really great. I saw the Dead Boys, and the Ramones, and Patti Smith, and the New York Dolls. But a lot of those bands had a lot of practice watching other New Yorkers, and it was not the most genuine thing. When I came back to Minneapolis in 1980, everything was just starting. And watching it all just sprout like this seed like Jack and the Beanstalk was just amazing.

Right away, the Replacements were so real, and in your face; what you see is what you get. They were the best band, ever, basically. Everything that they stood for was completely, one-hundred-percent valid. They didn't give a flying "F" about what anybody thought, and I've always lived by that.

Curtiss A: The Stinson family lived in the house [2225 Bryant Avenue in South Minneapolis] next to the house where my band practiced. I knew [their mother] Anita because she worked at the Uptown. Bob [Stinson] would come over and watch us, and the thing about him that I loved is that he hated us. He had this gigantic sneer, like Elvis. And he just sneered at us. I didn't know if he just didn't like us, or if he was just one of those kids like that, or if he was

maybe jealous that maybe his brother was showing some interest in what we were doing. At the time, I didn't know either one would be players.

Paul Westerberg: This could be cliché time: [I got into it to get] girls, and I had no other choice. I had no skill, and it was a way to get out of having a job.[23]

Jeff Culhane: I met Paul at a kegger in [the Minneapolis suburb of] Richfield. Everyone was in high school. This guy's parents would leave all the time and he'd bring in a bunch of kegs and invite every musician he could think of to come play. This one night, four or five guys were playing, and Paul was crammed in the corner. He wasn't as outgoing as the other guys, older guys, but he was really good. The next day I called my friend and asked him who he was. He goes, "Oh, that's Paul Westerberg." I got his number and called him.

Slim Dunlap: I remember seeing them at Oarfolk hanging out, and I just said, "Oh, man. They are *trouble*." I had met Bob a time or two. He'd come up to me for years, and was always very insightful in his criticism. It wasn't something you welcomed; he was always on Curt. If you ever got to thinking you were good, there'd be Bob with something to make you think otherwise. He would stand by the side of the stage and everyone else would be getting into it, but Bob would have that look of, "This is the same crap."

Jeff Culhane: I called Paul and told him I liked his guitar playing and told him I was really into Wishbone Ash, the double-guitar thing. He was into the idea of playing together, especially when I told him my brother could sing. We called the band Resister. I got him a job as a janitor, cleaning office buildings out by the old Met Stadium, where Mall Of America is now. He had an awful black Strat that would never stay in tune. I figured if we got him a job, we'd keep him out of other bands and he'd make enough money to buy a new guitar. He didn't have a driver's license—still doesn't. We drove him everywhere.

We were in Resister together for six or eight months. We both wanted to do something big, and we weren't very good. I remember him saying we should just be big and loud and do KISS covers or something and "I'd rather be really good at being crappy than really crappy at trying to be good."

Steve Kent: Resister was a power-pop band. I was the drummer. [Westerberg] did one show with us at the Longhorn, then he quit. He used to yell at me to not sing harmony on his songs; he didn't like that. I never got the

feeling that Paul was trying to take over the band, I just thought he wanted his own thing. I don't think he had a lot of confidence back then; I think he was looking for something less regimented.

Jeff Culhane: He left and started the Replacements. I recorded the demo tape that he gave to Peter Jesperson. I think we recorded it in Chris Mars' basement. It definitely wasn't the Stinsons' house. I've got mountains of tapes of Paul before the Replacements and of the Replacements that have never been released, and I promised Paul I'd never release them. One is of when the Replacements opened up for Resister at this place we used to play at—the Waconia Paradise Ballroom. They didn't go over very well.

A little while after their first record came out, he let us [Resister] open up for them at the [7th St.] Entry. By then I'd started playing in a cover band and I was making some pretty good money. He asked me what I was doing and I said, "I'm singing covers, but I get paid." He said, "I don't get paid at all, but I make records."

Terry Katzman: I remember going over to the [Stinson] basement and watching practice, drinking some really bad red wine that Smokin' [Bob Stinson] had procured. They were rehearsing in a place of about ten or 12 feet. Bob on one side of the exhaust pipe to the furnace and the other three of them on the other side. It was pretty revelatory, right away. They weren't your normal walk-in-the-woods punk rock band.

Lori Barbero: I would hang out in that basement all the time. I was addicted to it. That's how I first met those guys. I was seriously addicted to just seeing what would happen next.

Chris Mars: I had played with Paul once before I met the Stinson brothers. . . . He was real nerdy. When Paul first joined the band, he would be drinking orange juice while we would be getting really drunk. Eventually he broke down, though.[24]

Paul Westerberg: I was working as a janitor at Butler Square in downtown Minneapolis.[25]

Dave Ayers: I remember Paul telling me about being a janitor in [former Vice-President and U.S. Senator] Walter Mondale's office, or whatever local

office he would have had, and sweeping up under his feet. That's what he was doing as he was making up these songs in his head: sweeping up under people's feet.

Paul Westerberg: Coming home from work and my janitor's job, I used to hide in the bushes and listen. I could hear 'em from a block away . . . I'd peek in the window. And Chris called me up one day and he asked me to come over and play with his band. I was secretly thinking, "Oh, man, if I could play with this band that's playing here. . . ."[26]

Bob Stinson: Actually, there was no singer; we'd just get together, and just jam, and see what we could play. When I went over [to Westerberg's house] and heard him play, he was way too mainstream. He was doing Tom Petty shit, Bad Company, whereas we were just freelancing, fuckin' around and comin' up with stuff all our own, which probably lured him a little bit. We didn't have a format.[27]

Paul Westerberg: When I first met them they didn't have a singer and they had another guitar player. Then they got a singer, who was really shit—a hippie who had like a sheet, sat down, and read the lyrics. Then I just started yelling into the mike and stuff. Bob didn't like that. Bob wanted to get another singer. We tried another guy and they all liked him, and I sorta told him "The band doesn't like you. I think you're great, but the band says you're out."[28]

Bob Stinson: To tell you the truth, I don't think Paul—if I didn't ask him to play with us—would have done anything. He was always depressed. He didn't sing in his other bands. He'd just be working at Menards today or something, huh? Oh, I'm not taking no credit or anything like that, but he certainly started to smile. As a matter of fact, our first introduction—I quit smoking and he started smoking—his introduction was he gave me a joint from his brother. He goes, "Smoke this!" And for about the first two or three weeks, every time he came to practice he'd give me a joint.[29]

Curtiss A: It was very pointed fun. You could tell they were really serious about having what *they* wanted, rather than what somebody wanted them to have. The Sex Pistols and all that crap came out at the perfect time for those kids.

Oarfolkjokeopus, circa 1982, the nerve center of the 1980s Minneapolis music scene.
© *Joan E. Bechtold*

Lori Barbero: I knew Anita and I walked in and out of the house freely. It was just a huge rush. *What are they going to come up with? What's Bobby gonna do? Who's gonna get obliterated?* There was so much humor in it, and so much reality, and so much originality.

David Brauer: I thought they sucked. Friends who knew more about music than me were talking them up, but I just thought it was noise—plus, in my mind I was a sweet sensitive guy and the whole thrash thing just seemed too random to me.

Paul Westerberg: To like us, you have to try and understand us. You can't come in and just let your first impressions lead you. Because your first impression will be a band that doesn't play real well, is very loud, and might be drunk. Beneath that is a band that values spirit and excitement more than musical prowess. To me, that's rock and roll, and we're a rock and roll band.[30]

Rusty Jones: I saw 'em at the Longhorn. With all the hype, I felt pretty "unwowed," thinking, "This is just another clueless bunch of kids." I mean, we

[Jones' band Safety Last and the first wave of punk/new wave bands] were already twenty-four, twenty-five years old by then—but at some point I distinctly remember them kicking off "Milk Cow Blues" [a la Eddie Cochran], and I thought, "Alright, these guys know something beyond AM radio."

Gina Arnold: Whereas places like New York and Los Angeles were scene-driven and radio-driven, Minneapolis was store-driven: its punk-rock axis centered around a tiny "mom & pop" record store called Oarfolkjokeopus.[31]

Jim Peterson: Bob would show up at Oarfolk three or four times a week, either after practice or with his check from this Italian place he worked at in Dinkytown [near the University of Minnesota], ready to cash. Bob would hang out and chat, but he spent most of his time reading the rock magazines and books that we had—*NME*, *Rolling Stone*, *Rolling Stone* biography, whatever was handy. I can still picture him sitting on the ledge by the window, reading a magazine and biting his fingernail.

He would sit there for an hour just reading, and it would crack us up to see how studious he was, compared to the crazy onstage version of Bob. He would also spend some time going through the 50-cent records in back, and pick up the odd Yes record, or Michael Schenker Group, or Rainbow or something like that.

Terry Katzman: The store would close at 8. They'd go over to the CC [Club] across the street at about 5 and start drinking, and come over to the store at 8 and we had to play Thin Lizzy records or something. Sometimes we'd be talking and yakking to them and they'd be yakking to us, and we wouldn't close the till out for a while. That's when it was more fun to hang around a record store, and they were part of the reason why it was fun.

Jon Bream: Peter Jesperson is not a disc jockey for a far-reaching radio station or a columnist for a big-circulation newspaper. Yet he is the most important rock music taste-maker in the Twin Cities. He is the gatekeeper to the hip crowd, the guru of the underground, the godfather of the rock cognoscenti. Walk into Oarfolkjokeopus, that wonderfully eccentric record store on 26th and Lyndale, just about any afternoon. That's where Jesperson holds court. "Here's a great record you gotta hear," he says to any familiar customer. Today's pick is The Only Ones. They're from England.[32]

Peter Jesperson: Jon Bream did that article [on September 11, 1979], and Paul [Westerberg] gave me the tape in the spring of '80. I always thought that

was a very canny move on Paul's part. He must have seen that [article], and maybe he just targeted me. Who knows, maybe he'd come into Oarfolk before that, but the timing was such that they had just started playing together and he was probably thinking, "At some time I'm going to give this guy a tape." Without patting myself on the back, I was a good person to give a tape to: I was running [Oarfolkjokeopus], I had a record label [Twin/Tone], and I DJ'd at [The Longhorn].

Ryan Cameron: I had just moved to town, and I was a regular shopper there, and I'd overheard Peter going on and on, raving about this local band he'd just heard.

Peter Jesperson: I remember going through the tapes, and for some reason everybody in Minneapolis at the time sounded like the Stooges.

Mike Cisek: I saw one of their first shows at Jay's Longhorn. I was with [Jay Walsh] and our band, the Neglecters, had practiced that night. Since we were just beginning, we were always monkeying around with time [signatures] during our practices. How fast was good? Would people dance? Remember, bands rated their success by how many bar patrons were dancing in those days. We were watching the first band and Jay turned to me and said, "These guys don't play too fast, everything they do is controlled and people can dance to them." It was a controlled, paced, steady set.

Well, then the Replacements came on. They weren't controlled, paced, or steady. In fact, I had never heard a band play that fast and stay together. They didn't care if they were too fast to dance to. Everyone stopped dancing because they couldn't. You could tell that they weren't trying to empty the room in some kind of sarcastic maneuver; they could only play at that speed.

Peter Jesperson: Paul had given me a four-song basement tape, and I didn't play it right away because I was backed up. He called and came back into the store a time or two and asked if I'd listened to it yet.

Rick Ness: The Replacements are great musicians, and we're not. We have to practice four or five nights a week to sound like this.[33]

Tim O'Reagan: My first impression was, "What's all the fuss about?" It actually took awhile for me to appreciate them because I was listening to R&B

and blues and they were so far removed from that. Plus I wasn't really charmed by the drunken, sloughing-off on stage. I was into the very square practice of trying to play and perform as good as you can.

Tracie Will: The oddest thing I remember is that when we were growing up, [Paul] used to call people "puds." Like, "You're a pud." It was like, "What does that mean?" It was his own little slang.

Peter Jesperson: One day when I was feeling particularly guilty, I took a pile of tapes back in the office with a boom box and was just putting them in one after the other while I was doing paperwork, and the 'Mats tape came on. "Raised in the City" was the first song. For me, it was as magical as anything'll ever get. I called [friends] Steve Klemz, Bill Melton, and Linda Hultquist and said, "You have to come down here to hear this. I need some corroboration here," because I couldn't believe how good it was. I don't know about Bill, but Linda and Steve were both as blown away as I was.

David Carr: I was working at the Little Prince near Loring Park [in downtown Minneapolis] and I would just walk to the Entry from there without looking to see who was [playing]. I walked in and there was some kind of shoving match and a lot of laughing going off on stage and I asked a kid next to me when the band started. He told me that they were in the middle of the set. The next day I asked a pal at work who these jokers were—I think it might have been Michael, a tall, handsome gay man with a taste for Burberry and punk rock—and he explained that they were the future of rock music.

Lori Barbero: Besides like Led Zeppelin and Rolling Stones and Beatles, it was the new revolution of the new rock and roll at that time. It was after punk rock, and the Replacements were [a synthesis] of all of it.

Peter Jesperson: I called Paul and said, "Were you thinking of [recording] a single or an album?" And he said, "I was just trying to get an opening slot at the Longhorn."

Julie Panebianco: Who would you like to pattern your career after?
Paul Westerberg: Nobody. Isn't that horrible? We are trying to blaze this trail, and we have no one to follow. It is frightening and confusing. We are

blindly trying it and being as cautious as we can not to do what is usually done, which is throw yourself out there like some god or something. Our goal isn't to be the most hated rock band, our goal is to be the biggest, most natural thing that we are, and be as big as possible. We're just trying to be ourselves with as much gusto as we can.[34]

Jeaneen Gauthier: Being a songwriter and being a musical virtuoso are two completely different things, and you can be one or the other, but not both. The best songwriters are usually not the greatest musicians, from a technical point of view. They don't usually spend time practicing scales, killer guitar riffs, or drum fills. Some of them have singing voices that would wilt plants. They make a lot of mistakes on stage, or forget the whole song entirely. If they tried to play in someone else's band, they might not even be allowed in. And then sometimes they get really bummed out because they listen to a practice tape of themselves and say, "What am I doing? I call myself a songwriter and I can't even keep my guitar in tune."

On the flip side, technically good players can do just about anything on their instrument, but you'll rarely see them pull a song out of thin air. Maybe they can do a killer guitar solo or jazz thing totally on the fly, but the song structure has to be there already. And if an original song idea did come to them, they would probably tear it apart and analyze all the ways it wasn't good enough and how it ought to be changed or abandoned altogether. Any songwriter who knows the experience of showing a new song to their band knows how this works.

Peter Jesperson: I never fought to manage the band. Paul asked me to do it, and I did. Hartley Frank [manager of the Longhorn] took us outside [the Longhorn] one night and he was trying to get them to play this half-assed Tuesday-night show, and I was saying I didn't think they should do it. He was getting really pissed, and he said to Paul, "Do I have to talk to this guy every time I want to book you?" And Paul looked up at me and raised his eyebrows and said, "Yeah."

Jim Peterson: Bob handled a lot of his finances through [Oarfolkjokeopus]. One time he even asked me to cash his paycheck [$250 or so], but to hold onto the money and give him no more than $20 per day. I think that lasted about two days, before he asked to get the full balance. He'd also borrow some money from us personally, $5 or so at a time, saying he needed some money to go down to Hum's [Liquor Store]. But he would always pay it back on payday—he

always made sure he took care of any debts he had, and would leave money if he owed it to someone who was not working at the time.

Peter Jesperson: Nobody wanted to manage them. The closest anyone ever came was in '84, Robby Krieger [of the Doors] came to a Replacements show in L.A. once and he looked all skinny and old and speed-freak kind of guy, and he sauntered up and said, "Yeah, I've heard a lot about you guys. I might wanna manage you." We were all like, "Wow. Look at this guy. He doesn't look like he'd be a very good manager."

Dave Ayers: They were a band that hadn't made a mark yet [when their first LP, *Sorry Ma* was released]. They certainly didn't have the profile of the [Suicide] Commandos or the Suburbs.

Linda Hultquist: Paul was very dismissive of the Commandos. I said to him, "Listen, you little fucker. You wouldn't exist if it wasn't for the Commandos." But he didn't care, as didn't a lot of that next bunch, who just didn't get it. They saw the Commandos as so tongue-in-cheek as to not be a real band almost, they did covers and blah-blah-blah, and that really pissed me off. But I don't think Westerberg ever changed his mind about that.

Peter Jesperson: Once when a journalist asked Paul who they wanted to replace, he replied, "Everybody."

Slim Dunlap: Paul was not respectful of his elders, and Bob was not respectful of anyone, really. Paul was so cocky right off the bat. I told him once that he reminded me of a young Eddie Cochran, and he just acted really weird, like that was a really stupid thing to say. Early on, he was kind of unapproachable. You kind of got your head bit off if you tried. But Bob loved to spar.

Peter Jesperson: I think they were catching on right away, from those first couple shows at the Longhorn. I think there was a dedicated, small group of people who got it right away, and then it just grew in a very natural, organic way. And I know there was opposition. There was a resentment in the early days, people who really thought, "Why are they getting all these breaks?"

Kevin Martinson: I was at their first bar show at the Longhorn, when they opened for the Dads. After they played, I went into that bar in the side room,

"Low class rock." The band's first flyer, featuring Greg Helgeson photographs taken at the Walker Art Center in Minneapolis, November 1980. *Author collection*

and Peter Jesperson was having them sign their Twin/Tone contract right there in the bar.

Rick Ness: I taped [that first bar gig] on this crappy little Flatline tape recorder that people use to tape meetings or something. When Jesperson found out, he took the tape from me and kept it. He was just really excited, like, "Thanks! I didn't tape it." I was really pissed.

Peter Jesperson: Bob Mould said something to my face, about, "I suppose if you're involved, the red carpet's gonna roll out for these guys." Like it was unfair, like I should be paying attention to some other bands. And it hurt my feelings. I just said, "Bob, I think these guys are really great. Have you listened to these guys? This is amazing stuff. They're better than most of these bands."

Paul Westerberg: Where is it written? Where is it written that you have to pay your dues before [you make a record]?[35]

Jay Walsh: We were at a party in Kevin [Martinson]'s basement when our bands were just getting going—REMs, the Neglecters, maybe the Outpatience. Paul was there, too. People got up and played a tune and then passed the guitars around. I remember playing "Gloria" with Paul and a few others. I was so proud 'cause it was the one song I could play without looking down at my hands. Then Paul did "Johnny B. Goode."

He had the intro down cold and he knew all the words. He just ripped it. Sorta like that scene in *Back to the Future* when Michael J. Fox wows 'em at that dance. I got the same reaction when the 'Mats were in a bar, hitting on all cylinders. I looked around to check other faces, like, "Are you getting this? Are you taking this down?" It was like seeing [Minnesota Twins' Hall of Famer] Rod Carew when he was ten, playing at Lynnhurst [a neighborhood park in South Minneapolis]. He was on another level even then.

Bob Mould: I think there was a rivalry; I like to think it was a healthy one. I think at the end of the day, everybody helped each other out. It wasn't like anyone was trying to sabotage each other. From the Hüsker camp, there was a bit of a snub that Twin/Tone, which was the prevailing label at the time, wasn't that interested in the Hüskers. But the Replacements, on one gig, got an album [deal]. It was sort of like, "Hmm."

Advertisement for Twin/Tone's videotaped 1981 Entry "Soundcheck" show.
Author collection

Terry Katzman: The reason Reflex [Records, which released the first Hüsker Dü singles and LPs] started was because Twin/Tone didn't want to put out the first Hüsker Dü single ["Statues" b/w "Entertainment"]. Bob just said, "Well, we'll put our own stuff out then." I don't even know that there was any real jealousy. Bob [Mould] tried, they [Twin/Tone] didn't want to do anything, he thought, "Move on."

Grant Hart: Mould was intimidated by Twin/Tone liking them. There just seemed to be this all-or-nothing thing: We were going to get fucked by Twin/Tone because of the existence of this band, the Replacements.

Bob Mould: The Replacements were more rooted in traditional rock, maybe the Stones and stuff like that, and maybe with Hüskers it was more of a Beatles thing—more of a jazz thing. They were also doing a bit of blues, and [Hüsker Dü] was doing psychedelic stuff, so there was a bit of a contrast. It was funny, because there were periods where we were sort of trading little bits of ideas back and forth, around *Stink* and *Metal Circus*. We played so much together and saw each other's shows all the time, and everybody hung out.

Bill Schneck: The night Twin/Tone recorded the Neglecters, Replacements, and Hüskers [in the 7th St. Entry on September 5, 1981], I got all their autographs. This was before they started to get on my nerves, before I thought Tommy was a mean little fucker and Paul was an asshole to his crowd. I mean, we were all trying to make it, weren't we? But they didn't care. Paul was hesitant to give it to me but I insisted and when I looked at what he wrote he signed his name "Reg Presley." I remember thinking, "Who the fuck is that?"

Paul Westerberg: I don't think there's a whole lot going on in Minneapolis. There's the Suburbs, and a band that used to be called Loud Fast Rules—they're called Soul Asylum now—and then there's a couple sort of quasi-hardcore bands like Man-Sized Action and Rifle Sport. I'm not crazy about them, but they're my friends, so I feel like I should say something. A lot of people like 'em.[36]

Danny Murphy: There was definitely [a rivalry]. When they signed to Warner Bros., the Replacements signed first, but Hüsker Dü got a bigger advance. I remember sitting at the Twin/Tone office one day and Grant was like, "When the Replacements signed, they all wondered if they'd keep riding

bicycles or if they'd be able to maybe get cars. For us, we can get cars, it's just a matter of what kind do we want to buy?"

They were very, very competitive. I think it was fairly good-natured, but it was really two different schools of operating. Bob [Mould] was very career-driven and very much wanting to be the kingpin in the scene, and Paul didn't seem to really give a rat's ass about it. I would never see Paul at Hüsker Dü shows.

Terry Katzman: I think they were pretty friendly, really, but they definitely wanted to outdo each other. And those nights that they played together, that was like, "Wow, hold onto your seatbelts." I think they both might have blown each other off the stage at different points. I think it made them each better at what they were doing, but I think they become less related as the years go by. Which is a good thing, because they each had their great qualities. You never would want to say one was better than the other—they were both great for many different reasons.

Danny Murphy: Initially I was pretty—not in awe, really—but pretty moved and aspired to be that good and tenacious. The first couple years, I didn't think our band could ever compete, and then when we got successful ten years later, we'd go over to Japan and read some fuckin' Bob Mould interview and they were both [Mould and Westerberg] very dismissive of it. It was just sour grapes, mostly.

And the thing that they could gripe about is timing. The Replacements and Hüsker Dü were too early. I don't think Hüsker Dü ever made a record that sounded good enough to be on the radio, and the Replacements self-destructed before they [could have mainstream success]. But that's why people are still talking about 'em. You know, if they'd had platinum records and opened for Matchbox 20 [as Soul Asylum did], they wouldn't be as interesting.

Dave Ayers: If as many people saw the Velvet Underground as say they did now, [the Velvet Underground would] have a Saturday morning cartoon show.

Paul Stark: Ten years ago, there was a lot more interest in the Replacements. [In 2007] when it comes to interest in Twin/Tone, most of the recognition is for Soul Asylum. In recent years, when I get phone calls, it's Soul Asylum first, the Jayhawks second, and the Replacements a distant third. I get one or two a year now; ten years ago, it was one a week.

The kids out there now are much more interested in commercial success. Even though you find a lot of musicians who were inspired by them, you're now finding more local Minnesota people inspired by Soul Asylum's success story. You know, you see Winona Ryder with the lead singer in *People* magazine when you're eight, nine years old and you want to be a musician, and you see Paul Westerberg having problems putting a band together and touring and stuff, it's pretty easy to see which one you want.

Bob Mould: For me, personally, I think the influence would be more when Paul and myself would get together with Peter Jesperson at his place and sit and drink and do other stuff and listen to records and everybody would pull out stuff and play music for each other. That's the kind of stuff—more than Paul writing "Kids Don't Follow" and me saying, "Well I should write a song like that"—that influences you. It's more the personal things, like when Pete Buck first plays Nick Drake for you, it sticks with you. Or when Peter would play something and Paul and I would both perk up and go, "Whoa."

Grant Hart: Was there a rivalry? Put it this way: At the Rock For Karl thing [a benefit for late Soul Asylum bassist Karl Mueller in 2005], that was the closest I'd ever seen, in memory, to there being any kind of real tension. I was anxious to do it to be on the bill; Mould was anxious to do it because of what I perceived as some kind of rock-star B.S. between him and Westerberg. It was almost like Bob was gleeful to do it, because he was going to take Westerberg down a peg. And there was some obvious childishness going on. Westerberg and I were just acquainted through the music, and he was just bending over backwards to be friendly to me, like "I'll show Mould, I'll be really nice to Grant."

Ana Voog: All of my friends thought Tommy was so cute, but the person I always watched was Bill Sullivan. He was a roadie for the Replacements, and he would crouch behind their amps ready to put the mic stand back up when it fell down. I thought he was so sexy with his tossled Syd Barrett-y curly hair and scruffy look. But I never could catch his eye until almost a decade later and we went on a few dates. I loved his super intent look, twinkling eyes, and wry smile. In fact, I think it was because of him that I went and bought a pair of engineer boots, which are still my favorite boots to this day and are now all worn-in like his were at the time.

69

Danny Murphy: Karl [Mueller] and me were driving from Madison with [the Replacements] one night, and everybody was getting pretty fuckin' debauched. Bill Sullivan's driving, and Bob's sitting in the first row behind him, and he just covers up both of [Sullivan's] eyes on the freeway for like fifteen seconds. Everyone in the van was like, "This could be how it ends." Sully had his hands on the steering wheel, and he was like, "Are you sure this is how you want it to go, man? Is this what you want?"

Mary Lou Philipp Westerberg: I used to worry a bit when they were out traveling and doing the things that they did on stage and everything else.

Jim Mars: Chris would tell me that Paul would always yank the steering wheel when Bill Sullivan was driving. He said that those guys were in a van one time, driving from city to city, and they were bored out of their skulls. Chris grabs this fly out of the air. Bob was sleeping. He shakes it up, hits Bob, Bob wakes up, he sees this fly in Chris' hand, and Chris pulls a hair from his long hair, ties his hair somehow around the fly, and he times it for just when Bob woke up, and it flew around like a helicopter. Bob just flipped out: "How the hell did you do that?!"

Peter Jesperson: What occurred to me immediately was, "It's all there." It wasn't like, "This is good, and they've got to work on this"—everything was great already. And that was so overwhelming. It was almost like, "Is someone playing a joke on me? I really have the opportunity to work with this?" I kept expecting someone to come out of the bushes and say, "Ha! Ha! We were just kidding. This band has already been signed to Warner Bros." or something.

Paul Stark: Peter brought a demo tape over to the Twin/Tone headquarters, which was in my basement [445 Oliver Avenue in north Minneapolis] at the time.

Peter Jesperson: I told Paul Stark we had to do an album with these guys right away, and he said, "Peter, calm down. We have to do a single first, and see how it goes." I said, "I think it's bigger than that, Paul." He said, "Well let's do some recording and see what we come up with." And we went [to Blackberry Way Studios, a converted home in Dinkytown] in July '80 and did some two-track stuff and they knocked off fifteen songs in a half an hour or forty-five minutes. I remember Paul Stark looking at me and going, "OK, you're right. I guess we're talking album."

Curtiss A: I love Paul Stark now, but he was a nimrod. When we were recording [the song] "Sinister Forces," I wanted to put maracas in the middle of it. So I said, "You know, like on [the Rolling Stones'] 'Jumpin' Jack Flash.'" He goes, "What exactly is 'Jumpin' Jack Flash'?"

Paul Westerberg: Fuck, I think "Jumpin' Jack Flash" was written about me. I put myself in all the songs I love. The singer's singing to me, y'know?[37]

Lori Barbero: Paul's extremely sentimental, and that's something else I really admire about him. He remembers.

Tracie Will: I just remember [Paul] drumming all the time. I don't remember him ever taking out the trash, though. See, maybe he never did? You can have it on good record that his next-door neighbor never saw him take out the trash. But my mom has an autographed copy of *Sorry Ma* because I think she used to complain about the drumming.

Rock at Walker

Two Twin Cities rock bands, Curtiss A (fronted by Curt Almsted) and the Replacements, will perform at the Walker Art Center Saturday at 8 p.m.

Clip from *Minneapolis Tribune.*
Courtesy Peter Jesperson

Paul Stark: Peter was A&R, and I was more the technical side. So my questions were more, "Can they tour, how stable is the band, what kind of organization/management [operation is it], how much are we going to have to train them, how much work is it gonna be?" The question of their talent was Peter's job, mine would have been to see if these were guys we could work with, or is this an impossible, insane thing to do? I had no idea what would happen, but we'd had success with the Suburbs and it was worth gambling.

Willie Wisely: I walked into Oarfolkjokeopus on the day *Sorry Ma* was released, looking for my usual—anything in the used-vinyl section with an

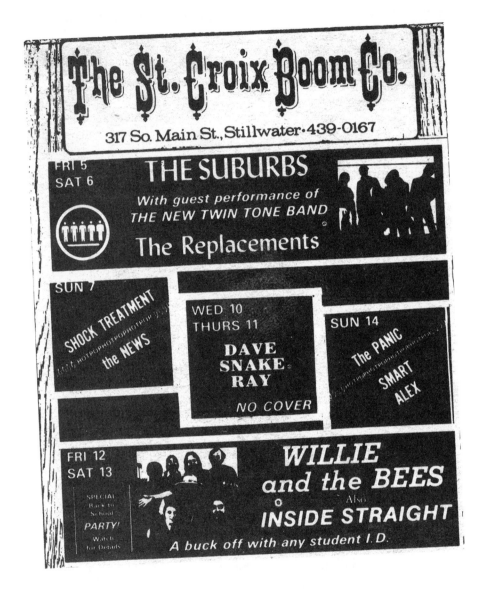

Ad for Suburbs/'Mats show at the St. Croix Boom Co. (Stillwater, Minnesota). *Sweet Potato*, September 30, 1980. *Courtesy Peter Jesperson*

Apple Records logo on it—when the clerk, Peter Jesperson, pointed out to me that today I should really think about buying something different. Well, me being in eleventh grade, and those clerks being the six hippest guys in the Midwest, I listened.

Peter Jesperson: The Suburbs were big shit, and everybody thought [Curtiss A] was going to make a splash, and Flamingo was a big deal, but everyone thought the Replacements were "Oh, that band with the twelve-year-old bass player." I think people thought they had potential, but I had to push to get stuff done and we'd go into Blackberry Way between bands that were actually paying with cash, so it took a while to make the record. We started in September, and it took six or seven months. We'd just get studio time when we could. It was wildly exciting. You'd hit "record" and they'd play like they were playing in front of an arena full of screaming fans.

Willie Wisely: The next day, I took my copy of *Sorry Ma* to Breck, my private high school, where generally, kids behaved, [but] that LP begat a couple months of skipping as many classes as possible, locked up in the music rehearsal room with an old turntable and my first bandmates-to-be, thinking about urinary infections.

Blake Gumprecht: I bought *Sorry Ma* at a record store in Lawrence, Kansas, before I had ever heard of the band, so it was a complete shot in the dark that changed my life.

Peter Jesperson: I remember sitting in the control room, calling out songs, and they'd do 'em and we'd record 'em. Tommy was in town [Los Angeles] yesterday [spring of 2007], and he came to the office [of New West Records, where Jesperson is now vice president of A&R], and I showed him this box I'd just had shipped from Minneapolis. His jaw just fucking dropped: There's the *Sorry Ma* tapes and all of our notes, my handwriting and Paul [Westerberg]'s handwriting and [engineer] Steve Fjelstad's handwriting. All the song titles and sequences and notes and all this stuff.

Dave Ayers: It's still my favorite [Replacements record]. It's the best American punk rock record ever. I've always felt that way. Song after song, in terms of capturing that thing—pure octane, terrified and fearless at the same time . . . leap into the future of whatever. . . . All that stuff that's wrapped up

in that moment in time of being a nineteen-year-old kid. I don't think [Westerberg] was ever stepping back and reflecting. Everything was very much in the moment, and it all sounded kind of reckless.

Ryan Cameron: I was hired by Twin/Tone to help do displays in the local record stores for *Sorry Ma*. I did a window at Hot Licks [a record store on Hennepin Avenue, in downtown Minneapolis] where I worked that was just a metal garbage can heaped with garbage [and] posters surrounding it. Even on the E Block, it raised some eyebrows.

Peter Jesperson: I remember one night they were really on a roll, and I was trying to keep 'em going, because we could have recorded every definitive version for the album right that second. What do you make 'em do next? You're not gonna get ten songs off 'em, but you can get two or three *right now*. And I said, "Kick Your Door Down," and they crashed into it, instantly. And it was phenomenal, and that's the version that's on the album. That was one that was so new that I don't think it was being considered for the record. It was so spontaneous.

Paul Westerberg: One of the standing jokes in the band is that we're not musicians, and we're sorta proud of that in that we don't wanna be. It's like, we can try to play music and try to play it tight, but we just don't have any fun, and then one day Chris said, "I hate fuckin' music, it's fuckin' crap". . . . [We improvised it] in the basement, we recorded it in the studio, but it was just like that—Chris said "let's do a song called I Hate Music [*sic*]", and Tommy went dadadada on the bass, and we all came in, and it was done in five minutes.[38]

Dave Ayers: It was one of the first records I reviewed for *The [Minnesota] Daily*. I was really curious about [Paul], because it was so profound in this really simple way. Right before *Stink* came out, I kept bugging Peter to see if I could do an interview with Paul, or a series of interviews, to try to figure out what it was all about.

Bob Stinson: [Being in the studio] is like being in the hospital. Everything's really clean.[39]

Paul Stark: Peter and I played good cop/bad cop. If someone had to be scolded, or someone had to be reckoned with, I was the one who did it—

whether it be money or recording or whatever. So I was always the fall guy. I was always the bad guy. The betterment of Twin/Tone and the betterment of the group was the overall goal, and those guys just were not capable of managing themselves.

They could barely hold themselves together to show up to the gigs, let alone the recording studio. Creative ideas, plenty, but as far as organizational skills . . . Chris Mars had some, and Tommy had hopes of it, but Paul and Bob really were rebelling against it.

Dave Ayers: Paul Westerberg is likable. Even on stage during his worst, shrug-shouldered, grumbling, half-drunks, he's magnetic and a little disarming. He's the same over his Manhattan at the CC Club—shy, a little smart-assed, a little mumbly. It's not that he's got a trumped-up, angry stage persona; he's still sorting himself out. He takes great pains to be honest, even if that means contradicting himself at times as he does in his conversation and in his music. In his words, "sometimes my mind goes a hundred different ways at once." He wasn't speaking on the topic at the time, but that's a pretty fair description of a young man trying to come to grips with his own raw genius. [40]

Tommy Stinson: I didn't know how to write songs before I met him. He's a total influence. Who better to learn from than Paul Westerberg. I mean, come on, he's written some of the greatest songs of the '80s. People will remember these songs for years to come. I'm proud to be part of that legacy. I think, beyond all the shenanigans and shit, the songwriting really holds up well. [41]

Jim Peterson: Paul and Chris came in one time and took a copy of *Sorry Ma* downstairs [to the basement storage/rehearsal space of Oarfolkjokeopus] and broke it in half and left it there. It was maybe six months after the record came out, and I think they had decided that it sucked. Peter totally picked up on how suspicious they were acting, and found the broken record in the basement after they left. He really was steamed about it, and let them know in no uncertain terms, then made them pay for it. I still have that record.

Terry Katzman: We'd all go over to the CC [Club], drink a few beers, come back to the store, and close the till and go to Peter's and listen to records. The CC was so involved in everything. Mars was the one who used to hang out at the store the most, reading periodicals. They would drift in and out. We'd let them have free roam of the place, or at least Peter would.

FRI. + HALLOWEEN
Oct. 30 + 31, 1981

flamin' oh's

w/ SPECIAL GUEST
OPENING ACT
The
Replacements

UNION BAR
507 E. HENNEPIN

MUSIC STARTS AT
8:45

Handbill for Flamin' Oh's/'Mats shows at the Union Bar (Minneapolis), October 30–31, 1981, two months after *Sorry Ma*'s release. *Courtesy Peter Jesperson*

Paul was drunk one time, coming back from the CC, and he went up to the "Replacements" section in the store, reached his hand in and snapped the corners of like five copies of *Hootenanny*. Skunky [Tommy] might have been the instigator, but Paul was the actual wrecker, destroyer, platter-breaker.

He just crunched them all, and you could see 'em sticking out [of the rack], broken. Half of me was laughing, the other was, "You know, you're destroying property that's not yours." But you couldn't stop laughing. You know, it was good ol' Paul; it has "Westerberg" written all over it, his cunning and diabolical side. Peter was pretty steamed about it, and he gave Paul a pretty good dressing-down about it.

Lori Barbero: Paul [Westerberg] loved it. He loved every minute there was any controversy. That was like, devil in a red dress. And who else didn't get off on all that stuff? Seriously, it's the epitome of rock 'n' roll, at its finest.

Lianne Smith: Rock is made up of mixtures of "I Don't Give a Fuck" and "I Give More of a Fuck than Anyone Else on This Planet," and somehow Westerberg found the perfect proportions for a cocktail that got us all high.

Paul Stark: Paul and Bob were both smart and they both could have done just fine in that department, if they'd wanted to. But they obviously made a choice early on that they wanted to rebel against the establishment, whatever that represented to them. So Twin/Tone became an extension of that, and I was that extension.

Lori Barbero: They just didn't care. They did what came out of their minds and hearts and whatever. Knee-jerk reaction to whatever.

Kim Walsh: At the last minute on the day of the [September 28, 1981] show, [First Avenue manager] Steve McClellan asked the Neglecters and Replacements to open for the Ramones. I was pressed into service at the last minute. The excitement about being an opening act for the Ramones was pretty intense. We moved all the Neglecters' stuff in my little Chevette from Podany's [a practice space on East Lake and 27th Avenue] and then picked up the Replacements' stuff. The Chevette made a few trips with the tailgate wide open and I had to help haul speakers and crap up and down all the stairs. I know I didn't get a thank you, but that will come back to all of the parties involved when their children reach the teenage years.

Paul Westerberg: The best band in the world is up next, and if you don't think so, fuck ya. [42]

Jim Walsh: [S]ince some young lovers of good music can't legally be admitted into some of the aforementioned establishments, REMs, along with The Replacements, would now like to bring their "dance music with a message" into various high schools around the metro area. So, if you like to sweat while you dance, as do both of these bands when they dance/play, and if you've had it with your basic "let's-get-stoned-and-make-out-in-the-bleachers" kind of bands that may have passed through your auditorium or gym, give these two young bands a chance. Let's get real, rockin', boppin', revved-up rock n' roll back where it belongs: into the corridors of your high school! [43]

Kevin Martinson: [REMs] played with them [in 1981] at the Sons of Norway [a bank building in Uptown Minneapolis] for West High School's prom. It was bizarre: all these high school kids in tuxes and formal dresses, and us in our T-shirts and jeans and basic grunge. They wanted to dance, but we weren't really dance bands. It was before punk rock was mainstream, so it threw everyone for a loop.

The next night, we all played at Regina [an all-girls Catholic high school in South Minneapolis]. We used our P.A., and they didn't help carry a single speaker or anything. They were prima donnas; they had all these people who did that stuff for them. The next time we played with them at Regina [in 1983], they were making out with their girlfriends and drinking in the classrooms before the show, while the rest of us were getting ready and setting up.

Wally Marx: Hot, sunny, dry, late September day in 1981. Carl Sandburg Junior High [in Golden Valley, a Minneapolis suburb] had started a few weeks before but summer was still definitely here, which totally sucked because it was still great outside but we had to be locked up all day in this Eisenhower-era bomb-shelter of a school.

It was eighth grade, and punk rock was big. These were the days when you could still get major hassle for wearing a fucking Clash T-shirt, seriously. Culture at the time was so backwards that if you got a crew cut you'd get punched. Any hair that wasn't feathered, any pants that weren't Levi's, any shoes that weren't ASICS Tigers, any back pocket that didn't have a comb sticking out of it, was a clear signal that you were a threat to society. So, naturally, we all got crew cuts, army pants, and Converse All-Stars.

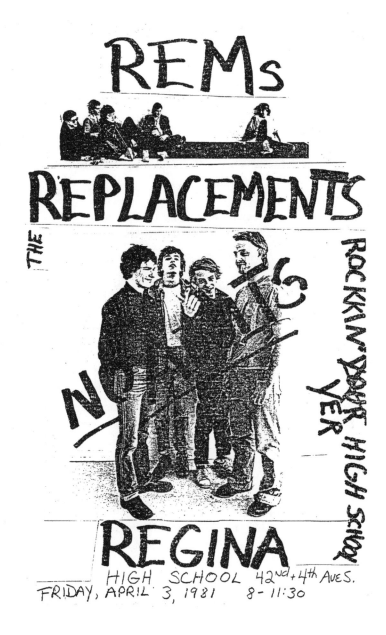

No Adults. Flyer for the REMs/'Mats April 3, 1981, show at Regina High, the erstwhile Catholic all-girls school in South Minneapolis. *Author collection*

We all had Sex Pistols albums, and Black Flag and Dead Kennedys were starting to make the rounds. I liked that stuff, but I had been brought up on a heavy dose of rock and roll. I liked the rebellion and aggression in punk, and I liked that it was definitely outlawed, get-you-in-trouble music. But in the end, I needed more *rock* in my punk.

There was a guy at school named Mike Attias—he was the king of the punks. His mom was French and, thus, permissive. He had every cool record and wore exactly what he wanted to which included black shirts, spiked wrist-bands, and Beatle boots. This is 1981, remember? So this guy was the para-mour of cool. We'd go to his house and listen to music and smoke Djarums.

Peter Jesperson: I remember cutting the acetate at Sound 80 [studio in Minneapolis], and Paul's scream on "Rattlesnake" actually threw a circuit breaker and stopped the cutting, and the cutting engineer at Sound 80 was so mad because he had to throw the acetate away and start again. He was an old guy, fifty or sixty. We kept telling him to push the volume, push the volume. We wanted it louder, louder, louder.

Wally Marx: One Monday, Mike comes into whatever class we had togeth-er and started talking about this band that he saw over the weekend, I think at some party or warehouse or something. He said they were fast and really loud, and that the songs were short. OK, three for three. Then he said that not only were they the best band he'd ever seen, but that they were from Minneapolis. Then he dropped the bomb: The bass player was thirteen or fourteen—our age. He turned to me and said, "You'd love 'em—you like rock and roll."

Peter Jesperson: I don't think Tommy even knew what was happening. I know [the release of their first single, "I'm In Trouble" b/w "If Only You Were Lonely," and *Sorry Ma*] was a big deal to them, but they wouldn't let on. And then there were all those clashing of ideas: Bob thinking Paul had taken his band away from him, Chris sitting quietly in the corner, drawing a cartoon or something.

Wally Marx: I begged Mike to make me a tape of their album, which he said he'd do that night. After a week of smuggling my contraband, new-technolo-gy Walkman into school in hopes of utilizing it, Mike finally showed up with the tape. His scrawled writing on the TDK label said "The Replacements (Mats): Sory Ma, Forgot to Take out THE Trash" [*sic*]. I held it in my hand and just kind of muttered, "Whoa." I held it in my pocket all day, with an eye on

my backpack, making sure no one kiped my precious lunchbox-sized portable, personal tape player.

Grant Johnson: I love the production on *Sorry Ma,* like how on "Takin' a Ride" the sound changes when he says, "radio blastin'."

Wally Marx: That afternoon I had practice for some sport. Probably football, maybe soccer. It was hot and dry and the ground was rock hard and the grass was tough and spiky. I can't remember why, but I missed the activities' bus home. Maybe because I was getting beat on in the locker room, maybe because the driver was a cock, well-known to take off without everybody on board. Who cared? I hated that jock-filled bus anyway.

Peter Jesperson: I had a lay-out of the artwork for *Sorry Ma* at Oarfolk, and when I wasn't looking they graffiti-ed it. The final artwork that was going to the printer. They drew a Hitler mustache on Chris on the insert, and I went, "You fuckheads. What are you doing? This is the photograph for your album cover and you've. . . ." Then I thought, "This is a perfectly Replacements-esque thing to do." I was mad for a second, then I laughed.

Wally Marx: I began the walk home, about a two- or three-miler. At the edge of the school ground I pulled out my Walkman and put in the tape and put the headphones on my head. Hoisted the backpack on and started walking. Pressed play.

> ### STAYRIGHTTHEREGONOFURTHER
> ### DONTGETADOCTORDONTGETMYMOTHER
> ### TOOFARTOWALKGOTTADECIDE
> ### TURNAROUNDWE'RETAKINARIDE

First thing I thought was, "OK, this guy is talking to me. Talking TO ME." The speed, the noise, the ROCK, told me, at the tender age of thirteen that *this was it, this was THE band.* Early on, I knew two things: that the lyrics were totally righteous, and that these guys were smokin' guitar players. And that drummer was definitely the fastest I had heard.

I kept walking and listening. I literally stopped walking—stopped in my tracks—when "Customer" came on, and I stood there on the sidewalk of Douglas Drive laughing my ass off. By the time ["I Bought a Headache"]

came on, I had one. The combination of the heat and the max volume of my headphones was giving me a real splitter. But the songs just kept coming. "Rattlesnake," "I Hate Music," "Otto." Then "Johnny." What a killer. At that point I rewound for the first time, listening maybe two or three times, something I still do to this day—just can't listen just once.

By the time my house was in sight the last few tunes were playing, "Raised in the City" and "Love You Till Friday." I walked in the house as it was ending, completely fried from the walk and the noise. Dropped my backpack, went down to my room, put the tape in the stereo, rewound, and listened to it again.

Craig Finn: I remember the liner notes to *Sorry Ma*. You know, "Could have been better if we'd tried harder." It was the first time, as a kid, I remember rock 'n' roll that was self-deprecating. And it was almost written in code: For "Something to Dü" it says, "Song for the Hüskers, our friends who have never taken drugs." I took that to mean that Hüsker Dü had never taken drugs. That's how far removed I was from the real thing.

Lori Barbero: I introduced Paul to Johnny Thunders [at Thunders' show at Sam's/First Avenue in 1981]. He was a huge, huge, huge Johnny Thunders fan and I used to know Johnny Thunders from when I lived in New York. He totally fucking didn't believe me, but when [Thunders] came to town I introduced them. Paul put out his hand and they shook hands and Paul couldn't even look at him. His tongue was just lying on the ground and everyone was stepping on it.

Jimi Nervous: "Johnny's Gonna Die" . . . conjures up grim prophecies concerning ex–New York Dolls guitarist Johnny Thunders, saying "Johnny always takes more than he needs . . . Johnny always needs more than he's got." You get the sense, though, that the band members themselves are aware that they are not immune to their own tale of excess and that the song could become a self-fulfilling prophecy.[44]

Paul Westerberg: When Johnny was playing, it looked like he was walking dead, it was pitiful, like watching a guy in a cage, it was like he didn't want to be up there, he was playing for pay.[45]

Jay Walsh: The weekend after *Sorry Ma* came out, we had this party in the hovel my brother and I had moved into on 36th and Harriet [in South

Minneapolis]. I think we started out making donuts on the stove and drinking Little Wally's. [Local art-rockers] Things That Fall Down were there and they didn't leave 'til 4 a.m. My girlfriend called the cops on our own party so we could get them out of the house. We called them "Things That Wouldn't Leave" after that.

Westerberg lived at his parents' house a few blocks away and he came and sat on the long radiator in the living room. We had *Sorry Ma* playing at 78 rpm when he came in. He grinned and said something like, "Sounds better this way." He looked bored and left pretty quickly. I always thought of that line from "Color Me Impressed" about people dressing funny at your party. I was into white T-shirts at the time. It had to be Things That Fall Down.

Peter Jesperson: The first time we went out of town was December of '80. We went to Duluth to open for the Suburbs. We probably did St. Cloud and then Sioux Falls, South Dakota. We played Madison, at a place called Merlyn's. And Milwaukee. And the first time we went to Chicago was with Hüsker Dü.

Lori Barbero: Years later, I found out the Replacements and Hüsker Dü had some big rivalry. I don't remember them saying anything about each other, because I don't absorb that kind of crap. I was friends with all of them, so maybe they just didn't shit-sling in front of me. Quite honestly, in the beginning, Replacements kicked butt on Hüsker Dü. Bob [Mould] always sang off-key. Now he's one of the greatest singers, but then I would just walk around going, "Ooh."

Brianna Riplinger: I am an only child. I do not pretend to know what the complex relationships between siblings feel like. But I think there is a direct correlation between that brotherly love/hate/competition relationship kinda thing and the relationships that exist in rock. Sometimes the intense sibling rivalry results in physical fights. But most of the time there is eye-rolling tolerance and unconditional love.

Jay Walsh: Paul and Bob [Stinson] got into a bloody fight one night on stage in the Entry. They were probably arguing over who was drunker or which song to do. They punched each other, rolled around on the stage and both got up bloody. Tommy and Chris kept whatever song they were playing going. Then they were like sailors reporting for duty, back at the mic and on lead guitar. I

Flyin' the flannel, circa 1982. Twin/Tone publicity photo shot at Duffy's (Minneapolis).
Author collection

Twin Tone
RECORDS
Twin Tone Records 445 Oliver Ave. So. Mpls., Mn 55405

The Replacements

think the set went OK after that, like they both needed to throw up and felt better after they did.

Bob Stinson: Some guy was fucking with me one night, and Paul stopped and started punching him. Me and Paul have had a couple tussles on stage before, too. One, he put a bottle (a broken wine glass) to my throat. The other one, I was playing a lead and he just stopped playing and jumped on my back and we started rolling around, and Tommy and Chris would not stop playing the song. Les Pauls and Strats, and just rolling around on the ground. It's pretty funny.[46]

Peter Jesperson: When *Sorry Ma* came out, Blake Gumprecht was at KJHK in Lawrence, Kansas, and he went crazy over the record. It went to number one on their playlist there, and they actually paid for us to come down there to do a show. We didn't have a booking agent, we couldn't, like, "route" ourselves down there, we just rented a vehicle and drove down.

Blake Gumprecht: I don't know the blues, but Westerberg's voice speaks the blues to me. Cigarette and whisky choked, it's rough, expressive, and so human. His unpretentious ability to capture the drunken loud and insane moments with the quiet and lonely, the frustrated with the angry, the smartass fun with the quiet empty solitude, is unmatched. There's a simplicity and honesty to his words that reminds me of Alex Chilton. He's no poet, his words just don't make it on paper, but when he spits 'em out . . . oh my. Soul.

To be honest, without Westerberg, the Replacements would be nothing. But for as much of a goon as Bob Stinson seems to be, his guitar speaks. Sometimes you wonder whether he has any idea of what he's doing, where his fingers are going even, or what he'd be like if he weren't stoned or drunk, but his bursting noise leads are sometimes chilling, and, somehow, almost always fit, y'know. It's all gone to the kids' heads a bit, but Tommy's nonetheless only gotten better on bass, like the rest of them, and Mars is as good a rock-n-roll drummer as you'll ever find. I'm moving to the Twin Cities in two weeks.[47]

Danny Murphy: I was nineteen and Karl [Mueller] was eighteen, and we shared a fake ID. We used to be able to get into Duffy's [on 26th and 26th in South Minneapolis] when we were underage, and they had strippers in the front room and they put [the Replacements] back in the back room. We saw

'em for the first time right after *Sorry Ma* came out. Bob had a fuckin' Silvertone P.A. system with a little light on the top for a guitar amp, and I just thought it was the weirdest shit in the world. It was like four guys that were completely in four different bands. It blew my mind. One night Bob wore a London Fog trench coat and was naked underneath. He looked like Chad Everett or something. I think it terrified Paul more than it amused him.

Jay Walsh: They played at Duffy's a lot, which was four blocks away from our practice space. Sometimes they used our rock room to practice in. I remember hauling their shit up the stairs one time. They kept their strings and wire cutters and other stuff in an army ammo tin and I thought, "These guys are tough." Once, Bob Mould and Paul and some other 'Mats were jamming with us after a gig in the rock room. Johnny Rath was our left-handed lead guitar player and his guitar was there. We snipped the strings off his Gibson and restrung it just so a right-handed Bob Mould could jam on it for one hour. Man, we were stupid star fuckers sometimes.

Grant Johnson: I was actually more of a Hüsker guy at the time. Hüsker Dü shows were amazing; Replacements a lot more hit or miss.

Jay Walsh: So I went down to Duffy's after practice one night with a guitar tuner and told them I wanted to tune their guitars before they played. They played out of tune almost all the time. Sometimes they'd start OK, then they'd beat the hell out of the guitars and spend countless boring, fruitless minutes trying to tune up. It was just dumb luck if all sixteen of their strings were ever tuned together.

After I'd tuned the guitars, Paul was suspicious and he came up and said, "Play a C." So I played a C chord and he hummed the same chord on a harmonica. He kinda shrugged and said. "OK. I guess." Like, "OK, maybe this being-in-tune bullshit will be something different."

Well, they went out and played and they sounded like an aircraft carrier. Big, magnificent, and in tune. I remember them exchanging looks with each other and shrugging. Like, "Wow, this is weird." After they played, Tommy said, "Man, we never sounded this good!" After maybe two years of playing around, they'd discovered that playing in tune could be fun too. But they reverted. I told them to buy their own fucking tuner. You could only baby-sit them so much.

Peter Jesperson: I still have the paperwork. It was signed by Anita and a notary public on 2/14/82. The specific language is that I was appointed "legal guardian in fact" [of Tommy Stinson].

Michael Welch: fIREHOSE came to town and was staying at our house on Lyndale, and Mike Watt was in the middle of the living room one night after their show, holding court and talking about how he had Tommy on his knee one night, crying about wanting to go home. You know, you couldn't have asked for a better babysitter than Mike Watt.

Peter Buck: Tommy seemed to quit the band, or wanted to quit the band, every other day when they first started touring. Can you imagine? He was like, fifteen or something.

Paul Westerberg: Tommy dropped out of tenth grade to go on tour. How many kids would die for that? They're sitting in a tenth-grade algebra class and Tommy's drinking from a bottle of Jack Daniels, going down the road. He's come out of it real good. If you weren't strong enough that would really screw you up. Like being a child circus performer or something.[48]

Lori Barbero: [Longhorn manager] Hartley Frank had a huge crush on Tommy. I was a waitress at the Longhorn, and [Frank] was gay and he drank fifteen chocolate cokes a day. He'd always be like, "Hey, why don't you bring your friend Tommy over for dinner?" He'd never invite just me over for dinner, but he'd always invite Tommy over for quote-unquote "dinner."

Linda Hultquist: There was a Turkish coffee place across the street from the Longhorn, and Tommy would go over there before they played and get wired on coffee. He'd also wear those basketball ankle weights around all day before [a show] so that he could jump higher [on stage].

Chrissie Dunlap: I remember Paul being really nervous backstage. He was always nervous before they played. And he always wanted an aspirin. Not hard-core drugs, just, "I need an aspirin."

Peter Jesperson: The first time we played Chicago, they played "Kids Don't Follow." It was the first time I'd heard it. I taped it on a boom box and we were driving back through snowy cold Wisconsin the next day, and it was one of

those moments where you just think, "This is my favorite song." It was instant. So I just begged Paul [Stark] and [Twin/Tone co-founder] Charlie [Hallman] to let us record some more, and they were really opposed to it.

Lori Barbero: I was there, at that warehouse party [the live recording of which opens *Stink*]. I'm the one who goes "Whoo!" at the beginning. I remember the Replacements being set up on the floor, and the cops coming, and there were only twenty-five, thirty people there. I was a little lit, and I was like, "You have to be kidding me. This is the most terrorizing thing going on in Minneapolis tonight?"

Paul Westerberg: The police said they could hear it from eight blocks away or something. I don't believe that, but they surrounded the place. ["Kids Don't Follow"] wasn't live; the actual police dialogue and the people yelling was authentic, but the song was live in the studio so we just tacked that on for effect. Everybody thinks it's fake; it doesn't sound real just the way it kicks in. We were pussies; we slunk away with everyone else when the police said, "OK, time to leave."[49]

Lori Barbero: That's Dave Pirner screaming ["Fuck you, man!"] at the beginning of "Kids Don't Follow."

Don Holzschuh: It was at the Harmony Building on 3rd Street and 2nd Avenue North [in the warehouse district of downtown Minneapolis]. We had a rent party at our studio there [in 1980], where the L73 and the Warheads and the Replacements were going to play. There were pictures of Stalin everywhere. About 500 people showed up right at bar closing. The cops came—twenty-two squad cars. It was on the fifth floor, so they had to climb up five stories and they were out of wind when they shut it down. And Katzman was doing sound and he recorded the whole thing.

Peter Jesperson: I said, "Look. We'll do [the EP] really inexpensively. I'll fuckin' hand-stamp jackets if I have to." Damned if they didn't take me up on that. So for the first run of *Stink*, we hand-stamped the jackets at Oarfolk, and we did some at the Modesto [Jesperson's apartment building, one block east of Oarfolk]. We had one stamp for the front that said, "The Replacements Stink 'Kids Don't Follow' plus seven" and the back, with the song titles and credits and Twin/Tone logo. We had three stamps. Paul did some hand-drawings on some, so there's some collectors' items floating around.

We recorded it fast, and we did it on the Q.T. With *Sorry Ma*, everybody knew about the songs and everything before it came out, and I remember Paul was really unhappy about it. He said, "Let's do this in a way that nobody knows what we're doing."

Dave Ayers: Before *Stink* came out, I interviewed Paul at Peter's apartment. As far as I know, it was the first in-depth interview with him. It was the first serious interview either one of us had done. Neither one of us really knew what we were doing. I remember the night going on very, very long, and Paul going from being awkward and not very forthcoming to, once he got the idea that I was actually seriously interested and we were having a serious conversation, it ended up being a fairly lengthy and pleasant conversation.

They played me all sorts of stuff I was never supposed to hear, and so transcribing the [interview] tape, I had all these still-unreleased songs with us talking over them. It made Peter nervous for years, but I've long since lost track of what the hell happened to those tapes.

Linda Hultquist. I was Peter's girlfriend at the time, and there were plenty of nights of staying up all night in his apartment with the whole band there. Tommy was never going to drink. He stayed clean during that whole initial part. I don't think he drank for a long time. He said, "I've seen what it's done to my brother, and I just don't want to do it." It didn't last, of course.

Craig Finn: What about "Dope Smokin' Moron?" Were they anti-weed? I thought everyone did that back then.

Terry Katzman: [Westerberg] may have been anti-weed; I certainly don't remember partaking in anything like that with him. He liked to drink. That was his thing. Though on "I Bought a Headache," he's obviously smoked before. That's first-person: "Smoking marijuana until it's coming out of my ears." You wouldn't likely write a line like that if you hadn't had some experience with it.

Peter Jesperson: I don't remember Paul reading at all, apart from the music mags and the occasional rock biography that floated around the van from time to time. Bob was the voracious reader of the band; he was always reading the music publications and weeklies we'd pick up in various cities.

Blackberry Way Recording Studios, Inc.
606 13TH AVENUE S.E. · MINNEAPOLIS, MINNESOTA 55414 · (612) 378-2466

Client ~Replacements~   Date 3/13/82

Track No: 4   Time 1:25   Title Fuck School

1	2	3	4	5	6	7	8
Kick	F	R	↓	↑	LOH	ROH	Guitar
9	10	11	12	13 Scream	14	15	16
Bass A,	Bass II	b Guitar	Voc	Voc Group	Voc Group		
17	18	19	20	21	22	23	24

Blackberry Way Studios session notes for "Fuck School," March 13, 1982. *Courtesy Peter Jesperson*

Linda Hultquist. I was certainly the only person at those all-night parties taking books off the shelf and trying to make people read things. At 3 a.m. I was going, "Take this home and read it." All sorts of things that people never read; I don't think I ever got Westerberg to read anything, but I think they thought they could talk to me about stuff other than music. A lot of times I was the only girl left standing at three in the morning, and to a certain extent I felt protective of them in a way, but not to any extent I could have done anything about it. Westerberg was an awfully smart cookie, and well on his way to thinking what he was going to think.

Peter Jesperson: So we booked the studio time under a fake name, and went in on the Q.T. We tracked everything in one session, did a couple vocal overdubs, and mixed it. It was done in a week. And with *Sorry Ma*, the rest of the band wasn't around for the final mixing. Paul and I ended up mixing it and finishing it, and this time the other guys were like, "Hey, we want to be around for this one."

They were around for one of the [*Stink*] mix sessions, and [engineer Steve] Fjelstad banished them from the mix session, just because when you had them all in one room, they became the Monkees or whatever.

We really kept it on the Q.T. And when the record came out, in June of '82, I believe [Minneapolis critic] Marty Keller wrote something like, "The Replacements have a new record coming out next week. How did this happen without anyone knowing it?" We managed to keep it quiet, and I remember

being really happy about that. When it came out, he gave it an A-plus, and wrote, "One of the greatest records to ever come out of the land of 10,000 guitars."

Doug Simmons: Unlike English punks, the majority of them working-class, America's hardcore youth and near-youth are generally well-to-do students, many of them in college, mooching off mom and dad and listening to numbers like "Fuck School." The only job worry they might harbor is the thought of having to get one. "God Damn Job" inspired me to search my collection for a hardcore song that approaches the explicitness of the Clash's "Career Opportunities" or any number of Crass or Oi tunes since. I couldn't find one. The Replacements are feeling the pinch of Reagan's missile-heavy budget, a preparation for war that Hüsker Dü are already railing against with astounding fury. Minneapolis has produced two great punk LPs. Hüsker's *Land Speed Record* and the Replacements' *Trash*, with *Stink* as a bonus. Boston's hardcore scene, by comparison, has been embarrassingly unproductive.[30]

Courtesy Peter Jesperson

City Pages:

Mark His Words!
Finally, someone with balls stands up and exposes local radio programming for the cancer it is. Thanks for an excellent piece. Let's hope someone will listen.

Now, I'd like to turn my attention to the incredible letter from Mark McHugh in the Dec. 23 issue of *City Pages*. McHugh sounds like he once went to see the Hüskers and stayed just long enough to hear them tune up. He claims that they are utterly devoid of hooks, tunes, beat, or singing worth a damn, as well as being "too cool" to talk to their fans. Wassamatter, Mark? Never heard "In

a Free Land" or "Old Milwaukee" (hooks), "Diane" or "Data Control" (tunes), "MTC" (beatus maximus) or "Ultracore" (singing worth your life)? And as for being "too cool" to talk to the crowd, collar Bob, Greg or Grant at the bar if you want conversation, not on the stage.

There is one point in McHugh's letter that I agree with. Although The Hypstrz have been the recipients of numerous reviews and items in *City Pages*, nothing gives the old publicity a shot in the arm like a cover story. Ditto REMs and L-73.

One last thing, Mark. Anyone with half an ear knows that The Replacements are not a hardcore band. They are, however, the best fucking rock 'n' roll band in the world! Just like the Hüskers are the best fucking hardcore band in the world!

Lou Santacroce
Mpls.

Du To-Du Redux
Re: "Du Don't Do It" (Letters, Dec. 23). To Mr. Mark McHugh: Drop dead, hosehead.
Tony Pucci
Mpls.[51]

CHAPTER 2

When It Began

Hi, we're the Replacements
Hi, we're the Replacements
Hi, we're the Replacements
And we're playing in a rock 'n' roll band
We're having a good time
We're having a good time
We're having a good time
Rock 'n' rollin' 'til the break of dawn

Hey, where's Tommy? Someone find Tommy
We're out on the road
Moving equipment, where's the equipment?
Soon we're going home

Then we'll have a party
Then we'll have a party
Then we'll have a party
Rock 'n' rollin' 'til the break of dawn
Hi, we're the Replacements
Hi, we're the Replacements
Hi, we're the Replacements
And we're playing in a rock 'n' roll band

—They Might Be Giants, "We're the Replacements

Bobby Stinson's guitar. Leif Larsen of Minneapolis owns the Hamer that Bob smashed in May 1984 (while wearing a tutu) at Grinnell College, Iowa, reportedly because the 'Mats were given the opening slot for Minneapolis accordion rockers the Wallets. © *Eric Dregni*

Chris Osgood: In 1983 I was working as a guitar teacher at Knut-Koupée Music in South Minneapolis. At the time there was a luthier from California working at Knut-Koupée named, coincidentally, Tommy Stinson. The joke at the time was that the Replacements' Tommy Stinson [a frequent visitor to the repair shop at Knut] broke the instruments and Tommy Stinson fixed the instruments. In the *Hootenanny* era, Tommy and Tommy's encounters occurred about weekly.

Bob shreds at Harriet Island, St. Paul, 1983. © *Joan E. Bechtold*

Bob, Harriet Island, St. Paul, 1983. © *Joan E. Bechtold*

It was not surprising to, early one week, have Tommy and Bob come into the shop with the pieces of a white 1965 Gibson Firebird guitar in their hands. What was startling was that the whites of Bob's eyes were bright, bloody red. They had played a gig the weekend before in Lawrence, Kansas. During sound check Bob did one of his usual stage moves and grabbed the mic stand to use like a giant slide, getting a nice, big noisy effect out of his overdriven guitar and amp. The other guys noticed that Bob stopped playing and couldn't let go of the guitar or the stand. After about ten seconds Bob fell forward onto his guitar and everyone realized he was getting shocked.

Bob went to the hospital.

When Tommy and Bob came in, they showed us how Bob had fallen, twisting the neck of the guitar into three pieces, breaking on either side of where his hand was. More amazingly, Bob held up his hand to show all of us the six burn lines across his left palm where the strings had seared him before they snapped.

We all agreed the shock would have killed a lesser person, but not bull Bob. The guitar did not recover.

Bill Flanagan: Maybe that's where new wave got lost. When they all started playing Strats. The Replacements' tone is a Les Paul tone—thick and dirty.[1]

Lori Barbero: I lived with Bobby for four years in the early '80s. We lived on Lake Street and James [Avenue], right above this place called Rolling Soles. He lived a very simple life. Every day, he'd listen to the Sweet. He'd play his guitar forever and ever, then he'd go fishing in that little channel between Lake of the Isles [and Lake Calhoun]. Then, because he knew [the train schedule], he'd run back, throw his fishing poles and tackle box down, grab his beer, and go sit by where the Greenway [walking and bicycling path] is now and watch the train.

Peter Jesperson: Linda Hultquist was my girlfriend at the time. "Color Me Impressed" was a Linda-ism. She used to say that: "Oh, color me impressed, Paul." I think she had a really huge influence on Paul in a lot of ways. Clearly, she was smart as a whip, and Paul was really impressed with her, and the fact that this woman was an academic, somewhat of an intellectual, liking him, gave him confidence from another side that he might not have had otherwise. When he wrote the song, Linda and I were just laughing: *Here's this thing you say, and the guy turned it into a damn song.*

Lori Barbero: The Replacements played with the Plasmatics at the Longhorn one night, and Tommy was fourteen or fifteen. I was like his big sister, but I didn't treat him like a little kid. He was more grownup than most of the guys at that bar. But Wendy O. Williams, with her duct-tape breasts and whatever she was wearing, was chasing Tommy around the bar all night long. He was so scared. I mean, here's this super-vixen, bleached-blonde, going, [in Vampirella voice], "Hey kid, get over here." Finally, I said to her, "Look, you're like thirty years old, and this kid is fourteen. You need to back off." She picked up a chair and whipped it at me.

Peter Jesperson, 1984. © *Daniel Corrigan*

Peter Jesperson: In the early touring days we tried the floor thing sometimes just to save money, even though the 'Mats weren't really suited to it, they were always a bit separate from the pack, didn't have the spirit of camaraderie that was so prevalent with other touring bands of the day. But we did stay with Julie Farman, who booked The Rat in Boston. She was great. And Danny Amis and friends or relations of Bill Sullivan's in Hoboken, New Jersey. [Replacements roadie] Tom Carlson's girlfriend had a sister who had a spare room in her Manhattan apartment. My best pal, Steve Klemz, had moved to Washington, D.C., and put some of us up when we were there. Various R.E.M.-ers and their girlfriends in Athens, Georgia. We stayed with the guys from Big Black in Chicago. Curt Scheiber, who ran the cool record store in Columbus, Ohio, let us stay at his house for days at a time when we were playing shows in that area. I remember he had a huge library of movies on videotape, which really helped while away the hours of downtime. We got hotels or motels most of the time.

RJ Smith: Everyone on the tour collects a per diem, usually $15, though either a packed house or an empty one the night before can alter that. Twin/Tone fronted the group $500 to get out of town, which, along with the take from each show, is what the Replacements are rolling on. A band like the Replacements can expect to make anywhere from $200 to $1250 a gig. Once in a while—a single time in the week I traveled—Jesperson sends money home, to pay off the studio time, the pressing and mastering of the record, the van. But after springing for hotel rooms (this is the first tour the Replacements have not depended on the kindness of strangers for lodging) and gas and instrument and van repairs, there isn't much scratch left. What they save up from their per diem is what the band members will take home. Out of this is born various strategies for economizing. Bob will politely ask anyone to buy him a drink. Paul sometimes eats about three bites a day. Occasionally there's a splurge—a band buy of food, say, or a case—which comes out of what Jesperson's been holding.[2]

Tommy Stinson: RJ Smith came with us on the road and saw how we slept, how we drank, how we loved each other, how we loved the band. He took it and made it look like something ugly.[3]

Peter Buck: They stayed with me for five days at my house in Athens [Georgia]. When they left, there were empty beer bottles and records out of the jackets everywhere. As their van was pulling away, they stopped and Paul rolled down the window and said, "Uh, Peter? You might want to throw

everything out of the refrigerator. Bob's been opening up all the condiments and pissing in them everywhere we stay." So I did; haven't been able to eat mayonnaise since. And for weeks later I was getting phone calls at all hours. Young girls' voices: "Is Paul there? Is Tommy there?" Apparently they got a lot of phone numbers.

Craig Finn: The other morning [in 2007], I woke up and called up [Dave] Ayers and said, "Did the Replacements get chicks?" You know, I just wondered if they were the kind of band that got girls, or if they even cared. And there was a pause, and he said, "They got exactly the chicks you'd wanna get, and nothing more." Which I took to mean, if it wasn't high-quality, it would just be a hassle. Which I thought was really cool.

Michael Hafitz: It has been over a month on the road. Gigs have been pretty steady for the most part, but during the last week they've been holed up in Boston, not practicing anything but hanky panky and doing a miserable job of staying out of trouble. Tommy Stinson, the 16-year-old bassist, pouts that he got kicked out by his hostess, "just for pokin'."[4]

Bob Stinson: We never ate before we played, so the deli tray was [tossed]. Then you didn't want to eat when you were done because you wanted to screw and do a couple lines of this or that. So we ended up being fast microwave boys. I mean that's the only time me and Paul ever ate. You'd go walking through the crowd and have a few drinks. We had nice dressing rooms (if you really want to know) and none of us ever used 'em. We'd sit in different corners of the bar, and "Pete, what time do we go on?" He'd tell us and we'd like come from different parts of the bar.[5]

Peter Jesperson: Linda and I lived together at the Modesto. She did lights for the Commandos and Suburbs. She was so smart, and so funny. She was incredibly stimulating to be around. She was not like any girl I had ever met. You know how sexy intelligence is? That's the crazy thing: not just a *Playboy* magazine thing. I couldn't stand it. And I think Paul was attracted to her for that same way. He wasn't trying to get in her pants or anything, even though everyone was sleeping around.

We hung out a lot. When Paul would come over to listen to records or whatever, she was there. She was there from the very beginning. They were close right away.

Dave Ayers: Peter had that free-association thing when he'd play records for you. He'd be so excited to share thirty new things with you, and Paul certainly was the beneficiary of that and was exposed to tons of stuff. Some of it I'm sure he had no time for, but some of it had to stick. Those [all-night listening] sessions were fueled by substances and enthusiasm and then, you know, "the Only Ones."

Paul Stark: I just recorded *Hootenanny* with the [Twin/Tone] mobile unit [a 24-track recording set-up on wheels]. I didn't pay myself, because we didn't have the money at the time. Because it was my unit, I was cutting the hours [charged back to the band]. They got away with murder on the project.

Peter Jesperson: The very first *Hootenanny* tracks were done at this practice space that the Suburbs had in Roseville. We started recording, and we weren't sure what was going to happen, because there were songs like "Junior's Got a Gun," and "Shoot Me, Kill Me," which became "Sex with a Goat." And "Willpower" came around.

"Ben": Buck Hill is exactly what its name says, just a hill. Its runs are way too small and the park is so small its [*sic*] not even worth walking to. The scenery is the freeway. (ugly) I do not recommend going here unless you realy [*sic*] love a palce [*sic*] with short line [*sic*] at the lifts (because no [*sic*] bothers with this place). I would recommend going to Hyland instead which is about 10 min. away.[6]

Keri Carlson: One of the most renowned surf bands of the 1960s is a Minneapolis group, The Trashmen. "On 'Radio Rumpus Room' [a roots-rock specialty show heard on KFAI-FM in Minneapolis—St. Paul], The Trashmen are our heroes," [co-host Ron] Thums said.

The Trashmen were greatly influenced by the early rock 'n' roll found in dance halls, as well as their [Dick] Dale records. The band, which started in 1962, actually went to California to establish a sound that would set it apart at home. While the members were there, Thums said, they attempted surfing, and one of them nearly drowned.

In February 1964, The Trashmen's "Surfin' Bird" hit No. 4 on the pop charts.

"It would have gone to No. 1," Thums said, "but The Beatles came out with 'I Want to Hold Your Hand' and stole the spot." The peak of popularity for

Coffman Union, University of Minnesota, 1983. *Mark Boquist photo*

surf bands began around 1962 and ended in 1964; "[The Beatles] stopped surf music," Thums said.

A second wave of surf music arose in the late 1970s, and Minnesota was again a big part of it. The Overtones brought surf to the punks and new wavers at the Longhorn, a club famous for its role in shepherding the birth of Minnesota punk rock. Danny Amis, of the Overtones, (who now plays in Los Straitjackets) wrote "Calhoun Surf," a song The Ventures eventually covered.[7]

Slim Dunlap: The Trashmen were like giant superstars to us. I saw them many times. "Surfin' Bird" just hit you like a ton of bricks—it was so damned weird. All of the other songs of the time had these chants that were about dances, like "Foot Stompin'." But then you heard this thing—"ba-ba-ba-ba-bird is the word"—and you thought, "What the fuck is that?"[8]

Peter Jesperson: Bob was MIA so ["Buck Hill"] was recorded as a trio, hence the writing credit Westerberg-Stinson-Mars. We'd been talking about surf music for some reason so Westerberg, contrarian that he is, said we ought to start a "Ski Music" movement. We did the vocals on another day when it was just Paul, Chris & I. I distinctly remember the three of us, gathered around a microphone, pretending we had poles in our hands and swaying our hips from side to side as if we were skiing, laughing our heads off and shouting "Buck Hill!" during the appropriate breaks. You can hear Chris screaming and his voice trailing off in a guttural sort of way at the end.

Paul Stark: We had the mobile unit in a rehearsal space that did not have a window going into the space. So I would sit in the truck, and I couldn't see what was going on in the studio. They would switch around: Paul would get on the drums, and Chris would play guitar, and all of a sudden the levels would be all over the place. We rolled it out and just had fun.

Peter Jesperson: We drove to Duluth to do a show with the Suburbs, and we had a bottle of whiskey in this car we'd borrowed. Paul got pretty loopy, and we got into this place called Grandma's, and Paul was liquored up enough so that he pulled me aside and said, "I gotta tell you, I wrote the best line I've ever written and I have to tell you what it is."

I said, "What's that?"

He said, "I could live without your touch if I could die within your reach."

I stood there amongst all these people, bar people, and Suburbs people, going, "Wow."

Paul Stark: Bob Stinson came to the [*Hootenanny* recording sessions] with three beers in him, and we realized his lead guitar playing was best between his fifth and seventh beer, and after the seventh he was worthless. If he hadn't had the four, he was worthless as well. That was a six-month period during his life that that was true; it probably wasn't true before then, and it probably wasn't true after that.

Luke Zimmerman: I love the bottle knocked over and dismantled ending of "Treatment Bound."

Peter Jesperson: We tried to record "You're Getting Married," and I remember Bob just moping. I think Bob always resented Paul, because it had been his band. And somewhere around that time, Paul had started to give me tapes of solo stuff that he was doing in the basement of his parents' house. Guitar and piano things. And it was really on the Q.T., and he swore me to secrecy, and "Don't tell the band." He was especially embarrassed to have Bob hear any of that stuff.

Paul Stark: On *Hootenanny*, I became what I kind of consider a partner with them. I was doing weird stuff and showing them things that could be done in the studio, and they were learning what they could get away with. I saw myself as a teacher more than anything, so from my point of view that was the perfect time to interject whatever influence I had on them.

Peter Jesperson: One time there was this song called "You Hold Me in Suspension." Paul [Westerberg] called me up and said, "I did this thing, and I sing the whole thing in falsetto. I gotta give this to you." And I said, "Well, great. Why don't you bring it over tomorrow or something? I'm busy right now." And he said, "No, no, I've gotta get it to you tonight or I'm going to erase it." So I told him to come by.

He came by the Modesto, and he had a little buzz of his own—some special beep-beep-beep [on the outside front-door buzzer] so I'd know it was Paul, because sometimes I didn't answer the door. So I cracked the door of the

The *City Pages* ad that inspired *Hootenanny*'s "Lovelines." © City Pages

apartment, and I heard him coming down the hall. I started going to the door and suddenly the door opened and just his hand came through with a cassette, not even in a case. I grabbed it and he turned and ran. Literally, ran away.

It's a beautiful song. I think that's the one where he sings, "All paint chips, and all love fades." I remember just being blown away.

Dave Ayers: Peter was just endlessly encouraging. I certainly learned something from that that I didn't know at the time. If you're on the other side [of the music business], or if you're a musician that's any good, you certainly see a lot of people blowing smoke up your ass, and being willing to buy you a beer, go fetch your dinner, make your plane reservation. All that crap.

The motivations for that are innumerable. Some people, it's to get ahead. Some people, it's just pure adulation. And with some people, it's just an unchecked desire to help. An instinct to help. And that's what I saw most purely with Peter: an absolute reflex to do whatever he could do to help. His enthusiasm is one of his great gifts.

Peter Jesperson: [Paul]'d been giving me solo songs for a couple years, going back to "If Only You Were Lonely." There was a point where late one night I was listening to a bunch of those songs, and I just felt like they had to be captured on better quality than just a boom box in the basement. So I called Steve Fjelstad and told him I wanted to book some time for Paul, and I didn't want anybody to know about it. I told him, "I'm calling you first, and then I'm gonna call Paul, and if he doesn't want to do it, I'll call you back and cancel."

I called Paul and said, "I've got studio time booked for you for Friday night, just you and me. Let's go over there and lay down some of these things." And he said, "Fucking right. Let's do it." And we didn't tell the band.

So like always, he came to Oarfolk to meet me. We were going to drive over to Blackberry. And he was sitting there on the radiator by the window with his acoustic guitar in its case, and lo and behold, Chris Mars just popped in. He looked at the guitar and said, "What's going on?" So we had to break it to him, and he ended up coming along with. We did a version of [Big Star's] "September Gurls" that Paul erased immediately. It wasn't very good. Then he did a song he called "Warning Sound," and I probably have it on cassette somewhere. That mutated into "We're Comin' Out."

Craig Finn: This is embarrassing, but I'll just say it: I first heard about the Replacements when I was playing tennis at Interlachen Country Club [in Edina, a tony Minneapolis suburb]. My friend asked me if I liked the Ramones and I said, "Yeah, the Ramones are my favorite band." They were the most punk rock band I'd heard. But his older sister knew one of the guys in the [Replacements] and he gave me *Hootenanny*. It was weird. It was like they were from the same place as me, but a world away. My friend, Eddie, and I, who got into music together, we were just dying. We felt like there was so much going on, but we just couldn't get to it because we couldn't drive. I heard "Raised in the City" and had a real "wish I was them" kinda thing.

Peter Jesperson: Paul had this great song, a rocker called "Lookin' for Ya," that had been around since the band's early days. They frequently did it live and we even recorded it for a Duluth radio station contest [and it ended up on a compilation they put out called *Trackin' Up the North* in 1982]. The band had a habit of doing rockers country style or slowing them down as a goof. "Lovelines" began as an example of the latter—it was a down-tempo version of "Lookin' for Ya" cut early on in the *Hootenanny* sessions when they were tossing ideas onto tape.

109

Replacements suk. Paul Westerberg, 1983. © *Daniel Corrigan*

I think the rough track had languished while we finished up the obvious, stronger songs. I thought the track was pretty cool. In spite of the fact that it had been done as sort of a joke, it had a nice swing to it. So I encouraged Paul, to try singing it. There may even be a take or two with him using the "Lookin for Ya" lyrics over the slowed-down track. But then he had the idea to just sing some random words so he picked up a copy of the latest *City Pages*, sat down on the floor with a microphone, and pretty much ad-libbed while scanning through the personal ads at the back of the paper. I think we did two takes and picked the best one.

Jessica Armbruster: Here's what I found in the archives for that [*City Pages*] issue [of October 13, 1982]. Cover: "Economics Rout Local Bus Agency: MTC's Fleet of Sinking Ships." Letters: Someone happy with a favorable concert review of the Who; someone slamming homophobia in the church. There's a story on the reproductive difficulties of frogs in Minnesota. Food

review of fast-food around town—Burger King, McDonalds, Wendy's. Film reviews: *Tex*; *My Favorite Year*; *Snack Canyon*. Music feature: T-Bone Burnett. Record Reviews: *Live Voodoo: The Jimi Hendrix Concerts*; REM, *Chronic Town*; Thomas Dolby, *The Golden Age of Wireless*. Music show reviews: Wally Cleaver, Howard Johnson, Richard Thompson.

Danny Murphy: They were very supportive [of Loud Fast Rules, which became Soul Asylum]. Paul used to always want to use my guitars because they'd always break strings and they didn't have a guitar tech back then. I used Les Paul Juniors, and I think that's how he got into those. They never smashed up our shit, which I always respected. They smashed up their own shit, but if they realized it was someone else's, they'd stop.

We played with them in Sioux Falls, South Dakota, a couple nights, Chicago, Duluth, and at Merlyn's in Madison, and that's how we got our record deal [with Twin/Tone]. I think Paul was a fan initially, and Bob and Tommy not so much. Tommy would always say to me, "You know, my brother might not be workin' out in the band, and we might try to find a younger guitar player." He would never actually ask me or anything, but it was like, *You better start practicing*. It was more intimidating than it was encouraging.

I used to have this Les Paul Junior that was pretty cool and had a hand-made pick guard. And at all the early Loud Fast Rules shows, they used to play it. It had this bridge tailpiece where the nut was supposed to be, and a screw that held it in and it had a really sharp point. Paul was like, "Hey, I broke a string. Can I use your guitar?" And he fucking cut his hand and literally lost a quart of blood on this guitar. And he was like, "Dude, here's your guitar." I think he thought it was the coolest thing; it was in the Entry. It was just wet and red. I should have just put it in its case and kept it like that for twenty years.

Peter Jesperson: We cut "Within Your Reach" during that secret solo Paul session. And Chris tried to play drums on it, and it just wasn't working. It didn't fit the song. And for some reason, [Suicide Commandos drummer] Dave Ahl had a drum machine there and we turned that on and Fjelstad mic'd it up and that's what we used for the song.

And that's the way *Hootenanny* came together. It wasn't like, "OK, we're going in to make the next record on Tuesday." It came in dribs and drabs. It's funny, because it was only their third record, but already we were like, "Well, let's not do it like the first two. We've got to break the mold."

Paul Stark: I'm not sure they understood what was going on; I don't even know if Paul has the kind of ego that would allow himself to think that somebody outside had some influence, and so on. Peter would help out with lyrics and say, "Shorten this or that." I was more interested in how you get the sound, how tight or how loose, be behind the beat, be ahead of the beat, those more technical types of things.

Paul Westerberg: We're very uncomfortable in the studio. I'm uncomfortable. This last album [*Hootenanny*'s follow-up, *Let It Be*] that's been the big pain. It was real uncomfortable this time cuz we went in trying to actually lay down something good. I mean, was, [previously] we went in and fucked around and stank, and we went in and got drunk and like in three hours did the whole record. And this time we tried to do it right, and it's not working as far as like the spirit; we're missing the spirit on a lot of the songs. The songwriting is as strong as ever and the musical performance is good, but it's missing a certain spirit. So what was the question?[9]

Peter Jesperson: The first time we went to New York was April of '83. I had a test-pressing of *Hootenanny* sent to me in Hoboken, New Jersey. We hadn't really toured before that. We bought a van. Tom Carlson said he wanted to help the band in any way he could, and he'd just been in a motorcycle accident and got a big insurance settlement and actually bought an old electrical company van for us. And around the beginning of '83, I started trying to figure out how to get the band out East.

I started calling people, distributors and stuff, I knew from the store, asking them, "Who should I talk to in New York? How do we get in to play CBGB's?" And out of the blue—big moment in Replacements history—I got a call from [legendary booking agent] Frank Riley, who said, "You indirectly helped get a lot of my bands shows in Minneapolis." And that was because [people who were booking the clubs in Minneapolis] would call Oarfolk and ask us if they should book certain bands, how much they thought we could charge for a cover, who would be a good opening act. At Oarfolk we were a team of experts. We knew what we were doing.

Craig Finn: I grew up in west Edina, over by [the suburbs of] Hopkins and Minnetonka. But you couldn't get a record out there. You couldn't go to Knollwood Mall or Southdale and get a Replacements record or Black Flag or anything. There was no Internet or file-sharing or whatever. You had to go to

Oarfolk. So to take the bus into the city to Oarfolk was like this journey to Mecca. My friend and I planned our purchases, and then we'd tape 'em for each other.

Bob Stinson: All the musicians, I don't know if I should tell you this, live from Franklin to Lake Street, Lyndale to Hennepin. Every dang one of them.[10]

P. D. Larson: South Minneapolis was kind of where everybody lived, and 26th and Lyndale was the Ground Zero for all of it—kind of the Haight-Ashbury thing. The after-bar scene in that area was pretty ferocious.

Craig Finn: *Hootenanny* has "Run It," which [references] Lyndale and Garfield [avenues in South Minneapolis], and I knew those streets and I was blown away that there was a rock band in my hometown. I mean, I knew there could be hardcore bands, or punk bands, but these guys were more rock. "Color Me Impressed" and "Within Your Reach" were real songs.

Paul Westerberg: "Run It" was me and Chris were drinking over at Bob Mould['s] of Hüsker Dü, we were drinking over at his house for a day and a half, and were on his motorcycle and we ran about nine red lights in a row. We were going on the wrong side of the road and played chicken with this car and it turned out it was an undercover police car. And they pulled us over. Chris pulled up next to them and said, "C'mon you little fuckers." Fuck, they chased us for blocks. We went up lawns and stuff, and finally Chris hit a bush. They handcuffed me and put me in the car, and Chris kept driving around the car. He didn't know they were the police; he kept like driving up and down. They called like the paddywagons and the squads.

Chris got arrested and lost his license, and I, they let me go. I told 'em I was hitchhiking and I didn't know him. They didn't believe that, but . . . I was real polite; Chris was the one that called them the names. He gets out of his head every now and then.[11]

Peter Jesperson: [Raybeats/Overtones guitarist] Danny Amis was living in Hoboken with Ira [Kaplan] and Georgia [Hubley], and Yo La Tengo was just starting. He went into Manhattan and dropped off a copy of *Stink* at Frank Riley's. At the same time, a guy from Faulty Products, which was a distributor and part of I.R.S. Records, had messengered a copy of *Sorry Ma* over to Frank, and another guy from [distributor] Dutch East India sent a copy of *Sorry Ma*.

First trip to New York, April 1983.
Susan Kohlsaat-Turnquist photo

All three said, "Word is that these guys are trying to get out East. This is an amazing band, and you should keep an eye on them."

So in one fell swoop, Frank got three people [bending his ear]. He called [First Avenue manager] Steve McClellan, who gave him my number at Oarfolk. [Riley] called and said, "I understand you're working with a band called the Replacements, and I'd like to help them." Suddenly we had a booking agent. In New York. You can't overstate how important that was.

Jack Rabid: I DJ'd their New York debut at Gildersleeves on the Bowery, opening for Hüsker Dü, also making their New York debut. The crowd was 100 largely disinterested and unimpressed hardcores who were out for the Gildersleeves "punk Sundays" series they were doing with an outside promoter who'd hired me. The [previous] Sundays had bigger crowds for Black Flag/Minutemen, TSOL, Naked Raygun, Void, Minor Threat, D.O.A./Toxic Reasons, et cetera—i.e., bands much more accepted by the hardcores of that time.

Neither band went over at all, but myself and about ten other people were really blown away by both bands and couldn't understand why these lunkheads couldn't just drop their prejudices—for one thing, neither band dressed punk at all—and just feel how incredibly intense and fast and exciting and powerful both bands were.

I met Paul and Peter Jesperson before they went on. They and I think Tommy came up the ladder to the DJ booth to give me a test pressing of the just-completed *Hootenanny* because they loved the stuff I was playing while they were killing the time before starting. Paul suggested I play the first song, "Hootenanny," and the hardcores started booing and throwing things up into the booth thirty feet off the ground.

Bob Mould: That was a funny show, because the Young and the Useless were on the bill, and I believe that Steve Martin was the singer, who is now [head of] Nasty Little Man publicity, and the other three guys in the band were the Beastie Boys. The main thing I remember is we were doing "Eight Miles High," and I was having one of my usual screaming fits—eyes popping out of my head and bellowing—and the guy sitting right in front, five feet away, getting the best of it was Christgau.

Robert Christgau: I count maybe seven up-and-comers [in the 10th or (11th) *Village Voice* Pazz & Jop Critics Poll], the fewest in many years, with Aztec

Roadie Bill Sullivan behind the kit for sound check, Harriet Island, St. Paul, 1983.
© *Joan E. Bechtold*

Camera, Culture Club, and the Replacements the only ones that inspire much hope in me.[12]

Mike Hoeger: Tommy Stinson overhears a group planning their trip to Folk City, the Hüskers' next N.Y.C. appearance. He comes over to the band as they pack up, lowers his voice and imitates what he's heard: "You guys are fuckin' incredible. A fuckin' hurricane." Everyone laughs.[13]

Jim DeRogatis: The first time I saw the 'Mats was during their first trip to New York, after the release of *Stink* but before *Hootenanny*, in the spring of 1983. I could lie and tell you I was the hippest twenty-four-year-old in the Hoboken, New Jersey, rock scene, but the truth is, I hadn't yet heard *Stink* or *Sorry Ma, Forgot to Take Out the Trash*. At the time, I just went to Maxwell's every Friday and Saturday night, regardless of who was playing. I remember that these guys had drawn an unusual crowd, heavy on the Mohawk-sporting, *MaximumRocknRoll*-reading punks you'd see at CBGB's hardcore matinees, but the set proper struck me as a louder, faster, sloppier version of a wannabe Rolling Stones, without any good songs. The Mohawks didn't like it, either, but then Paul Westerberg did something that really impressed all of us: Everybody else left the stage, but he stayed, and he turned the tables on the punks who'd been taunting him: "You think you can do better? Get up here!" He sat down behind the drums and a couple of leather jackets grabbed the guitars and bass. Then this instant band proceeded to play the worst version of "Louie Louie" you've ever heard for twenty minutes or half an hour. As lousy as it was, it was better than what the 'Mats had given us that night, and I suppose that was one of Paul's points. The others, I thought, illustrated two of Lester Bangs' central maxims about the glories of rock 'n' roll: *Anybody can do it*, and *There shouldn't be any separation between audience and performer.* The Replacements and their fans were the same people—the same as me, no cooler or any more clued-in but just as eager to make their mark—and I was hooked.

Brian Gomez: Lead guitarist Bob Stinson took control with some sharp note-bending on slower songs like "Johnny's Gonna Die." He also gets a striking visual citation for his smart attire of suit, shirt, tie, pleated mini-skirt, tennis shoes, and anklets.[14]

Danny Murphy: They came back from the East Coast and they were all wearing make-up and overalls and glitter boots. It was kind of like this glam

Westerberg performs in the side project Jefferson's Cock, with Max Ray in the background. Duffy's (Minneapolis), 1984. © *Joan E. Bechtold*

119

thing, and I thought it was hilarious. Then they had that Jefferson's Cock band—Bill [Sullivan] and Carton [roadie Tom Carlson] and Girard from Rifle Sport—and then we did Spider Byte, the Alice Cooper [cover band] thing, all in those same years.

P. D. Larson: Pete Buck loved Minneapolis, and whenever he had time, he'd come and hang out. And one night there was something going on at First Avenue, and everybody was pretty lit up and ended up in the women's bathroom. One of the band's many female admirers did the, "Let me put make-up on you."

At that time, glam wasn't really in vogue, and your basic indie band was into flannel. And this was also a time when, if you were crossing over from the Entry to the main room, you risked getting your ass kicked for, you know, "Hey, fag." And lo and behold, here come Paul and Peter walking around like no big deal, like Alice Cooper in 1972.

Well, within a half hour the eyeliner and mascara starts running and they both look like hell. Kinda cool hell, but hell. So after the bar, we decide to go to my house over Northeast [Minneapolis] to listen to records and drink, but beforehand we stopped at White Castle on Central Avenue.

It was 1:45 in the morning, and we walk in there and it's rush hour. As I'm walking up to the counter, it suddenly dawns on me that Paul and Peter are still in costume. And this was two hours later, they looked even worse and were even three more sheets to the wind, and at this time Northeast was not the hip place it is now, but more like headbanger/heavy-metal territory.

So right away it was, "Who are you? What's your problem? Hey, faggot." And Paul was not terribly confrontational, but Peter for some reason, who was bigger than Paul, he was taking umbrage to some of the comments directed towards him. Then he started talking, and he had a fairly noticeable Georgia accent, and that caused some friction as well.

Next thing I know, it's rumble in White Castle. There's swearing and voices raising and people being pushed and panicky-looking employees behind the counter reaching for the phone. And I'm standing there going, "Well, I could run out the door and pretend it never happened, and I'd be responsible for two of the key figures of '80s independent rock getting killed." But I corralled 'em and fortunately got 'em out of there.

I distinctly remember dragging Buck towards the car. I mean, he wanted to go. He was screaming, "You're lucky . . . you're *lucky*." We went back to my house and listened to Alex Chilton records or something until the next afternoon.

Grain
BEE

erfect Br

Twin Tone
RECORDS
Twin Tone Records 445 Oliver Ave. So. Mpls., Mn 55405

Duffy's flyer by Chris Mars, October 15, 1983. *Courtesy Mary B. John*

The Twin/Tone publicity
photo—taken outside Hum's
Liquors (Minneapolis), circa
1983—that accompanied
Dave Ayers' *Hootenanny*
review in *The Minnesota Daily*.
Author collection

Peter Jesperson: I don't know that I recall exactly when the make-up period began and/or ended. Or if there was any link to "Androgynous." I could be wrong but I always thought it was a Peter Perrett thing, after Paul finally fell for the Only Ones.

Jon Ginoli: The most honest song on *Hootenanny* is the closer, "Treatment Bound." They're sitting in the basement at the end of the night, with the drums already packed away, singing in an endearing way about how they get shit-faced drunk and are treatment bound. They know they're assholes, but their admitting it makes them a little easier to take. You help them out the door, and admit they've been fun to have over, but are glad you don't have to see them very often.[15]

Steve Perry: [Seeing the Replacements] didn't change my life, honestly. They were doing a lot of post-punk shtick and other things that I just thought would be destructive to [Westerberg] in the long run.

Paul Stark: The touring was really heating up, and they were really starting to take off. It was more of a press thing and a cult thing. We weren't seeing any dollars, and they weren't seeing the dollars, and we wouldn't for nine or ten years after that.

Lori Barbero: Remember when they'd say [at the end of a set], "Just throw money!" You know how much money they got? A lot. Everyone would empty their pockets, everyone was drunk, and everybody worshiped these guys. And [the band] wanted that money. They [scrambled] for it. I think there might have been a couple fisticuffs because there were bills.

Paul Westerberg: We barely escaped with our lives in Richmond, Virginia, Sunday night. We pulled a hootenanny on 'em and they didn't buy it at all. There was a little altercation: they wanted their money back. We played in Nashville the night before, and they didn't understand us. And we had a weird time in Ann Arbor, Michigan, too.

In Richmond, there were three other bands on the bill, and two of them were hardcore bands, so we went the other way, playing some country, folk, and blues. Plus the P.A. was so bad we didn't want to play loud.[16]

Roscoe Shoemaker: Another great show was in Norman [Oklahoma] at the

Subterranean. Michelle, Wayne [Coyne]'s wife and former manager from the Flaming Lips, owned the place. It was an all-ages sold-out show and Tommy got arrested backstage for drinking as a minor and got thrown in jail.

Paul, Chris, Bob, and Sully were across the street at a bar getting hammered and they run over and tell us. Paul winks at me and says, "They're going to get a real Replacements show tonight." They went on as a three-piece, Paul playing bass. Third song, Paul puts me in a headlock and wrestles me up on the stage and puts the bass around my neck and tells me to take over.

I never played bass or guitar in my life. Me, Bob, and Chris do Alice Cooper's "I'm Eighteen" and "Memphis, Tennessee" I think. Paul stood in front and shot me the finger all the way through the two songs. They played about thirty [songs], did no Replacements songs, and royally pissed everyone off. What a wonderful night.

Dave Ayers: It figures that a band dealing heavily in energy, passion, and humor might be irresistible live, irresolute in the studio. So why is it that the Replacements have just released their third terrific record and I haven't seen them turn in a decent set in a year? The most convenient explanation for their whirlyblur shows is that old demon alcohol, but I'm guessing that's just a symptom of a commonly fetching weakness. Despite singer/songwriter Paul Westerberg's mumbly-teen machismo, Tommy Stinson's punk histrionics, and brother Bob's fashion flair, these guys are just plain shy.[17]

RJ Smith: Their fuckedupness and frustration aren't so far from [Hank] Williams'. But they know how much of a cliché being fucked up is, and how much of a problem it can be too. They end up acting fucked up about being fucked up—metafuckedupitude!—and grabbing at anything that might serve as a bouy.[18]

Kathei Logue: My impression is that a lot of work and caring went into each individual song but very little into the overall concept [of *Hootenanny*]. Maybe the next record will fit together better or maybe the band's problem is that they really don't know how to put the puzzle together.[19]

Paul Stark: I think everyone realized with *Let It Be* the band had a perfect chance to do something major. And I think Paul felt the pressure on him, and he did quite well with it.

Rick Fuller: While in college in Eau Claire [Wisconsin] in the early '80s, I was a member of the R.E.M. fan club. One of their newsletters mentioned that Peter Buck had played on an album from a Minneapolis band called the Replacements. Being a hardcore R.E.M. fan at the time, I bought *Let It Be*. I remember being shocked that something on that level could come out of Minneapolis.

Peter Jesperson: We'd sold boat-loads of the first R.E.M. single at Oarfolk and the band hung out there when they were in town so we naturally became friends. Peter [Buck] was a record hound, like me, so we hit it off especially well. He was also a Replacements fan. The two bands did some touring together in the summer of '83 and the idea for Peter to play on a new song of Paul's was hatched then. The Replacements were going into the studio to start their fourth album in August so Peter flew in and hung out for a few days and ended up doing that cool little guitar thing on "I Will Dare."

Jim Sullivan: Opening for R.E.M. at The Paradise [in Boston] Wednesday, they were hit and miss: a little slow and sloppy when they were off, but speedy

Peter Buck and Linda Hultquist, Harriet Island, St. Paul, 1983. © *Joan E. Bechtold*

and full of conviction when they were on. Bets are that when the stage is theirs to headline, they'll open up the throttle and burn.[20]

Craig Finn: A friend of mine and I were watching an R.E.M. video the other day [in spring 2007], and he goes, "R.E.M. just wishes they could be the Replacements." I was like, "I don't think so."

Paul Stark: In those days, college radio was a huge thing. We were able to mail out [promo copies of *Let It Be*] to three or four hundred college radio stations, track them, and really work the record. And two years earlier, we wouldn't have been able to do that much. We had doubled our staff, and we were working directly with the stores. Plus, Peter [Jesperson] had toured with the band and had gone to most of the stores. Everything was in place. *Let It Be* came out right at the right time.

Todd McGovern: September 1984. Walking down East Liberty Street in Ann Arbor, I saw a large black and white poster announcing the release of *Let It Be* and an upcoming live show at Joe's Star Lounge. That performance was a transcendent experience for me. For me and everyone I was with that night, the Replacements sang the soul of our unnamed generation and what it felt like coming of age in the Reagan years. In the coming months I bought and wore out copies of both *Let It Be* and *Hootenanny*. In those records were the anger, fear, abandonment, and boredom, but also a sense of freedom like anything was possible. A volatile cocktail for a twenty-three-year-old, and in certain respects I've been reckoning with that juice ever since.

Craig Finn: When *Let It Be* came out, I was taking guitar lessons from Chris Osgood, and the record started doing well, and he stopped teaching me and went over to work at Twin/Tone. I got into them the summer of eighth grade, and *Let It Be* came out that fall. One of my chores was to mow the lawn, and I did it early that week so I could go to Oarfolk and get it.

My dad sensed this was really important to me, and he said, "Why don't I just drive you up there." And he bought the record for me out of his money, not mine, and whoever it was behind the counter rang up the record, turned on the music [on the turntable behind the counter], and he looks at me and points at my dad and goes, "Cool dad." Then he points at me and looks at my dad and goes, "Cool kid."

127

City Pages:
So-Called Punk Rockers

When a friend and I first asked the administration of Regina High School whether it would be possible to invite the Replacements back to R.H.S. for a performance in February, there were several reservations. These doubts stemmed from the fact that when the band originally played at Regina in April of 1981 as an opening act for the Rems [*sic*], there were various problems with crowds, groupies and friends of both bands.

However, after much discussion on how we could eliminate these problems, we called Peter Jesperson (manager of the Replacements) and set the date for Feb. 24, 1984. We thought that with five months of planning to the last detail, we could have things running smoothly. We were wrong.

Things were running smooth until the Replacements hit the stage and all the so-called "punk rockers" started slam dancing. When we signed the contract with the band, we knew that there would be slamming and that we would have no real control over it, short of pulling the plug on the band. We also thought that if people knew what they were doing, things would not get out of control and no one would get hurt.

On Friday, a vast majority of the large crowd was not slamming. The problem was that the people who were slamming had no understanding of what they were doing. The idea behind slam dancing is to have fun, not to see how many people you can maim or step on when they fall to the floor. If the person next to you is on the floor, it's your responsibility to help them up. Several of the "week-end slammers" didn't seem to know or care about this little detail.

It was first evident to me that things were out of hand when I noticed "veteran" slammers that I have seen various times around the cities, standing up against the stage or just trying to get out of the way of the pseudo-punks. Was this phenomenon occurring because it was too dangerous to slam with the amateurs, or had they all just forgotten their dancing boots at home?

The people dancing acted like a bunch of no-minds with nothing better to do than step on each other and slam to the floor others who tried to watch the band perform. I don't care if people slam dance, and I understand that in a place like The Entry bystanders are liable to get hit once or twice. However, in a gym that can hold up to 700 people, there is no excuse for people standing 50–60 feet from the stage to be

leveled or slammed against a wall. When Paul Westerberg asked that the "fake punks settle down," these idiots responded by slamming all the harder.

By the time the Placemats left the stage, tempers had risen. A lot of people were ready to do some serious slamming to all the pseudo-punks.

Mariann Wolf '84
Regina High School, Mpls.[21]

"Fake punks settle down." Flyer for the February 24, 1984, show at Regina High. *Author collection*

Replacements

with
LAUGHING STOCK

FEBRUARY 24

8:00 PM

OO   NO I.D.

REGINA H.S.
4225 4th avenue south mpls

129

Chris on the bill with
R.E.M. at Harriet
Island, St. Paul, 1983.
© *Joan E. Bechtold*

Dave Ayers: I started working for Twin/Tone around this time, and Paul [Stark] was reluctant to have me work for the label, because I had been doing stringer stuff for *Rolling Stone*, *CREEM*, and the *NME*, and people outside of Minneapolis weren't paying attention to them yet. And for me to go on payroll, suddenly they were going to lose that mouthpiece. *We're gonna have this guy here doing data entry and mailing lists and lose that?* Which was pretty smart on Paul's part. It quickly went from that to [Twin/Tone publicist] Blake [Gumprecht] leaving and me becoming their publicist. By the time I started that job, people were just calling. People were starting to pay attention, because the promos of *Let It Be* were obviously striking a chord with people.

Steve Fjelstad: They were a lot of fun to work with [on *Let It Be*]. Paul was more focused than the other guys, and that helped. Sometimes you'd be pushing bands, trying to get a little tension going, and with them it worked because if they got a little bit pissed off, they played harder.[22]

Peter Buck: We had been playing together a lot in those days. Paul sang "Color Me Impressed" with us [R.E.M.] at the Orpheum [Theater in downtown Minneapolis], and I just remember him being really nervous. But it was the total hometown crowd, he was this local hero, and it was just great. Around then, the suggestion came up that I come to Minneapolis and help out. So I did, and I ended up playing [mandolin] on "I Will Dare."

Bob Stinson: I was not there when he did his overdub. He was in town and they decided to put his you know . . . if you listen close, there's another lead underneath it. I did that way before we ever made it. Yeah, Pete came into town and they did an overdub with him. What I remember then was when we toured with them, and that's when we became friends.

They did give us like beer and we'd wait until they'd go on stage and . . . their dressing rooms—there was no lock, boys. We ate all their food and drank their booze. They're like doing one of their real pretty hit songs and we're just sitting there drinking their booze. And they're playing in front of a thousand people. You can't stop and come and grab it from us. We really had mean fun with them.[23]

Peter Buck: The thing I remember most about Bob [Stinson] is that he didn't know the names of the songs. Paul would just say, "The fast one," or "The sorta fast one," or "The one that goes like this, Bob," and with the other guys he'd call out the [song] titles. But Bob would just rip into 'em. It was like this little thing they had between themselves.

Craig Finn: I had grown up on KISS, but I understood them to be so square. And I was so blown away to hear them covering "Black Diamond." Because I didn't have the perspective that of course they liked KISS. I was still figuring it out. They were certainly embraced by critics and elitist people, but not for being elitist. Putting "Gary's Got a Boner" on the same side as "Unsatisfied" may be exactly why they're a great band. That may say it all.

131

Casey MacPherson and Bob Stinson
on Lyndale Avenue, April 1984.
© Joan E. Bechtold

Burl Gilyard: When *Let It Be* came out, I'd only seen the Replacements play live once—at a poorly attended all-ages show one Saturday afternoon at First Avenue. It was sloppy and halfhearted, but I thought it was magically great.

I kept calling Oarfolkjokeopus to see if the album was out yet. I'm guessing it was either Terry Katzman or Jim Peterson who kept patiently telling me "not yet," until one day, it was out. And I made a beeline for the northeast corner of 26th and Lyndale Avenue.

I remember it as a cool fall night. I remember it was dusk. It seems to me it was a Wednesday night. And maybe it was none of those things, but that's the way I remember it. I just couldn't believe that the album was finally out.

Dave Ayers: They weren't interested in doing interviews, and Peter was smart enough to know that things had to be really controlled by ideal circumstances to go well, so they just didn't say yes to much of anything. So my relationship with the band was like, collecting names for guest lists and clipping reviews out of publications and building relationships with members of the press who would go see them and be transformed and become lifelong fans and supporters.

Burl Gilyard: *Let It Be* hit me at the right time: my senior year in high school. "Sixteen Blue." I was seventeen at the time. Close enough. It was all there: the joy, anger, confusion, and the self-deprecating sense of humor. *Let It Be* is full of throwaway classics and classic throwaways, but it is perfect in its imperfection.

"I Will Dare" was a swingin'-for-the-fences, shoulda-been-a-hit pop song: the most upbeat, hopeful song Westerberg had ever written. As far as I know, it still is. But it was "Unsatisfied" that was my theme song.

My senior year of high school was not one of my all-time favorites. My kid brother Bret was dying of a rare disease that no one had ever heard of—and no one could do anything about. Beyond the usual high school confusion and awkwardness, I felt like I had more reasons than the average kid to be angry at the world.

Through it all, *Let It Be* was my soundtrack. Those were my anthems, my slogans, my touchstones. They weren't just a local band, they seemed like the neighborhood band for a South Minneapolis kid, even amid the talk of the band getting "signed" and going on to take over the world.

Peter Jesperson: I'm guessing it was February or March of '83. I remember being at Paul Stark's house, where we had the first Twin/Tone office in the basement. Paul [Westerberg] called me saying he had just written the best song he'd ever written, he thought it was "a hit" and he wanted to record it immediately. I could hear the excitement in his voice and that got me excited. But I had to tell him that recording right then was probably not in the cards as *Hootenanny* was done but not out yet so we wouldn't really have a place for a brand-new track. And it wasn't like we had any money to splurge on paying for studio time ourselves, either.

He was, of course, disappointed but understood what I was saying. I didn't actually hear the song until maybe a week or two later. The band was doing a show at Goofy's Upper Deck. About five or six songs into the set, I heard the opening chords to a song I'd never heard them do before. It was unusual for them, bouncy and instantly catchy and I knew immediately that this was the song Paul had called about. And that was "I Will Dare."

Peter Buck: More people bring that up to me than anything else. And I mean *way* more than anything else: "You played on 'I Will Dare.' What was that like?"

Ralph Heibutzki: That shimmering, propulsive A-side, "I Will Dare," became *Let It Be*'s keynote song. Jesperson recalls Westerberg lobbying him to release it only a week after *Hootenanny* had been on the store shelves: he labels it "the hit that never was."

"I Will Dare"'s soaring romanticism ("Meet me any place, or anywhere, or any time now, I don't care/If you will dare, I will dare"), shining guitars and bopping bass "should have been a monster, mega, super, gigantic hit for the band," asserts Jesperson. "I remember thinking, 'This is a crime against

humanity here. This is one of the greatest tunes anybody's ever done anywhere.'"

To Jesperson, *Let It Be* proves the Replacements were maybe too far ahead of their time: "Everybody has *Let It Be*. It's the college rock album of all time. At that time, we were doing okay, but it was not like [the 'Mats] were accepted to anywhere near the degree they are now. Those records became famous long after they were done."[24]

G. R. Anderson, Jr.: I've been playing in bands playing Replacements songs for damn near 20 years, and I can honestly say that in all the times I've been a part of covering "I Will Dare"—probably no less than 300, but who's counting—all the various combos I've played with have really nailed the song maybe five times. That song is a bitch. The rest of *Let It Be*, wisely, I've rarely ever tried.

None of this was apparent to me when I first heard it 19 years ago. My friend Jean, who, alas, was decidedly not my girlfriend at the time ("Fifteen Blue," anyone?), was in the throes of a mad crush on Tommy in early 1985, which I found pretty damn annoying, frankly. For this, I dismissed the record every time I hung out in her bedroom and she put it on.

It sounded tinny and grating, and what the hell was with the half-assed ending of "Androgynous," anyway? *Tommy this, Tommy that,* Jean would say, *blah, blah, blah.* So in a fit of jealousy, I swiped the cassette out of her boom box one day, hoping never to hear—or never let her hear—the record again. At least that's how I remember it. But a funny thing happened on the way to my adolescent envy: With Jean being frustratingly unavailable, I fell in love with the 'Mats.[25]

Daniel Corrigan's "classic basement-band-in-the-basement" photo, taken at the Stinson home on the same day as the famous "roof" shot, 1984. © *Daniel Corrigan*

On the Stinson roof for the *Let It Be* photo session, 1984. © *Daniel Corrigan*

Blake Gumprecht: I remember hearing "Favorite Thing" for the first time at Duffy's; Peter Jesperson and I looked at each other knowing the world had changed.

Daniel Corrigan: I was hired by Ayers to do promo pictures [for *Let It Be*], and they were being their usual selves—they weren't cooperating, and all that stuff. So they were playing a show at the Great Hall [of Coffman Union at the University of Minnesota] and I was supposed to go there and do a portrait of them. And they wouldn't do it.

So I told 'em I had coke, but, "We can't do it downstairs here. We have an office up on the top floor. Let's go up there and we can all do lines." I didn't have any coke, I just wanted to get 'em in the elevator because they'd be trapped.

My friend, Iver, was kind of assisting me, and we stopped the elevator between floors. And that's where I got that sort of crazy picture where they're all packed together. I really like that picture; out of the twenty or twenty-five frames I shot, that's the only one that turned out.

The most enduring 'Mats photo: the *Let It Be* cover shot, 1984. © *Daniel Corrigan*

But Ayers didn't like it. He wanted me to reshoot it, which was fine. That was Ayers' call.

Dave Ayers: I don't recall any of that, but I've always been pretty forthright about my two cents' worth. And if I didn't like some shot, I'd always be candid. And Dan and I fought about plenty of photographs over the years, when we worked at *The [Minnesota] Daily* and I was the editor [of the arts and entertainment section] and he was the photographer. I have always been a fan of candid, editorial-style photography in the world of rock 'n' roll. It just makes more sense to me than studio shots.

Daniel Corrigan: So we reshot it at [the Stinsons'] house. They were having a practice and I did portraits of them and all that. I made some great pictures that day; the classic basement-band-in-the-basement—cramped, asbestos-coated heating pipes. And then I thought [about shooting on] the roof, just for something different.

They were a little more cooperative that day. Bob was always a little jinky—about people in general. Paulie didn't quite have the [big] head on him yet. But that day, he was being OK. I don't think Tommy cared one way or another, and Chris just knew he had to do stuff like that. We crawled through that bedroom window, Bob's bedroom I think.

Dave Ayers: He captured a moment. The one overriding thing that's always been in the back of my head: It's a great shot, and it's become iconographic and it says "the Replacements" and everybody recognizes it. And from a completely pedestrian, clinical point of view, from the very first time I saw it I was like, "What the fuck are they doing on a roof?" You know, this "candid" moment, and they're on a fucking rooftop. They had to crawl out a window—there's nothing candid about it.

The shot Corrigan felt would make the better *Let It Be* album sleeve. Coffman Union elevator, University of Minnesota, 1984. © *Daniel Corrigan*

Daniel Corrigan: Ayers picked that one, he really liked that one. And I said, "You're making a huge mistake. This [elevator] picture is better." But, you know, he's the boss, and thank God. That's my classic story of "What do I know?" If it had been left to me, my most famous picture wouldn't have happened. People have analyzed it way more than me, stuff like "It captures the alienation of youth that was necessary for a band like the Replacements to happen."

Tommy at Macalester College,
St. Paul, circa 1984
© Joan E. Bechtold

I think Paulie's got a chip on his shoulder about that picture. Paulie's just been rude to me for years. I don't know. Maybe that's just me thinking I'm more than just another fuckin' photographer that Paulie's had to deal with over the years. I suppose I shouldn't think it's anything more than that, but I think he resents it because it's something he didn't make. It's so entwined with them, but it's not his product. I've never talked to Paulie about it, so I don't know. It could just be me, but my last couple dealings with him, years ago, he was really unpleasant to me.

Paul Stark: *Let It Be* has sold a quarter of a million [copies]. It's been Twin/Tone's biggest seller. I've got about fifty or a hundred vinyl copies left [in 2007]. I sell about one or two a week via the Internet.

Darren Jackson: I first heard of the Replacements from a friend's older brother. He returned from college one summer with a mix tape that seemed to be sent directly from the gods. This may sound extreme but growing up in western South Dakota severely limited my exposure to new music. This tape changed everything for me. Sandwiched between the Violent Femmes' "Blister in the Sun" and the Suburbs' "Heart of Gold" was "I Will Dare" by the Replacements. This new music, and especially the Replacements, resonated deeply in my teenage ears. It was wild, sexual, heart-wrenching. It made my mother cringe a little. It was the most important music of my youth.

Matt Fink: Prince never talked about those guys with us, per se. I know me and [Revolution drummer] Bobby Rivkin did, a little bit. But we were so pre-occupied with what we were doing that I did not pay a whole lot of attention to what was going on around us. We were so busy doing the Prince thing and getting ready to film [*Purple Rain*], and going to acting and dancing classes and recording. Prince wanted to be at the top of the heap, so to speak, and always felt, at that time—once we became successful and being on tour and selling out all over—that we were one of the top groups at the time. But there were a lot of great groups at that time. I'm guessing he was aware of them. I'm sure he had to be, because he kept up with what was going on, but he never discussed it with us, like *Hey, we're going after the Replacements*.

Peter Jesperson: Paul and Tommy never talked about "Sixteen Blue" to my knowledge. But I remember the first time they played it, summer of '83 in Boston at The Paradise at sound check. They had just learned it at practice

that afternoon. We had borrowed the Del Fuegos' [practice] space for a couple of hours. I remember very clearly, walking around the big, empty room, checking out the sound and suddenly connecting with the words—it was very heavy. I don't recall Tommy acknowledging or Paul saying anything explicit, it was always just understood [that it was penned from Westerberg for Tommy].

Paul Westerberg: [I]n a way 16 (*is* the hardest age). If you're a misfit, it is. Although I'm beginning to believe if you fit in perfect when you're 15, 16, 17, you're gonna tend to be a little fucked up when you're our age, or in your early thirties. I think that maybe you reap the things that you didn't have when you were unpopular or when you didn't fit in. I mean, I certainly have "gotten more" in the last two or three years than I had when I was a teenager. You can't tell a person who's 16 that, 'cause when you're 16 you don't think you're gonna ever be anything or make it to anywhere. The cheerleaders and the quarterbacks and shit, they tend to be the ones that get married quick and get fat and work for the refrigerator company or something.[26]

Steve Albini: This is a sad, pathetic end to a long downhill slide. The Replacements are now little more than four guys trying to be what their press releases said they were. Self-consciously "gut wrenching" in its pandering sensitivity and pathos, this record is irretrievably lost in the maudlin cabaret of Westerberg's folk music blatherings. The jokes aren't jokes, they're copies of jokes pulled off for effect. I hate it. Except "I Will Dare," which for some reason rings truer than the rest of this. I used to love these guys, now I hate this guy.[27]

Terry Katzman: Bill Sullivan grabbed a bootleg tape [of a Replacements' performance at the Bowery Ballroom in Oklahoma City, recorded on November 11, 1984] from a fan, which Twin/Tone released in limited edition. It featured slaughtered covers, including U2's "I Will Follow" and Robyn Hitchcock's "Sleeping Nights of Jesus" and all that. The tape didn't do much for me. The fascination of watching them do "Misty Mountain Hop" [while] smashed wore pretty thin for me after one gig. As much as I loved them, I didn't see the romance in them being that fucked up and playing. It frustrated me, because I knew how good they could be.

Roscoe Shoemaker: I was the manager and DJ at the Bowery in Oklahoma City. We did the Replacements numerous times because they would play at the

start of the tour and also at the end of the tour, usually just for gas money. The Bowery was a huge place. It was an old church and used to be a gay disco also.

The night [*The Shit Hits the Fans* was recorded] was a Sunday-night gas money show, so I asked Paul or somebody if he minded that I record the show. He said, "Why? We suck." Typical Westy response.

I hung two microphones from the front of the deejay booth and there it is. There was nobody at the show—maybe twenty, thirty people—and we yelled out requests all night long. It was a great show. They had a new soundman that night. I was used to Sully being there and in charge. So after the show we went to a party and they headed out to Minneapolis. I went back to the club and the tape was missing. I thought a customer stole it.

Twin/Tone put it out [in January 1985]. If you read the actual liner notes it says that it was yanked from a fan and confiscated. On the liner notes Paul promised "there's 3.95 in it for you brother," or something like that. I'm just glad I witnessed the show and a lot of other people got to enjoy the show. Back then it was all about the music, and the 'Mats were our band, their songs were our real lives. I actually had to buy a copy of the tape but I will always love the 'Mats.

Emily Boigenzahn (*née* Dunlap): I saw them play the first time when I was in seventh grade. My mom was working at First Avenue, and there was an all-ages show, and it was great. *Let It Be* was just out. I listened to it all the time in my little attic refuge of a room, and all those songs are so poignant for a teenager. Paul Westerberg just really captured teenage angst the way no one had before.

Chrissie Dunlap: That band was for the youth, and it really meant a lot to me, as a mom. [My daughter] Emily played it over and over, and I was so glad she found someone to speak for her.

Iowa City, Iowa, circa 1984. *Dave Conklin photo*

Author's note: Other than journal and diary entries, the following is my first piece of rock journalism. Not knowing a thing about newspapers and deadlines, I submitted it to The Minnesota Daily's *arts and entertainment section a week before the five-night record release stand for* Tim *in October 1985. The editor, David Adams, looked at me like I was nuts, but he said he'd read it. It was never published, but here it is—warts and misspellings and green writing and all:*

The Replacements: Highlights 1980-1985--A Fan's Notes

By Jim Walsh
October 7, 1985

One summer night five and a half years ago at the now legendary Jay's Longhorn in downtown Minneapolis, a far from sellout crowd saw the first bar performance of four boys who will live in infamy. The Replacements were playing "Tiger" night—a sort of showcase for new and upcoming bands—and were warming up The Dads, a post-punk outfit whose members have spun off into bands such as Summer of Love, Red House, and Good Joe as well as the USMC. The Replacements that night were, and to this day still are, the best rock 'n' roll band ever to come out of these parts. They've made me laugh and cry in the same breath and shout and yawn in the same night. I've lept to their defense and lept from my seat in the bar to leave out of sheer boredom. It's not easy being a Replacements fan.

But like the song/book/movie says, that was then and this is now. A lot of water has gone under the bridge since that first night, and the band has grown, though you may need a Richter scale to measure it. Covers have gone from standards ("Slow Down," "All Day and All of the Night") to uncool ("All My Rowdy Friends Are Coming Over Tonight," "Yummy, Yummy, Yummy"). Simple three chord originals with basic messages ("Shut Up," "I Hate Music") have given way to introspective "life" songs ("Sixteen Blue," "Swinging Party," "Here Comes A Regular"). And the guy who used to ride the MTC cuz he had no place else to go in "Hangin' Downtown" has now found true love on old big red in "Kiss Me On The Bus."

The Longhorn is closed now and these days, First Avenue's Main Room is the only venue that can hold them locally. Over the

past three years, the Replacements have zig-zagged across the states and will embark on their first European tour sometime before Christmas. And last but not least, they've cut the apron strings of Twin/Tone, their record label of the past five years, and signed with Sire/Warner Brothers. So on this, the eve of the Mats' first major label release, *Tim* (in stores Monday, October 14th), and with an unprecedented five night homestand (October 15–19) at the 7th St. Entry to celebrate the event, it seems like a good time to gaze into some of that sky blue water that's gone under the bridge.

If Ed Sabol was a Replacements fan, he'd have a bitch of a time in the cutting room. For each live highlight, there are at least as many lowlights, and for each slow motion shot of Bob mooning the audience to the strains of "Flight Of The Bumblebee," there's another of uninspired apathy. Keeping this in mind, the following can be considered a somewhat colored retrospective as many of the bad moments have been mercifully blocked from my mind and only the good memories remain. So let me play Pat Summerall for a moment as I give you Tommy and Bob Stinson, Paul Westerberg, and Chris Mars—*The Replacements' Highlights Film (Local Shows Only) 1980–1985*.

7/2/80: First gig at the Longhorn, opening for the Dads. Covers by 999 and Johnny Thunders along with some now forgotten originals like "Off Your Pants" and "Toe Needs a Shoe (Problem . . .)," which Bob sang in his own Stinsonesque falsetto. The focus, however, was on the thirteen year old bass player who would drop to both knees, blonde hair in his eyes, and yell "fuck you!" to bar patrons. Westerberg wore a green and white football/baseball shirt, drank water, and mumbled embarrassed "thank you's" in between songs. Some people danced, some people gawked at Tommy, but mostly everyone there agreed that this was a good new band.

2/14/81: Walker Art Center, warming up Curtiss A in a "St. Valentine's Day Massacre." Paul opened the evening by saying "We're the Replacements—don't ask why and don't forget to tip your waitresses and bartenders," an allusion to the foreign, non-alcoholic turf on which they stood. No one laughed. The band responded with a furious song-to-song set that previewed material from the soon-to-be recorded debut album *Sorry Ma, Forgot to Take Out The Trash*.

4/3/81: Regina High School. Band went on at 8:30 and due to an inadequate P.A. and the fact that Mars started the wrong song after the four count, the first thing the nuns and all-girl student body heard from the Replacements clear as a bell was Paul screaming, "What the fuck happened?!" Sound and tuning problems marred the first set, but the second was one of their best up to that time. The school administration griped about the booze and non-student element that had seeped into their hallowed halls, but as we shall see, their memories grew faint when an even more profitable second coming was offered three years later.

4/8/85: West High School's "Sno-Daze" semi formal, the night after the Regina nightmare. I danced to every song at the Sons of Norway as the band redeemed themselves in a big way.

5/16/81: Front steps of Coffman Union, U of M. An open air afternoon show that drew Minneapolis' finest boys in blue to the scene as neighbors and students from Wilson library had called in complaints about some horrible noise coming from the campus. Even as the cops came on stage the band refused to quit, turning volume and blood pressures up higher and higher. The police finally pulled the plug by cutting off the electricity in CMU.

8/3/81: Loring Park. Another outdoor show, playing before "The Long, Long Trailer" with Desi Arnez and Lucille Ball as part of the WAC's Music and Movies in the Park series. Prince sat on the grass wearing a confused smirk throughout the set.

9/5/81: Twin/Tone records the 7th St. Entry. Sandwiched between the Neglecters and Hüsker Dü, amidst video cameras and sound equipment, the Replacements played the best set of their young career. Though out-of-tune guitars sabotaged the latter half, inspired versions of much of the *Sorry, Ma* and *Stink* material as well as some long gone nuggets ("Junior's Got A Gun," "D-E-A-D Dead," "Staples in her Stomach") more than made up for the lack of a tuner.

9/24/81: A Thursday night at the Entry and the opening band didn't show up. Forced into action so early in the evening, the Replacements pulled bar stools up on stage and did jazz versions of "Rattlesnake," "Customer," and made a half hearted effort at "If Only You Were Lonely," but stopped midway so as not to completely maul it. That night, Paul sang like Michael Franks, Bob played like George Benson, and a die was cast for future "poop" sets.

10/12/82: The first headline at the Cabooze. Hypstrz opened with one of their patented power outings. Much of the Mats's set consisted of fulfilling audience requests and took on a laid back, happy-go-lucky complexion. Until the very end.

The last song, "Rattlesnake," moved the few dancers in front to new heights of slam-dancing, the likes of which the Cabooze and its bouncers had never seen. The goons stepped in, using muscle to break up the dancers, and stood, arms crossed in the middle of the pack like some guardians of goodness, might for right, and all that. Westerberg witnessed what was happening to his partners in crime below, sensed the bigotry behind it, and something snapped in his head. He screamed out the last verse with a vengeance, whirled around and skewered the neck of his guitar on his amp, almost breaking it in half as Bob grabbed hold of the mike stand and did a manic metal slide solo. The band hit the last chord, Mars kicked over his kit, the bouncers glared at the stage, and I threw both fists in the air, heart pounding, wondering if they'd ever play at the Cabooze again. They would and did four months later.

1/21/83: Goofy's Upper Deck. Another plug puller. This time not because of the volume, but because the band was so drunk and enjoying themselves so much that they wouldn't leave the stage. A feable go at "Treatment Bound" was introduced by Paul as being the "ballad of the Replacements." The encore included the first "hoot" locally—Paul on drums, Bob on bass, Tommy and Chris on guitars doing "Hootenanny," etc. until 1:15 a.m.

9/23/83: Duffy's. This is it, hands down, no doubt about it, the winner of The Worst Replacements Show in the History of the

Typical Bob stage apparel.
The Cabooze on the West
Bank (Minneapolis), 1984.
© *Joan E. Bechtold*

World. Auto pilot. Going through the motions. They did not want to be there. They wanted to be at home, at the fair, in bed, watching tv, anywhere but on stage in front of a bunch of rock fans with high expectations. The reason I love these guys as much as I do is because they don't put on a show and they don't pretend. Any emotions put out are as real as real. But tonight was a night when I wanted my money and time invested back. Loud Fast Rules opened and closed doing obnoxious covers of "18" and "Smoking in the Boy's Room" with Westerberg on guitar as the encore. I left before the finale and vowed never to see the Replacements again.

2/24-25/84: Ahem. Where was I? Back at it . . .

My most memorable Replacements weekend, one that served up the best of both their worlds, started out with the return to the scene of that 1981 crime at Regina High School. Unlike the first time, this was a young, capacity crowd that chanted, "fuck school, fuck school" before the last encore. The band came back out and Westerberg spun around to face them, middle fingers on both hands thrust into the air, half-mocking, half-saluting. After leading the pack through this universal pep rally rouser, Tommy, in a fit of hormonal overload (all those Catholic girls his own age), raised his Rickenbacker bass over his head a la Pete Townshend and brought it down on the stage taking a good chunk out of the body. Paul went up to the mike and said "Thanks a lot. See you again in three years." Right.

The next night at Duffy's, the other shoe dropped as the Replacements, drunk and hilarious, did mostly covers and attempted "Answering Machine." Then they went into a particularly awful version of "Jumping Jack Flask (sic)" and were pelted with plastic beer cups and bottles. A garbage can was strategically rolled up next to Westerberg—a trophy to the ambiance of the evening. Next, Bob got up on the drum riser and climbed into the garbage can as the band went into "Customer." He stood like the statue of liberty until he lost his balance and the garbage can, with all its contents, including Bob, spilled out onto the stage. He jumped up and never missing a beat ripped off his skirt revealing baby bare buttocks for all to see. The night ended with a plea for money from

151

our heroes who scurried around the stage like crazed panhandlers, stuffing bills and change into their shirts and pockets.

10/21/84: Cabooze. Another stellar performance complete with versions of "Kumbaya" ("Yeah, we go to church . . .") and "Go." End of set donation requests produced a wad of bills and a baggie full of pot which Bob stashed away on top of his amp for future considerations. Then as Bob was preoccupied with a lengthy solo, Paul put his fingers to his lips and slyly tucked the dope into his pocket. Bob never knew what hit him.

12/26/84: This was the first night in a series of "who would've ever thoughts" started running through my head. The Mats, playing the main room at First Avenue for the first time in a while, sold the joint out by 10:30. WWTC (pre-two-song format) was giving heavy airplay to "I Will Dare" and when Paul started strumming those first few opening chords, squeals and bopping, normally reserved for out of town national acts, took hold. It was weird and out of focus, but ultimately a victory for all of us because no matter what the future holds for Minneapolis's favorite sons, they've provided us with some of the best moments and memories rock 'n' roll can give. And if the past five years (and *Tim*) are any indication, the Replacements will be writing and growing up in public for many years to come. The next five may not be the same as the last, but for a preview of the 1986–1990 Highlights Film we've got five nights at the Entry next week. See you there.

CHAPTER 3

What's That Song?

Well the old people
They love to tell their stories
About the world and
About what it all used to be

And the young folks
Are sick of hearing all them stories
Their mind drifts away
In place of history

Because a story gets old
If a story's never told
Oh oh it gets old
It stays untold

Well us old folks
We sort of live in a kind of dream world
To us, life has always been the same
To you young folks
You don't like to think of that
You prefer to hope that
Somehow your lives will change

And the stories they get told
They get old and they get cold
But there's nothing worse than
A story must be untold

So take some time and
Listen to an old feller tell
You his tale
Hell, you can even pretend
That you're slightly interested
And who knows?
Someday you may grow old
And you can tell that story
And tell that kid
That it all happened to you

But those stories they get old
As a story gets untold
There's nothing sadder than
A story untold

—Slim Dunlap, "Story Untold"

Dennis Pernu: The summer before my senior year of high school, three or four guys from the group I hung out with built this little one-room shack next to a creek in the woods behind the municipal airport. They used mostly, uh, "scavenged" lumber and it was actually quite nice. We called it "The Lodge." I mean, it had bunk beds and a woodstove and everything.

Anyway, there were like ten or twelve of us in this group we called "the Beer Brothers," and I can tell you we took our license for our behavior from the legends we heard about the Replacements. I can't tell you how many Friday and Saturday nights various combinations of us spent at The Lodge after football and hockey games, being wiseasses and listening to "Fuck School" over and over and over again. It was exactly like "Bob Dylan's Dream" and the lines about "the old wooden stove where our hats was hung" and "Talkin' and a-jokin' about the wicked world outside."

The Beer Brothers' sort of de facto leader was Glen Mattson. His older brother, Rich, had moved to Minneapolis, and Glen was the conduit between Rich, in the city, and us teenage rubes on the Iron Range. A lot of music trickled down to us from Rich and one of his housemates, this record-collector dude named Jimmy the Sloocher. By that time, *Tim* and *Pleased to Meet Me* were out but I mostly remember listening to *Sorry Ma* and *Stink* and *Hootenanny*. I doubt any of us even knew Bob was out of the band by that time, we were so isolated. I mean, this was twenty years ago. No Internet, and the cable up there didn't even have MTV. There was *SPIN* and a weird music show on USA Network called *Night Flight*, but I don't remember hearing about the Hüskers, and I don't think I even had a sense of who Alex Chilton was, even though some of my first musical memories are "The Letter" and "Cry Like a Baby." Never put two and two together. We only got what Glen passed on to us—mostly third- and fourth-generation dubbed *cassettes*. Which was fortunate, because if Pamida didn't have what you wanted, tough titties.

Anyway, I think what most appealed to us about the 'Mats was a sense that they were rebelling against their peers as much as anyone. That was pretty appealing in a backwater high school run by jocks who listened to Ratt and Poison. The Beer Brothers were all smarter than those guys and their girlfriends. Not just book smart, but stuff like making Replacements silk screens in art class—that was a way *cooler* kind of smart than straight A's. It was also ironic, though no one ever pointed it out, that the guys who'd call you a "fag" for listening to the 'Mats were listening to music performed by hair bands dressed like friggin' drag queens—and Judas Priest, for that matter. I mean the 'Mats wore *plaid* flannel shirts and reportedly drank their asses off, just like

working stiffs, which is what we were surrounded by—steelworkers and shit—and which that culture told you were prerequisites for masculinity. Immature, I know, but think about it—"They laugh in the middle of my speech" or "Goin' to the party though we weren't invited." Barreling down gravel logging trails on Friday nights in our parents' cars, we all believed Westerberg wrote those songs for us and that for all practical purposes *we* were Replacements, too.

Anyway, the sheriff got wind of The Lodge and tore it down, and Glen moved to Minneapolis literally the day after we graduated. A few of us went to the local junior college for a year or two and continued with the antisocial behavior we thought Paul would require of us until I'm sure *we* were the dicks. In fact, for me this continued after I moved to St. Paul and fell in with like-minded 'Mats fans at school *there*.

Chris Dorn: The Replacements led me to Big Star, and after I discovered Big Star it was all over for me and the Replacements.

Craig Wright: It was many years ago, maybe even twenty, and I was working at Coastal Seafoods, and through a coworker there I got invited to a party at Slim Dunlap's. I didn't know very many people there, so I wandered a lot, moving from room to room, pounding beer after beer.

Somewhere along the line, I found myself in the backyard standing across from Alex Chilton. I gave him a few general compliments and then gave special attention to "Hey Little Child." I told him I loved the rhythm. Alex smiled and said, "Yeah, the old cha cha cha." Like it was one of his first girlfriends.

A few seconds later, he told me he was going downstairs and he invited me to come along.

Soon I found myself in a crowded basement, seated on an old couch surrounded by Alex Chilton, Freedy Johnston, and Slim Dunlap, and everyone but me and Peter Jesperson had a guitar. The guys were trading songs and riffs in a gentlemanly way, but the aural dance floor cleared when Alex started playing transcriptions he'd done of Nina Simone solos and then, mind-blowingly, of Wagner overtures. It was amazing.

Watching Alex's fingers crawl up and down the frets like a family of crazy spiders, I got the impression he could do whatever occurred to him to do on that guitar, that anything was possible, and that every note he chose to play had a green glow around it, the glow of having been chosen among millions of options.

It was magical, virtuosic, gracious, infinite, unexpected, and completely perfect.

Carleton College, Northfield, Minnesota, February 1985.
© *Joan E. Bechtold*

Alex Chilton: Minneapolis was, in those days, sort of a great refuge. In the middle of the Reagan '80s, Minneapolis was fun and very pleasant and unlike the rest of America for me. It was a great breath of fresh air. I'll always be thankful, in the middle of Reaganomics, for Minneapolis. It was just one of those places like New Orleans used to be, and maybe still is, and like the East Village was in the '70s. It seemed like the whole town was one of the few places in America where a person like me or the Replacements could be themselves, and not be hauled up on charges.

Paul Westerberg: This is the truth: The war in Kuwait or a zit on my cheek—which worries me more? You know, my fuckin' cheek! My hair or global warming? It's like, yeah—that shit is all bad, but I'm not gonna talk about something I don't know about.[1]

Peter Buck: Minneapolis was like Athens [Georgia] for us then, just this oasis of sanity or something, where you could get away with anything and not feel like a total freak. It had tons of great bands, great record stores, good college radio, and papers and fanzines—and that was not like the rest of the country, believe me.

Paul Westerberg: The point [of "We'll Inherit the Earth," from *Don't Tell a Soul*] is that the meek shall inherit the earth. Well, it's ours already, but we don't want it if you continue to do with it what you're gonna do. It's my feeble attempt at social commentary.
Burl Gilyard: I thought that was [the 'Mats' B-side] "Election Day" (jokingly).
Paul Westerberg: Nah, that was just 'cause the bars were closed.[2]

Rosanne Cash: The '80s still felt like anything was possible. Or maybe I just felt like that. There was good and bad. We were all way too influenced by the synths on "Bette Davis Eyes," which was a great record, but we should not have all gone crazy trying to recapture those synthesizers. The Reagan years felt like a wall we were banging against, which was exciting. It all feels different now [in 2007]. There's no wall, only a virus, and you can't bang against a virus.

Alex Chilton: Politically, it was such a wretched period of time. It was sort of like now [2007]. It's like the '60s were great, the '70s were a nightmare, and the '80s were worse.

RJ Smith: Greil Marcus writes approvingly about Sonic Youth making rock so crude it was almost noise, but at JB's the Replacements made Sonic Youth sound like the Dillards. This was gap-toothed noise laughing at music.[3]

Peter Buck: Two years after we started, we'd be driving through towns and we'd hear all these bands that sounded like R.E.M. [on the radio]. The next year, or two years later, they all sounded like the Replacements. But not nearly as good. A couple years later, it was Sonic Youth.

RJ Smith: It had been a while since the people who had thrown lit cigarettes and cans of soup and toilet paper had left, and everybody else now was either just tired, or, I think, subtly pacified. And happy, too.

"My Sharona" came then, and when I looked over, I saw the bartender shaking a tambourine and bopping from one end of the bar to the other. Eventually they got to "Breakdown," and Jesperson sang every word from the back of the room. And then, pretty quickly, they found a way back, maybe found a new way to being Replacements once again

And when they wailed on "Johnny's Gonna Die," it was maybe more fucked and more moving, than ever. A friend in Ann Arbor a night later would tell me the Replacements were great because they had so many "objective correlatives" poking out of every song, like shrapnel in some Vili nail fetish, and maybe here was the biggest example of all. Westerberg at 20 writing about role model Johnny Thunders, how his update of Hank Williams's life was appealing, and terminal.

Built on the chords to "So You Want To Be a Rock and Roll Star," "Johnny" is a kid meditating on what's not a kid's theme: that what he loves—and it's not really junk, it's speed, wide eyed and no pauses—may kill him. The Replacements are crucial because they proclaim their hunger, and they don't shut up. From the mournful din of "Johnny" to *Let It Be*'s expansive, calamitous variety, they have been even smarter than they have been stoopid.

Nobody else left once things got interesting, but the band was getting tired. Still, the set never really "ended." Somebody left the stage, Tommy and Bob sat down on the edge, and roadie Bill Sullivan took the mike to say, "Once again we'd like to thank you for that big Ohio welcome." It cleared out briskly after that.[4]

Glen Morrow: Alternative rock music as it was called in the mid-'80s was really about British bands. They seemed to understand how to work MTV with big hair and make-up and synthesizers in a way that American bands

had trouble grasping. We're talking before the grunge era here when there was a new band coming out of the UK every week. Flock of Seagulls, Thompson Twins, Spandau Ballet, ABC, Human League, they just kept coming.

This was what was being played by the more adventurous commercial radio stations, with a little R.E.M. thrown in. It's why the Replacements wrote the song "Left of the Dial"—because the only place you could hear American bands was on college radio stations that were clustered at the lower end of the radio dial. The major labels picked up these stylized British bands for the U.S. and put their marketing dollars behind them, leaving most American bands to languish, most often unsigned or failing when they did get signed because they were not properly promoted.

This was the atmosphere that the Replacements had to deal with as they first started getting noticed. Even though they were very dysfunctional on a number of levels, their greatness could not be denied. They quickly rose to the top of the indie rock heap, and they did it in flannel shirts and jeans and the occasional dress.

George Regis: I was doing legal work for Twin/Tone and Hüsker Dü, and being from Stillwater [Minnesota], I would get back to the Twin Cities [from New York] on a regular basis. I met Westerberg, and I'm sure Peter Jesperson had something to do with that, because I'd done all my record shopping at his joint when I was in law school and journalism school at the University of Minnesota.

It was right after *Let It Be* came out, and it was starting to blow up and they found themselves needing counsel. Economically, it was starting to matter more; they were starting to make a buck, and major labels were starting to get very interested. I tried to give them a sort of primer education on what might be expected with a major-label relationship, and weighed the pros and cons of it versus doing another record at Twin/Tone. And it became pretty clear that they had pretty much exhausted the potential at Twin/Tone with *Let It Be*.

Michael Hill: Andy Schwartz, was from Minneapolis and started *New York Rocker*, and I had first started hearing about the Replacements through a review someone wrote for *New York Rocker*, where I worked. We started following them then. I had gotten to know Peter [Jesperson] and the band through Folk City stuff. [Yo La Tengo's] Ira Kaplan and I had done this three-bands-for-three-bucks night at Folk City, and when they first came to New York they stayed with Ira and Georgia [Hubley], right around the corner from my place. We had a Jonathan Richman cover band that we would practice for there.

When [the Replacements] first came to New York, I just remember stepping over an inert Bob in a sleeping bag every day. I loved the band, and when I went to Warners in '83, it was my personal dream to sign the Replacements. But I had no juice whatsoever; I was the young tape-listener guy. [Legendary Warner Bros. talent scout] Karen Birg hired me; I was the junior guy, and I didn't know jack shit about the record label other than I thought this band was great.

George Regis: Back in that day, a major label deal was the gold ring. That's what bands were pointed towards, as opposed to today, where a lot of bands are not interested in major label deals, for good reason. So what I tried to do is educate them fundamentally about what they could expect, and put them in situations where they could meet people from different labels and start to get a handle on who they liked and who they didn't like, and what sort of presentations made more sense to them than others.

Dave Pirner: There's music lovers in the music business, but for the most part there are other *types*.
Martin Zellar: It's like Sammy [Davis, Jr.] said: "It's two words—'show' and 'business.'"
Dave Pirner: That's right. It's an unholy mix of business and pleasure.
City Pages: What do you mean?
Dave Pirner: I don't know. . .
Paul Westerberg: Yes you do, explain it to us.
Dave Pirner: Frustrated musicians and business people that want to get involved in a hip business instead of a square one—you know, people that don't really know shit about music in general, but are involved in the business because of some other reason. There's good people in the music business, it's just that you're lucky if you come across 'em.[5]

Michael Hill: I was their A&R guy at Sire and Warner Bros., and in Paul I saw this sensitive singer/songwriter who could write both really personal material and incredibly anthemic material, in the context of this band that was just this side of punk rock. That seemed incredibly exciting, and it seemed to me that if that energy could be harnessed in a particular way, they could be huge. And I don't mean huge like Green Day today, but like a really meaningful band.

To me, Westerberg was like Bruce Springsteen or something. The whole thing seemed to have this enormous potential in this romantic rock and roll way which, looking back on it, was something of a different era. You know,

they were the Rolling Stones, or wanted to be the Rolling Stones or the Beatles, or whatever. I think everybody aspired to those.

Alex Chilton: A lot of people see rock and roll as a real movement that's headed somewhere good, or something. But I was thinking the other day that I really never have felt [part of anything]. I mean, I saw some unity in style and music and all that kind of stuff in the mid-'60s, but that's like the last time.

Michael Hill: With the Replacements, there was this critique going on of pop culture as we knew it. And what were our expectations? I know for myself, as an A&R guy who was brought into a major label because I had quote-unquote indie cred, when I got in there you begin to adopt a value system that's pretty different from the one you walked in with. And the thing is, those guys played both ends against the middle: they laughed in the face of stardom, yet got really pissed off at you if you didn't treat them like a star.

Westerberg really set a tone for the rest of them, and carried it even further to his audience: If you like me, you're a fool. But if you don't like me, you're equally a fool. There was incredible self-regard and very low self-esteem issues going on at the same time.

George Regis: *Let It Be* had hit its peak in terms of critical acclaim and commercial availability, and I was a young lawyer with a serious music firm for the first time. I had a real mentor, Owen Epstein, who was a real legend at the time. So my first big moment with the Replacements was showing them off to the various major-label A&R people that I was getting plugged into through Owen. It was at a CB's show where they were just as loaded as they could possibly be. They did not get a third of the way through anything they attempted to play. It was one of those nights.

At one point, they stopped a song and there was a lot of kicking around and drinking going on onstage and Westerberg sort of mumbles into the microphone, "Have we got a major label deal yet?" Soon afterwards, four or five of these very senior record executives who I had just met and only knew me because Owen had introduced me as the Replacements' lawyer, they all started filing out. And to a man, they patted me on the shoulder and said, "It'll be better than this. It'll be better than this." Almost offering condolences.

Michael Hill: I did take the entire Warner Bros. staff to see them. A lot of people didn't get it, particularly because they'd do something to alienate every-

body in the middle of the show. People looked at me like, "What is it you like about them?"

RJ Smith: The point in running down this bad behavior isn't in the details. I had heard many of these stories before, but it wasn't until I was on the road with the Replacements that I began to see how depressing their untenable heap of ambitions and energy can get. *Hootenanny* sold only about 6000 copies, and they're deep in the hole financing *Let It Be.* The record industry isn't going to look at this band and see a sack of Krugerrands. When the Replacements came to New York and played for some A&R people at CBGB, they flopped. To me it seemed meaningful.

New York was where they figured they'd be heard by some big label representatives—Warner Bros.' Michael Hill was coming out and, because he was a fan, he had set up a meeting with the band once they got to town. According to Paul, nothing in particular happened. "I wasn't expecting to sign a deal or nothing, at all. Basically we're talking 'in a few years.' He didn't say anything specific at all. He just wanted to know if we had half a brain or if we were a bunch of loads. At this point he'd be embarrassed, it would be too much of a risk to bring some bigwig down and see these guys who could possibly fall on their face.

"Last night [at CBGB], was a classic example. We went up there, we did what we wanted to do, and they [the record industry wanted us to play our best songs as best we could. And we didn't feel like it. And so they figure, 'They're a small-time bunch of amateurs.' That's one way to look at it, and that's partly true. But I think it's also the spirit that makes rock exciting and immediate."

But if Paul and Jesperson say there were no big hopes for the meeting, I remember the argument outside the gyro restaurant. Bob was complaining about the size of Twin/Tone's operation. And I remember Paul saying, "Well, just wait until we get to New York. We're going to talk to somebody from Warner Bros. there." He wasn't just placating an angry Bob. And then there was the show the night of the meeting with Hill.

Shortly into the set Paul babbled, "You may have guessed tonight that we don't want to play any of our own songs." This was big-league self-abuse: not the rocket ride that can make their covers go bang, more like an extended submarine fart. The audience was howling at them, and the band couldn't come up with anything to shout back. Finally, they stumbled into the Stones' "Start Me Up," with shit-eating grins I would swear were slapped over some raw feelings. And then Paul said into the mike, "Do we get a record contract now?" No,

but Hill did say he had tried to get Rod Stewart to cover "16 Blue" [*sic*].[6]

Jim DeRogatis: By the time *Let It Be* was released, I was writing for a couple of fanzines—*Matter*, *The Bob*, and *Jersey Beat*—and I'd road-trip with those publications' editors, Liz Phillip and Jim Testa, whenever the 'Mats played anywhere in New York, New Jersey, Connecticut, and sometimes even as far as Boston. I'm pretty sure I was with them when I saw one of those incredible gigs in '84 or '85, with the Replacements playing the songs from *Let It Be* at Maxwell's, and proving that they could be amazing, inspiring, tight as hell, and absolutely transcendent. The next night was the memorable one, though: They played CBGB and it was a complete train wreck, and of course that was the show where all of the record company people turned out, as well as the radio and MTV folks and all of the big-deal New York rock critics. The band truly sucked: I don't think it finished a single song, and not even the fact that Bob Stinson had dressed for the occasion by wrapping himself head to foot in aluminum foil could turn things around.

Alcohol always gets blamed for these disasters, but don't underestimate the Replacements' very Minneapolis-like ability to choke under pressure when they really wanted to impress, because on top of playing to all of the industry bigwigs, they were sharing the bill with Alex Chilton. On the New York rock scene, this quickly became known as "the night Paul met Alex," and fans there sort of took credit for the song for that reason.

P. D. Larson: Those were heady, heady times. I was on tour with those guys for three weeks of that tour. We stayed with Ira Kaplan, and we had some downtime. Bruce [Springsteen] had just filmed the video for "Glory Days" at Maxwell's, and the 'Mats were playing there right after, and the Fall or somebody was playing there the night before so we decided to go. It was me, Peter, the band, Maggie [Macpherson], Sully, and maybe Carton.

Before we went out, I'd been talking to Bob, because he had discovered that in a past life I had listened to some prog rock. He was a huge Steve Howe fan, and, being the anglophile record-collector geek that I was, I started telling him about bands that Steve Howe had been in before Yes. The night we were all going out to Maxwell's, he stayed in because he wasn't the most social guy; he was happy just to stay in and watch TV and hang out.

So we go to the show, and after the show we're walking around Hoboken and we got the bright idea to go find Frank Sinatra's birthplace. At this point, common sense had long gone by the side and the alcohol and drugs had taken

over, and we started walking around and didn't really find anything. We stayed out all night and went to an all-night diner that served booze, and when we got back to Ira's place it was light out.

There were people sleeping everywhere: floor, couches, chairs, whatever. And Bob was sitting pretty much in the same spot he was seven, eight hours earlier. He wasn't drunk or anything. I was gonna hit the hay, and out of nowhere he goes, "So that band Steve was in before Yes was Tomorrow? That was what they were called? Or The Syndicats or something?" He completely picked up [the conversation] like I'd gotten up and gone out of the room for five minutes to go get a beer.

George Regis: You always knew when you saw one of those [bad] shows you wanted to be at the next one, because you knew they were going to tear the roof off the place, wherever it might be. And that's what happened two nights later at Irving Plaza. Owen brought Seymour [Stein], and I went with Steve Ralbovsky, who was and is one of my oldest friends, and he was doing A&R for Columbia [Records], and he desperately wanted to sign the band.

They did a transcendent show. They treated their own material with all the respect it deserved, and the covers were great, and they played like motherfuckers. Seymour was knocked out of his socks, committed to signing them right then and there, and met them and charmed them in the way only Seymour can, and ultimately that's where it ended up.

Michael Hill: Seymour really liked them. I think Seymour is a real music lover and can cut to the chase very quickly and see the value in something. I think Seymour thought they were cute and they were fun and getting in everyone's face, and so on.

Owen was hyping the Replacements to Seymour, and Seymour basically said, "Michael, if you can bring them in here, I can sign them." He trusted me because I came from their side of the tracks. Bill Sullivan just introduced me to somebody by saying, "Michael was the guy we knew who went to work at the major label. And we thought, 'Well if he's there, then maybe it's OK to go take a meeting or something.'" And that was really the spirit of things. Seymour was just good to go, because he could sign with impunity.

Alex Chilton: To me, the Replacements were always a great live band. I don't know if a record did them justice. They were completely fun at a gig. My bass player at the time was very interested in the Replacements, and he

always talks about once, in the dressing room, and I wasn't here for this, it's just hearsay.

But there was a big spread in the dressing room—dip and chips and that sort of thing. I guess it was in Miami. And Paul walked into the dressing room and said, "Mmm, what a nice bunch of little stuff." And there were about eight or ten people in the dressing room, and he just upset the whole table immediately; knocked the whole thing over. That greatly impressed the bass player, Ron Eastley. I wasn't all that impressed with that sort of thing, but I guess that might've been a good enough one if I'd seen it myself. I might've liked that.

Paul Westerberg: You saw us in some weird circumstances when you open for a bigger band, you're sort of treated like baggage, and it's almost like, "Well, you're damn lucky to be on this bill." And we don't like being told what to do. So in those events, we would rather blow a show completely to flip them the bird than play the game. We'll come out and give them a circus.[7]

Michael Hill: Seymour is very much a collector—he collects antiques and various things—so once he's got the band, he was on to another one. So we were lucky that we had this relationship, where there was actually someone who they could talk to on a daily basis while Seymour jetted off to his next rendezvous.

I think [the Replacements] reminded him of what he saw when he went to see the Ramones and a lot of other bands not quite a decade earlier. I think it reminded him of both the bands he saw in the CB's era and in England around the same time—the late '70s. I think he saw that Ramones energy, which is one reason why Tommy Erdelyi got involved [as the producer of *Tim*]. But I think he also saw the one-two punch of Paul and Tommy: the songwriting potential in Paul, and the teen idol potential in Tommy.

Bob Stinson: Seymour Stein is a genius. He saw immediately what he got himself into. It was a good joke for awhile. I was always asked not to go to the interviews with him, but he saw right away what we were up to and where we were going. And there was no way it could've gone on for very long. Ten years is good enough.[8]

Michael Hill: I can't honestly say that I ever got to know Bob. He'd call me by a different name every time he saw me. I remember we were recording one time, and he came in and said, "Are you my lawyer, man?"

Peter Kohlsaat: They signed their Warner Bros. contract in my apartment. I was staying in a house on like 24th and Girard [Avenue in South Minneapolis]—one of those great big duplexes. They needed someplace to do it, and I had this great big dining room with this great big table and I said, "Why not here?"

George Regis: I was staying with Pete [Kohlsaat], and everybody knew Pete because he was a cartoonist and the dentist to the rock stars. There was some excitement, but they were careful not to betray too much excitement. They would much rather come off as renegade, or dismissive of it. But the whole ritual is to go through it, and from my point of view, it's important that they all show up when the sun is high in the sky and we go through it one time so that I'm assured they've had a proper opportunity to know what it is they're signing, even though it might not be sinking in. I can simply present it to them and hope for the best.

Peter Kohlsaat: They all came over to the house, Jesperson and everyone, and I just happened to take a few pictures.

George Regis: Their attitude was either snotty at times or sober, believe it or not. Interested, curious, and willing to be informed—as opposed to the public persona they liked to project about not giving a rat's ass. Behind all of the shenanigans, they really did want to know how it would work and how it would push them up that "ladder of success." But at the same time, their propensity for shooting themselves in the feet was always there.

One foot in the door. Inking the major-label deal (with Jesperson and attorney George Regis).

Paul Westerberg: We're making money, but we don't see it because you got like lawyers and accountants and fuckheads.[9]

George Regis: There was some genuine excitement. It represented a major step in their career. We toasted the whole thing; we had some champagne on hand. And they were really excited to be with [Warner Bros. subsidiary] Sire and Seymour. At that point, Seymour's track record was impeccable. They were part of a long line of A-plus-level rock and rollers that Seymour had signed, and they were absolutely an appropriate addition to that roster. They fit right in with the Ramones, the Talking Heads, the Pretenders, the Smiths. It was that pantheon. It was all cool stuff, and there was nothing cooler than the Replacements at that time.

Peter Kohlsaat: George loved my little red TR-6 [Triumph convertible] so much he bought one when he got a little more disposable income. But he and Westerberg spent the rest of the day driving around town, celebrating. Paul changed lawyers a few years ago, and that's been a real sore spot with George. Because he really likes Westerberg, and he was a big fan and personal friend. And I don't think he ever really explained to him why he cut him loose.

Paul Westerberg: They see it as there's a hundred bands like us who would die for our chance, who are starving hungry and would do whatever they're told. And they don't understand that we want to go as far as we can, but we don't want to be like AHa and shit. We're not like the Cult.

Peter Kohlsaat photos

We don't have a strong, hip image that's going to sell right now, and they don't know what to do with us.[10]

Tommy Stinson: They think we're trying to piss them off, but we're just being ourselves. This isn't like a job. Or a big thing to make us popular and pick up chicks. We just like doing this—it's fun. They just sit there and go, "You guys are just trying to piss us off. You want to be the bad kids of the rock business."[11]

Michael Hill: I always said to Paul and all of them, "It's not you against everybody. It's really all us against everybody else. Don't make us all the enemy, because we're all in this together. We're a force, fighting the good fight together." And I thought we needed to be more communal in that sense, rather than hostile to the very people who were key to not only our survival, but the survival of this whole aspect of popular culture.

Paul Westerberg: And [producer] Tommy Erdelyi, for all the help he gave us, did a pretty crap-ass job at mixing the thing [*Tim*]. I mean, he mixed it on headphones 'cause he was deaf from playing with the Ramones. So it didn't help us a whole lot. But it's got some great tunes on it.[12]

Tommy Erdelyi: What grabbed me was their intelligence. It was refreshing to see an intelligent group.[13]

Casey Greig: I was in seventh grade when *Tim* came out. My older brother Tim, the black sheep, gave it to me. He just handed me the cassette and left the room. I put it on and looked at the cover: "Tim." I wondered why he put his name on the side. *This is MINE now*, I thought. I left "The Replacements" on the cassette cover, scratched out "Tim," and defiantly wrote in "Casey."

When my brother got back, I asked him, "Why did you put your name on MY cassette?" After a second he said, "You dumbfuck, that's the name of the album."

Is it possible to point to the moment life starts? I can: the first seven seconds of "Bastards of Young." First that guitar, then that Howl. Rewind. Play. The guitar and then the Howl again. I felt like I was being born.

Paul Westerberg: We named it *Tim* for no reason at all. We had other titles kicking around: this was the first time we named an album after it was done.

Uptown Bar & Grill (Minneapolis), Summer 1985. *Mary B. Johnson photo*

We sat around a bar, we were gonna call it either *Whistler's Mammy, Van Gogh's Ear*, or *England Schmingland*. I think I said *Tim*, and we sat and laughed for a few minutes and then we said, "Why not?" When somebody asks, "What's the name of your album?" "*Tim*." No one's really done that. It took us dumbos to come up with it.[14]

Casey Greig: To me, music in 1985 was my parents' country station, KQ's classic rock, and whatever Top 40 station was around then. *Tim* had pieces of all three but sounded more RIGHT NOW than anything I had ever heard. My brother told me they were from Minneapolis. I couldn't believe it. Twenty miles south. Why wasn't anyone playing this on the radio? If they wouldn't play this, what else was out there? I had to find out. Thanks to the two Tims, I went to look and never came back.

171

Steve Albini: I'll be honest. I didn't listen to much of [*Tim*], which is why I'm not gonna saddle them with a grade. What I listened to didn't appeal to me at all, and I saw no point in wasting the better part of an hour to listening to a record I obviously wasn't going to give a shit about, especially when there's shit I know is gonna be tits just sitting there by the Hi-Fi unheard as yet, like that Live Skull LP and the new Buttholes EP and the Amor Fati LP and anyway, you get the picture. This isn't my kind of shit, and there are people who do it much better anyway (Squirrelbait for one) so I don't see the point.[15]

Brad Zellar: All sorts of people from my world, and from the fringes of my world, knew the Replacements after all the *Tim* buzz, but that didn't really bother me much. It would be hard for me to overestimate what an impact that band had on me, though, as a guy who'd grown up listening to crappy AM radio in southern Minnesota, in a town without a real record store. I always thought there was this relatively small conglomeration of real bands—all of them, of course, from someplace other than Minnesota—and a million cover bands that played versions of the real bands' songs at weddings and on weekends in local bars. The Replacements turned that whole notion completely on its head. Seeing them the first few times was particularly astonishing in that, at that time, I was in a band that played almost *un-ironic* versions of the same sorts of schlocky covers the Replacements butchered purely for ornery sport and fuck-you yucks.

George Regis: I was in town when they were finishing it up, and I'll always remember sitting on the floor [of Cookhouse Studios on 25th and Nicollet Avenue in the Whittier neighborhood of South Minneapolis] listening to the first playback of the thing. There were only a half-dozen people in the studio, and I'm sitting next to Paul, and we listen to this thing in its entirety. And it was just amazing. So wonderful. And he was in a real reflective mood, and I'll always remember him just surprising himself at how good this turned out.

Jon Pareles: "Time for decision to be made," Mr. Westerberg sings in the opening song of "Tim"—and the Replacements have decided to hang tough. "Tim" was produced by Tommy Erdelyi, formerly the drummer for the Ramones; it cleans up the band's attack just a little, while bringing Mr. Westerberg's voice forward. It also shows how well they use Beatles-flavored pop and rockabilly ("Kiss Me on the Bus"), skiffle ("Waitress in the Sky") and folk-pop ("Here Comes a Regular").

There's something missing, though—humor. The Replacements always had a streak of wild-eyed, tolerant slapstick, in such songs as "Androgynous" (about consenting adults) or "Take Me Down to the Hospital." On "Tim," however, they concentrate a little too hard on making a statement, defining themselves in one song as "Bastards of Young" and asking in another for a "Dose of Thunder." For some reason, their put-downs are also addressed exclusively to women for the first time.

Doubtless the band felt some pressure. "Tim" is the first Replacements album many people will ever hear—and those that do are likely to be impressed by the ingenuity that goes into such heartfelt songs as "Lay It Down Clown" or "Kiss Me on the Bus." But it's worth searching for the albums "Let It Be" or "Hootenanny," with a different style in every track; they offer a far better sampling of one of America's most cantankerous bands.[16]

Robert Longo: Paul's a great songwriter. His songs can rip your heart out. But I also like their self-destructiveness. And the way the band follows him is kind of scary.[17]

Brad Zellar: God, I hated that [photographer/visual artist] Robert Longo cover [artwork for *Tim*]. *Hated* it. I looked at it and looked at it and it just seemed so artsy-fartsy. I guess that was the first indication of how much things had changed with the move to a major label.

I bought the record the day it came out. In fact I bought both the vinyl and a cassette, because I couldn't wait to hear it and the best and truest test of a record for me then and now was how it sounded in the car. I was also working in a parking lot at the time and wanted to be able to play it in my boom box.

I remember picking up a six-pack of Milwaukee's Best at John's Superette on Como and then driving over to Siebert Field at the U. There was a railroad yard back there, and it was a good place at the time to park and hang out at night.

I sat there and listened to the tape a couple times. I have to admit that I had sort of conflicted feelings initially. It was definitely a huge departure from *Let It Be*, or at least a seriously cleaned-up version of the band. It grew on me in a hurry, though. There were a bunch of great songs on there, a lot of them sort of atypical of the Replacements at the time, but an indication of the direction Westerberg in particular was headed: "Kiss Me on the Bus," "Waitress in the Sky," "Swingin' Party," "Left of the Dial," "Little Mascara," and "Here Comes a Regular," which I still think is (along with "Unsatisfied") Westerberg's masterpiece.

Outside 7th St. Entry at the beginning of the *Tim* five-night stand. October 18, 1985.
© *Joan E. Bechtold*

Molly Walsh: Do you remember the time they had a five-night stand at the Entry? I think I went all five nights. Were you with me?

Laura Poehlman: We weren't old enough to go all five nights. It was fall 1985, but you didn't turn nineteen until December; we only went to the all-ages show. That was when we discovered the greatest sightline was the steps by the bathroom and the bar, and as a result Pete Jesperson pushed past us several times carrying cases of Heineken downstairs and we both fell in total lust with him. That show was the day before *Tim* came out. Since we'd heard all the songs live the day before it seemed like we knew all the words the first time we listened to the record.

Molly Walsh: You are completely right. Was this the same year you asked Bob Stinson to go to prom? I remember seeing Bob Stinson at Oarfolk that one night and we gave him a ride, dropping him off by the train tracks near Lake Street. We didn't realize 'til after he was in the car that the paper bag he had actually contained a can of beer.

Laura Poehlman: That's right, the ride was the summer before the Entry show. Bob was gallant enough to try to refuse the ride because he was barefoot, but didn't mention the beer, probably because it wasn't open yet. I found out later that he walked from his house to the train tracks almost every warm night to watch the sunset, which sounds impossibly romantic.

The same year [*Ed. note: The* SNL *broadcast was the January following the October 1985* Tim *five-night stand.*], we saw the Replacements show at First Ave. the day after they broadcast their musical appearance on *SNL*, which was shown Sunday night in Minnesota for some reason—the [First Avenue] show was a

This page and following: Paul beats the heat on night two of the *Tim* five-night stand at the Entry, October 19, 1985. © *Joan E. Bechtold*

Monday, and after they were finished, we saw Bob, and Harry Kaiser dared me to talk to Bob, so I said, "Should I go ask him to the prom?" and I did. He said yes right away, and then added, "Unless we're on tour." What ended up happening was, since it was still winter, he was on tour and forgot too, plus he got married that spring before my prom at the same manor on Park Avenue where Regina *had* their prom. . .

Molly Walsh: I am still so bummed I didn't get to go to that dance. I was grounded from getting caught shoplifting at Target. You probably don't remember that I also waited on Paul Westerberg at Snyder's on Hennepin and Lake when I worked there. I sold him the *SPIN* with Iggy Pop on the cover, and I decided it would be cooler to not be fannish and "recognize" him, but I totally traded out of my register to keep the $20 he paid with and kept it for as long as I could afford to.

Laura Poehlman: Too bad we don't know how to get in touch with Jessie whatshername who had pieces of Tommy's bass after the Regina show, and then ended up hanging out with him. What was her last name? She was in your class, went to Annunciation, but she was on my bus because she lived over by the Osterbauers.

Alex Chilton: We did a lot of gigs together. Fifteen dates or something, and

every one was just great. Magical. They just really had it on stage. I never saw 'em not set an audience on fire. I was opening for them most of the time, and we did some one-offs and a tour through the Southeast. Most were in Florida.

I never saw a bad Replacements show. I can remember a show or two that wasn't very long, and the audience had a big response to that. But even then, they got a big response—both negative and positive. I remember some pretty explosive audience reactions, but from my tastes they were great every time.

Paul Westerberg: Lately, we've been trying to go get a happy medium. We got a lot of people coming now to see us for the image shit. And it's not something we contrive, it's what we are. But we'll try to play some of the songs good. It's like we won't try to purposely mess up. But there are some songs we'll just wing. . . . And sometimes we're going for like a big kamikaze thing. I'd rather have them hating our guts in some circumstances, so they can at least go "Who the fuck was that band?"

Tommy Stinson: But the people are here to see us tonight. The fucking Replacements. The fucking Mats.[18]

Jon Bream: The good news is that the Replacements, the critically acclaimed rock quartet from Minneapolis, will get a big break this weekend

Graffiti in the legendary 7th St. Entry restroom references the fire that had gutted Oarfolk just prior to the *Tim* five-night stand, October 1985. © *Joan E. Bechtold*

with a performance on "NBC's Saturday Night Live." The bad news is that WUSA (Channel 11), the local NBC affiliate, will not broadcast the program live because of a previous commitment to carry a syndicated telethon for cerebral palsy.

"It's one of those things," Art Ludwig, WUSA program director, said Tuesday. "We've had the telethon scheduled for over a year. We didn't know a local band was on it (Saturday Night Live). It didn't come to our attention until two days ago."

Channel 11 has made arrangements to broadcast a tape of the "Saturday Night Live" installment shortly after midnight Sunday.

"It's pretty cool," said the band's manager, Peter Jesperson. "We had talked about it in California when we were talking to Warner Bros.' video guy." That record-company official, the director of creative marketing, wrote a letter to the producer of "Saturday Night Live" in early January pitching the Replacements. After checking with several sources in the music industry, "SNL" invited the group on the show.

"I don't usually book bands that way," said Michele Galfas, "SNL" music talent executive, by telephone from her New York office. "I usually see them myself. But they (Replacements) got a great reputation in L.A. (after their performances there Dec. 16 and 17). Their album is No. 6 on the college charts, and the college charts mean a lot to me.

"They (Replacements) came out of nowhere. I wasn't aware of them until the middle of December. I think it's exciting and fun to have new bands on the show instead of consistently booking (hitmakers) from the charts."[19]

Peter Jesperson: I remember there was this controversy because they were drinking beer in the green room, and they said that was against the rules. We were like, "Really?"

Abbie Kane: Harry Dean Stanton was the host, and they got drunk with him. They were drinking and watching hockey. I flew out to New York with [Twin/Tone co-founder] Paul Stark. For many years I've been friends with Bobby Z, Bobby Rivkin, Prince's drummer. And at that time, we were really tight. And his wife was about to deliver a baby any second. I remember being a little hesitant to go, because I wanted to be home for that, but it was the Replacements in New York and *Saturday Night Live*.

And Paul Stark is really good friends with Al Franken and Tom Davis, who were writers on the show at that time, and he mentioned that Bobby Z was

"Kiss me on the butt." The poster for the infamous
1986 *Saturday Night Live* guest appearance. *Terry Katzman collection*

gonna have a baby. And it just so happened that they were doing a skit about a pregnant woman and they changed the character's name to "Mrs. Rivkin."

Bob Stinson: It was '86 and we were doing "Saturday Night Live," staying at the Berkshire Hotel. I caused all the trouble on that one: I broke the phones, put a hole in the door, threw an ashtray out the window. Lorne Michaels put food and flower baskets in our rooms, free bar tabs—we went to town. I think I'd have to say I abused it more than anybody. They swore no band from Warner Bros. would play on that show again unless we paid the tab on the $1,000 worth of supposed "damage" we did.

We were picked up to go to the studio at 10 in the morning in a limousine stocked with booze, and from 10 to five you couldn't leave that floor. Anything you want they'd send for. Before we played we were completely just out of it. Harry Dean Stanton was in there drinking booze with Tommy. They were all fucked up. I was in the bathroom getting high. I had no idea those three had switched clothes, I didn't even know until I saw the playback—didn't even occur to me. I was wearing something Lori, ah, Mrs. Westerberg, gave me. It was something like "I Dream of Jeanie" [*sic*] would wear: stripes, big bell-bottoms. But on stage I bent over when we were playing and Paul stepped back from the mike and said "fuck you." As long as it isn't audible they couldn't do a damn thing. Lorne Michaels was pretty pissed about that.

We played "Kiss Me on the Butt, er, Bus" and "Bastards of Young." That was the original name of it: "Kiss Me on the Butt," but we changed it to "bus," or Paul did—take your pick. As soon as we went to commercial Lorne Michaels came to us and said "that was a cheap shot."

We had to sign like a $20,000 agreement not to swear on national T.V. The cheap way around it is to mumble. It was like our record contract: it never said we had to be in the videos we made, so we just had Paul's shoe and a cigarette in one of 'em. It just seemed the harder we tried to piss off everybody the more they liked us; I'd have to blame that on our demise, on what led us to walking away from each another (sic), anyway.[20]

Pat Whalen: I had only seen the Replacements once: in Detroit at the stunning Fox Theatre. It was 1986. They were a surprise opener for R.E.M.—The 3 O'Clock had the third spot of the bill—and I was thrilled. As music director at the Traverse City [Michigan] college radio station I had arranged to record ID's with the members of R.E.M. after the show . . . "This is Mike Mills of R.E.M. and you're listening to W-N-M-C 91.1 in Traverse City" . . . plus a pre-show interview

with the main singer/songwriter from The 3 O'Clock. All one-sentence answers to amateur questions, one of my first and worst artist interviews.

As I was standing outside The 3 O'Clock's tour bus with my friend/recording engineer—he owned a brand-new TEAC four-track cassette recorder—the Replacements pulled up in their van and U-Haul trailer. I could see Paul Westerberg in the passenger seat. A guy I would come to know seven years later was driving.

The 'Mats' van pulled half up on the curb behind the tour bus. The sliding door opened and a couple dozen crushed beer cans of various makes fell to the pavement as the band stepped out. They looked just like they did on the cover of *Let It Be*, one of my favorite records at the time. I exchanged smiles and a "hey" with Paul Westerberg as he walked by.

A brush with greatness, I thought, stained with a dirt-rich reality that, as a small-town Midwest kid, impressed me a great deal. The show was stellar. The band was relatively coherent, playing a mostly straight, fun, *Tim*-driven set, spiced by a few abortive covers. Definitely surpassed The 3 O'Clock. And I actually like The 3 O'Clock.

Years later, soon after I moved to Minneapolis to join [writer/critic/promoter and *Your Flesh* publisher] Pete Davis' fledgling booking biz, I was shopping for a desk to put in my itsy upstairs room at the big house on Colfax upheld by Lori Barbero, who led me to a junk store somewhere between Lyndale and Hennepin on Lake Street. As we made our way down the sidewalk I heard a band practicing in the basement of one of the many storefront businesses there. I recognized some muffled riffs rising from the grates. It was the Replacements at practice. Lori confirmed it. No big deal to her. It was to me. "I'm in Minneapolis," I repeated to myself. Officially there.

Then, years later, I came to know a very nice and talented guy named Eric Pierson through various bands he worked with and some recording projects and endless shows. He was the driver of that van that pulled up to the Fox Theatre in 1986: the 'Mats' tour manager. I told him my tiny tale, my Replacements story. He then clued me in: The band would purposely chuck their empties into that ditch where the door meets the van as they made their way from city to city. It was a shtick.

Luke Zimmerman: I have an unconfirmed report [from] a friend of mine at First Avenue, where they had the lights down low and announced the Replacements and you could see the band walking out. Westerberg walked out and grabbed the mike but just kept walking off the end of the stage, crashing

to the ground. Immediately the lights came up and a roadie says, "OK, show's over" and everybody had to go home. Not sure if it's true, but from what I've heard, not out of the question for that time.

Bill Holdship: Before concluding the interview Paul tells us that he's "as happy now as I was when we started—we don't have any money, but we've been at the bottom and it doesn't scare us at all." We tell him we can appreciate his attitude. He thanks us, adding, "I think we're doing something that no one did before. The Sex Pistols pretended to do this. But this is just naturally us. We don't want to be stars and shit—but we're sort of slipping into it."

What if the money becomes real good?

"I don't think so. . ."

That's a powerful incentive.

"No. It really isn't when you see the ramifications that are going to come along with it. Because we are uncomfortable now with the little tiny stardom of signing autographs. That's cool, but I would not like to be . . . even like Michael Stipe or something. . ."

By the time we [Holdship and fellow writer J. Kordosh] re-enter the auditorium we are both seeing double (and maybe even triple). The place is packed.

"We can't find Bob," Paul says into the microphone. "Has anyone seen Bob?" (Bob is actually sitting with some fans in the audience—but no one knows this until later.) "Oh, well, this might be fun. . ."

The Replacements begin playing, replacing the lost Bob with a roadie—and later an usher—during the opening part of their set. They begin with a dynamic "Color Me Impressed," followed by an *incredibly* sloppy "Johnny B. Goode" that couldn't have been any more powerful if it were Chuck Berry playing it in '58 or the Stones in '66. "Bob! Bob!" chants the audience. "Bob?" asks Paul. "Fuck Bob!" He is obviously a bit perturbed.[21]

Jim Walsh: June, 1986. The Replacements are roaring through one of their patented skittish sets at the Ritz in New York City when singer/guitarist Paul Westerberg belly flops into the crowd. The sea of bodies part; Westerberg goes down hard to the floor, where a combat boot stomps on his left hand, breaking the ring finger. As he returns to the stage, the band makes a valiant effort to finish the set, but the pain proves too debilitating. They abort the set and saunter offstage.

This was the last the world heard from the Replacements for almost a year. By the time they resurfaced in April with their new *Pleased to Meet Me* LP, the

band had fired guitarist and band clown Bob Stinson and split with longtime manager/mentor Peter Jesperson.[22]

Slim Dunlap: I can recall Bob and the janitor problems at First Avenue. I was a janitor there, and Bob was . . . Bob was not the world's best employee. They wanted me to get rid of him, but I couldn't do it because I knew what was coming down for him. Kind of more than he did. I remember one night coming to work and Bob showed up late, and he was really drunk and I knew then that what I was worried about was coming down.

He came up to me and he goes, "I bet you anything that they won't find anybody, and sooner or later they're gonna come knocking on my door."

And I go, "Let's hope for their sake that day doesn't come, Bob," and we both laughed about that. And I completely put it out of my mind. I didn't tell anybody or try or say anything to anybody. I kind of prayed that I wouldn't be the last in line.

Paul Westerberg: I'm not sure if [Bob] was lazy or maybe a little intimidated. And that was sort of degrading to him and to me, because he's a better guitar player than I am and I never wanted to sit down and show him things that he could already do.

I think he enjoyed touring, because of the "fringe benefits" aspect of it, but he wasn't really willing to work for it anymore. We got tired of it, because it got to be kind of like dead weight. We gave him chances. For a long time we were saying, "Bob, c'mon, get your shit together," and we'd try to help him and have patience, but it got to the point where he'd miss practice or he'd show up in a state not ready to work or play.[23]

Slim Dunlap: Bob was angry one night, and he was telling me that the way it came down wasn't right. I didn't argue with him, but I tried to make him feel like, "This isn't the end of the world." It was really hard to be around him at that time. Loving Bob, that was really mean. Letting Bob go for the reason they let him go was mean.

Chris Mars: The band was getting screwed up with cocaine and Bob was a scapegoat. Everybody said, "Well, we did it for Bob's sake," but we were all doing it just as much. After Bob left, I didn't see how we were going to fill his shoes.[24]

IN CONCERT
Replacements
WITH SPECIAL GUEST
alex chilton

ALL AGES
FRIDAY
APRIL 24
8 PM

Tix:
$10.
advance
$12.
door
Available At All Bass
Ticket Outlets

Call 672-7226

CAMEO
THEATRE

1445
WASHINGTON AVE.
MIAMI BEACH

CROSSOVER
CONCERTS

Children by the millions. The flyer for a 1987 Miami Beach show with Alex Chilton in support utilized a band photo depicting Bob, even though he had departed by this time. *Author collection*

Paul Westerberg: Bob didn't have a clue. He didn't know the key of A from his left foot, so I'd sort of show him where to put his hands. "Just kinda start there, Bob."[25]

Bob Stinson: I went to treatment when, hell, everybody should have.[26]

Paul Westerberg: It's tough, but Tommy was right there with me and Chris. We didn't want to go down the toilet with a guy who wasn't willing to play. Tommy wanted to see Bob straighten up, but he wasn't and he wouldn't and he's gone.[27]

Slim Dunlap: Recounting this story is ugly. Ugly on so many fronts. And people don't know that, because the gossamer of time shields everybody from the reality of things. I don't really ever want my story to be heard, because I don't like to go back and think about it. It was not all pretty. The world doesn't work that way. But I don't want to be the one who pops that legend. I benefited so much from it that I can't be spiteful about it.

Paul Westerberg: Slim's played for everybody around here. If your guitar player got sick you called Slim. He's better than me but he's not a virtuoso. We thought about getting a real hot player, but then we thought it was better to get someone we got along with, and Slim fits in good. He's a real humble guy and he likes to take a drink and he owns a gun. What can I say? He's in the band.[28]

Slim Dunlap: That day, Tommy had come to see Chrissie [Dunlap, Slim's wife and First Avenue band booker], and I was going to record with Curt[iss A], who was being produced by Big Al [Anderson of NRBQ]. I was all worried about that, because I didn't really have anything to play. I didn't really want anybody to hear it, because it was so bad. I remember recording with Big Al [at Cookhouse Studios], and he was not very encouraging in my contributions.

And somehow Tommy had heard I was there, and he came in and said he'd been looking for me and asked me to come to rehearsal. I told him, "Maybe later tonight, if I can get down there I'll get down there, but don't count on it." And I started thinking, "God, should I go down there, or is this a horrible mistake?" Then I thought, "What have I got to lose?" How could you not take that opportunity?

So foolishly I walked to this little spot below Torps Music there. Tommy had that little room. I don't know why they had been rehearsing at that time.

Paul and Slim, November 1987. © *Daniel Corrigan*

Maybe they were auditioning people. I don't know. I never really asked them what the story was, how I ended up there.

But I remember ending up at J.D. Hoyt's [in downtown Minneapolis] after. And [practice had been] so blisteringly loud, that I didn't really hear anything they said. I just remember having one too many cocktails, and they were bugging me, "What would it entail for you to do something like that [join the band]?" And I just kind of thought they were messing with me. I never really got a straight answer out of Paul, especially. I can't really remember that night ever coming to any conclusions. Then I think I dropped 'em all off and went home. And Chrissie called me the next day that she'd heard a rumor that I had joined the Replacements.

Tommy Stinson: I figured it out after we got down to Memphis to record, after we'd talked to Slim about playing with us. The reason I wanted Slim in the band was to *replace my brother*. I've known Slim for years so it was a good thing. We couldn't have some guy from L.A. with hair down to his butt come in. It had to be someone I liked.[29]

Eric Lindbom: Were Bobby and Tommy good babies? How much did they weigh?

Anita Stinson: Bobby was 7 lbs. 3 oz., Tommy 6 lbs. 8 oz. and they slept a lot.

EL: Either of them play little league baseball or collect things?

AS: Bobby won a trophy in softball.

EL: Which one cut the lawn?

AS: Bobby, till I finally had to replace the sod.

EL: Did they play guns or army?

AS: Tommy did—he'll never forgive his sister Lonnie for breaking his bazooka.

EL: How'd she do that?

AS: He was running down the alley and Lonnie and her girlfriend tackled him.

EL: What were the best presents they ever gave you?

AS: Tommy made me a frog and Bobby made me a leather hanging planter with his name on it.

EL: Are you a proud mom?

AS: Yes.[30]

Tommy Stinson: My mom was totally supportive of the right move. We mentioned it to her before we mentioned it to him. When he was in treatment. She said, "You guys have to do what's right for you guys." She's not really got-

ten involved in that sort of stuff. When it came to contracts she wanted to know what I was getting into. When it comes to what we do, it's not really her place. She likes to know what's going on.

Bob kind of dug his own grave. The family—and everyone—tried to help him for God knows how long. After a point it got to be a real futile effort to even get him out of the garbage. But now that he's doing it on his own I think he's probably wised up a little bit about what's going on with his life.[31]

Paul Westerberg: You guys summed up Bob perfectly in the last story. I can't remember exactly. . .
Bill Holdship: "Eyes like cherries in a vat of buttermilk."
Paul Westerberg: Exactly. It makes no sense to talk about Bob. You've met him, you've seen him. Anyone who's met him knows what Bob is like. We don't want to tell everyone that doesn't know.
J. [Kordosh]: He's in another band?
Tommy Stinson: Yeah. And he's a lot happier. And he's spending a lot more time with his wife, which was causing him personal problems. He'd leave town, and he wouldn't be happy. So he's happier now. I don't see him much, but I know that he is.[32]

Amy Buchanan: After Bob was out of the band, he used to come see me sing all of the time, and one night at Lee's [Liquor Lounge, in downtown Minneapolis] he slipped his phone number into the pocket of my skirt. I remember that skirt; it was a full floral skirt, and I wore it with my high-top Converse. There's a picture somewhere of him and I showing off the chip each of us had in our front tooth—the result of stepping on the mic stand base, and having it smash back into your mouth.

Jim Peterson: Bob was totally loved at [Oarfolk], but even if he was hanging around for awhile, it was a few hours, tops. It's not like we had to travel around in a van with him for a couple of months at a time. I'm sure his Mr. Hyde nickname was well-deserved. I know some people thought it was a sellout or something like that to get rid of Bob, but replacing him with Bob Dunlap was pretty well-received, and it wasn't like they hired some young pretty boy. It was never the same for me after Bob left, though, mainly because they had ceased to be a band that I could see on a regular basis, and turned into someone who played in bigger places. They always seemed uncomfortable there, I think especially when it was in their hometown.

Michael Hill: Bill Sullivan was kind of a savior. As crazy as he might have been, Bill always understood what was going on. He was able to translate. And I knew if he was around, things wouldn't go completely awry. And when things began to get crazy with Jesperson and all the managerial things were happening, I think Bill always had a clear idea of how far the boat was rocking. He's one of the smartest people I've met from Minneapolis. He's incredibly insightful. I mean, he should have been the big record executive, but he was probably too smart for that.

Peter Jesperson: We brought in that new management team—Russ Reiger and Gary Habib, [who owned] High Noon Management. I helped find them; when [the band] went to Warner Bros. Everybody knew we had to get some formal kind of managers, because I was as informal as it got.

Jim Walsh: May. The month his life changed forever. The month when, in 1986, six years after he was first possessed by "Raised in the City," the Replacements fired Jesperson and band co-founder/guitarist Bob Stinson. "In many ways," Westerberg said at the time, "Peter leaving was harder to take than Bob. Peter was like a fifth member of the band, and in the beginning, I'd give him a lot of credit for our success. He was invaluable. But we didn't need a 'dad' or a 'big brother' anymore. We needed someone to guide our career.[33]

Paul Westerberg: In the beginning, I'd give [Jesperson] a lot of credit for our success. When we had no money at all, he would always buy us drinks and lunch and things like that. He kept us together in the beginning. And then we grew up a little. We were young when we started—I was 19, Tommy was 13, and he was six or seven years older, and he could calm us down when we needed it. Consequently, we grew up to the point where we could call 'em ourselves.[34]

Jim Walsh: "I've said this before: When Bob and Pete left, things just didn't feel the same," says Chris Mars, the former Replacements drummer-turned-solo-artist. "I took it hard. I know it was a different thing with Bob, but with Pete I think it could've been handled differently. I was not for it as much as the other guys. Definitely, I wanted Pete to stay. But it's like one of those things with the way the 'Mats were: You just went along and took it on the chin, like Slim would say, and then just stumble on. But that's how we were. We never really handled things in the best way."

The firing devastated Jesperson. The 'Mats had become increasingly difficult to work with—he felt as if they were trying to make him quit—and he even contemplated doing so several times. But when the axe came, "it was like having," he says, "your stripes peeled off." He'd put all his eggs into the band, to the point of going on hiatus from his first passion, Twin/Tone, to join the 'Mats full time. It all went up in smoke that May afternoon in 1986, when the band informed Jesperson he was done. Jesperson, Westerberg, and bassist Tommy Stinson sat in a booth at the Uptown Bar, as Westerberg tried to soften the blow. "I'm really unhappy with the way things are," he told Jesperson. "I want to start swinging when I'm mad, and I don't want you to be in the way catching any punches."

He was cut off. Ostracized. Not coincidentally, the Replacements's first recording in the post-Jesperson–Stinson era was "I.O.U. Nothing" from *Pleased to Meet Me*.[35]

Michael Hill: [The song "I.O.U." and the chorus "I want it in writing/I owe you nothing"] could have been directed at anybody. I never took any of that personally, myself. I always felt like I was in their camp, in the sense that I never felt totally comfortable within the system I worked. I felt always like I was on [Westerberg]'s side, while at the same time I knew enough to not want to sycophantically want to hang out with him.

I value him as a human being and like him as a guy, and I really valued him as an artist. And Tommy, too, man. I think Tommy should have his own television show or something. I really liked each of those guys, and really felt like we were all part of something; that we all found ourselves in a particular place. And I never—for better or worse; I could've probably had a multimillion dollar career—I never identified myself as a major label guy, rather I identified myself as someone who had somehow gotten in there and was trying to promote certain kinds of music.

Paul Westerberg: I like to write a song that someone understands, but if I want to throw in a phrase that makes sense only to me, I'll do that. I'm not doing it to tease or to confuse. What you get, I guess, with my voice and the way I write is. . . . It comes across as pissed off and "Don't cross me or you're going to get your ass kicked!" You know me, I'm not that kind of person. But it tends to come across like that, whereas it might be exuberant and full of life.[36]

Jim Walsh: It was cold, and there was a pot-calling-the-kettle black subtext to the firing that put the blame squarely on Jesperson's drinking and drug use: "My drinking intensified while I was with them because it was such a whirl-wind," he admits. "One of those guys would say I was responsible for them drinking as much as they did, but I just think they enabled each other in a lot of ways. And then when I was booted it was just like, what's the point?"

Spirit broken, Jesperson took a job at a friend's dad's warehouse. It was the first straight job he'd ever had, and for the first time in his life, he wasn't working in music. He stayed at the warehouse for four years, and dabbled in some music projects, most notably as part-time manager for the local group A Single Love and as manager for the Toronto band 13 Engines. But the Replacements had been his baby, his family, his life. In the end, he found solace in his two addictions: music and booze, the latter of which almost killed him.

"Frankly, I don't know that I really cared too much if I actually died, you know? It didn't really matter too much, because I had been stripped of my self-esteem, is pretty much what I think happened. It was just flushed down the toilet. And I don't want to sound whiny here, because I mean, I certainly was partly responsible for it."

Bad as it was, he never contemplated quitting music. "That thought process never occurred, but I was pretty well medicated at the time, so maybe I wasn't thinking all that clearly. I just thought I was going to die. I just thought I'd rather, at that point, be dead, frankly. It seemed to me that you do something for the pure love of it and you put everything you've got into it for no other reason than to help people you thought were good, and then to get tossed out the back door . . . It was more than I could deal with.

"It was just the whole feeling of being kicked out of a club that you helped start. It was like one of the most horrible things that you've heard someone doing to someone else and then going, 'Someone did that to me.' But I really don't want to blame someone else for my problems, because I had as much to do with it in many ways as anybody. But there's also the addictive part of it, too. Until you've known full-blown addiction, you can't imagine it in a million years."

Things went from bad to worse in the autumn of 1990. Jesperson quit his day job to travel to California for the recording of 13 Engines' *Blur to Me Now* at Neil Young's studio ranch, but parted ways with the Engines over artistic differences. Around the same time, Jesperson and Westerberg began the recording of the Leatherwoods' *Topeka Oratorio*. Then in January, Buck flew

him down to Athens, where he saw the Dashboard Saviors for the first time. The two bands would serve as his guiding light out of the pits.

But right now there was something terribly different. In the preceding four years since the Replacements dumped him, Jesperson's records had soothed him, given him a lift, wretched him from his gloom. He was able to turn to his turntable to snap himself out of even the deepest depression. As it always had been, music was his lifeblood; the most important thing to him. And now it barely mattered.

"It got to the point where it was more important to make sure I had enough beer in the fridge and more important to keep the eye on the clock for last call than it was to listen to a record," he says. "That was when it really got bad. There was a point in my life where even the music wasn't all that important. I was just biding my time. It was sort of a chickenshit attempt at committing suicide, I guess."

It almost worked. After a couple of close calls, he was admitted to the intensive care unit at Hennepin County Medical Center, and went through the county's three-week treatment program. He hasn't touched the stuff since.

"I just had to get myself sick enough that I could put three weeks between me and a drink and then I didn't want to have a drink again. I was just anxious to have the 21 days over with, because I didn't feel they told me anything I didn't know. They have all these classes and lectures and groups and all that stuff. If I could have just fast-forwarded to the 21st day and gotten out I would've been happier.

"But I guess the experience was good for me. And there again, why should I complain about the situation that caused me to lose my self-esteem, because at this point in my life I couldn't be happier. Like in my bitterest moments, I can say they tried to flush me down the toilet and all they did was make me stronger, ultimately. I just had to bottom out enough to wise up. Once I got out of that, then, off to the races."[37]

Slim Dunlap: How cool is it that they wrote a song called "Alex Chilton?" I mean, what if the Rolling Stones had written a song called "Chuck Berry"?

Paul Westerberg: I'm saying "babe," there [at the end of the verses]. That's what everyone says down there: "Hey, babe." "How you doin', babe?"[38]

Alex Chilton: I heard about it first, and I was very worried and scared about what it would be like. When I heard it, I was so very relieved and thought it was

193

Photo taken in the band's Minneapolis practice space for Bill Holdship's September 1987 *CREEM* interview. © *Robert Matheu*

a great, thoroughly pleasant, positive song. I was in Memphis when I heard it, we were both recording around that time, in the same studio [Ardent Studios, which is owned by Jim Dickinson who produced Big Star and *Pleased to Meet Me*], so I imagine that is where I heard it. But it's not like the Kennedy assassination. I don't have a visual record in my brain. It certainly helped with people knowing my name, and becoming a famous name in this world.

Paul Westerberg: Memphis is like that. You can go to a doctor and say "I want to lose some weight," and he'll give you speed. Or "I need to relax," and he'll give you Valium. All this shady bullshit.

Bill Holdship: Did you go to Graceland when you were recording in Memphis?

Paul Westerberg: No. Elvis used to live there. It was too depressing. I thought it would be in bad taste. I didn't want to go in there.

Bill Holdship: Well, the Beastie Boys went there when they were in Memphis.

Paul Westerberg: Yeah, but the Beastie Boys are crass assholes. C'mon, I'll fight 'em right now, goddammit![39]

Alex Chilton: A lot of times people will just come up and be excited about it. The words they say are maybe not all that informative or interesting. It's just the excitement that's the main part of the message: "Dude! Alex Chilton! Wow!" That sort of thing.

I don't think Paul and I ever had a conversation about it. I don't think we ever had a serious conversation about anything, really. The drummer was the only one who could have a conversation it seemed—at least in those days.

Chris Mars: Up to *Pleased to Meet Me*, no one told anyone what to do. We would suggest things and were very democratic. Until then, we just went in and did what we did, and let it rip. Then, the last couple, it started getting, "You should do this beat"—people telling you what to do, so that kinda sucked.[40]

Bill Flanagan: "But [Dickinson] pretty much let us do what we wanted," says Westerberg. "The main thing he did that was different was he got Chris to play in time. Before we would get bored after two or three takes and if there were drum drops we wouldn't give a shit. But Jim would make us do a song three or four times for two weeks. 'Alex Chilton' being the prime example of one Chris couldn't get a handle on. Chris finally did, but by then Tommy and I were drunk or bored so we had to wait another week. Jim had a sense of the thing that we didn't understand: 'It has to be in time and in tune!'"

The Replacements played by Dickinson's rules—better they figured than getting into click tracks or drum machines or heavy overdubbing. Westerberg says he played all the guitar, "except when Dickinson had his fifteen year old son in and play the Van Halen noises on 'Dirty Pool.' We didn't say anything. The consolation we got out of it was that there was no Lead Guitar Solo, just the noises. Dickinson's a nice guy. He's the best producer we ever worked with . . . and the first.

"I don't want it to sound like I run the whole show, but I do come up with all the major ideas. 'Alex Chilton' will be the best example. They're credited as writers on that. In actuality they did not write the song. But when I came up with the three chords I said, 'This sucks!' And they said, 'No, this is good, let's do this!' They were excited about it, they got me excited about it, and I went on to write the rest of it. To me their willingness to be into something and to pull me along and say, 'Paul, this is good, let's do this,' constitutes writership. They're entitled to a third of it."[41]

Jon Pareles: In "The Ledge," over a guitar riff that alludes to Blue Öyster Cult's "Don't Fear the Reaper," a teen-ager stands on a ledge, looking down as a crowd gathers. From the room behind him, a girl he knows begs him not to jump; on the breeze, he smells coffee and doughnuts "for the press." A policeman reaches for him from the windowsill. "I'm the boy they can't ignore—for the first time in my life," Mr. Westerberg sings. Soon, with a bitter laugh, he amends it—"for the last time in my life!"

"The Ledge" is an unusual song for the Replacements. For one thing, it tells a story instead of delivering a manifesto; more important, its narrator gives in. For most of his other songs, Mr. Westerberg hurls himself into battle against liars, snobs, phonies, sellouts, cowards, cheats—and, lest he become too self-righteous, against his own failings. What he asks for, as he did on "We're Coming Out" from the "Let It Be" album, is "one more chance to get it all wrong." At a time when pop culture is busy worshipping yuppie success, and the standard-issue rock singer is as slickly packaged as a new brand of detergent, the Replacements aren't just another band with good tunes—they're an obnoxious, confused, boisterous slice of real life.[42]

Emily Boigenzahn (*née* Dunlap): Junior high into high school was a really hard time, as it is for everyone. Becoming an adult, becoming a woman, worrying about not having a boyfriend or what you're going to be when you grow up. And when it's a guy singing, as a teen especially, you can always imagine yourself as the girl he's singing about, and definitely romanticize it that way. But I wasn't in love with Paul Westerberg or anything—I was in love with the music. The ironic thing is, when Bob Stinson left the band I was crushed because they were my favorite band, and in my mind they were disbanding. And then my dad joined them.

Slim Dunlap: I think it was hardest on Emily. It's never a good thing when your dad joins your favorite band. That should not happen. Of all the bands to have your dad join. . . . But nobody could sit in my shoes and regret it. I have incredible guilt about being on the road so much. Mostly because of the burden it put on Chrissie. But it wasn't years at a time on the road; it was like two months at a time. I seem to have finally recovered.

Delia Dunlap: I remember well the day I found out Dad joined the band. I was in fifth grade. I remember knowing that it was an important achievement in Dad's career. He would be gone for months and then back for a couple of

days only to leave again. During those short stints at home, Dad would be exhausted and would mostly sleep.

Slim Dunlap: I remember one night, playing a ballroom somewhere, and Paul was really angry at the light man. He kept saying, "Yay, yay, yay" to the light man, and the light man got so upset he was crying. Then later, Paul completely disappeared. And suddenly he was saying, "Come on, light man, light me." And the spot light was going all over the building, looking for where he was.

Delia Dunlap: I missed him because he was a really wonderful dad. When he wasn't touring, my dad was always one of the kids. He was the most popular dad in the neighborhood because he actually liked having fun with us. We would have water-balloon wars in the summer and snowball fights in the winter.

I would always come home from school and hear Dad play the guitar in the basement, the sound of music under my feet. I remember noticing one summer that my dad actually changed the neighborhood. He would always play baseball and basketball with us while all of the other dads were doing who knows what? And then suddenly, when you looked around, other dads were out with their kids, too. The neighbors never would admit this, but it was clear that my dad inspired them to be better parents and to take an interest in their kids.

Slim Dunlap: I have thousands of scars. . . . It's similar to [post-traumatic stress syndrome], where, unwillingly, shards of memory come flying through your head from it, because you kind of endure a psychological shock to do that. Memories occasionally come back. I remember wonderful gigs where, god, it sure felt good to be in that band. And other nights, it would be a blushing embarrassed feeling, but it lasted for like, two hours. You just felt really bad for the people out there, and there was nothing you could do about it. It was hard to stand there and smile some nights. It was so awful.

But that's kind of what made it good for so many people, were those bad, bad, bad nights. But the bad nights on my end weren't fun, because I didn't want to be bad.

Chris Osgood: Bob Dunlap is my hero.

Scott McCaughey: Once, as we [the Young Fresh Fellows] came off stage in Santa Barbara, Paul told our guitarist Chuck Carroll how awesome our set had

Young Fresh Fellows perform at the Bizer–Westerberg wedding, 1987. *Author photo*

been, and Chuck replied: "We sucked." "Fuck you!" said Paul as he turned and walked away.

Paul Westerberg: We mentioned 'em last time and you didn't write anything about them so you should mention the Young Fresh Fellows from Seattle. If you think we're good, then they're the best band in the world. They're like the new NRBQ, only sloppier.[43]

Scott McCaughey: Paul's girlfriend, Lori Bizer, who worked at Twin/Tone, had somehow discovered and become enamored with the first Young Fresh Fellows album. I was working at Cellophane Square records in Seattle and we struck up a friendship over the phone, by coincidence really, I think. The "indie rock" scene was sort of claustrophobic then, but in a good way, with a lot of cooperation and camaraderie.

Lori turned Paul onto us—or maybe shoved us down his throat. I believe I said "Hi" to Paul and identified myself after 'the Mats absolutely mind-blowing show at Astor Park in Seattle in '85. Then when we had an open date on tour, and noticed the 'Mats were playing the Living Room in Providence, Rhode Island, that day, Lori wrangled us onto the bill through Paul. We were pretty damn excited.

Paul Westerberg: The song ["Things," from Westerberg's first solo album *14 Songs*] says a lot about what I am, and essentially says that what I do is the most important thing in my life. And no matter who you are, you can be in second place, but you're never going to replace my first love.[44]

Scott McCaughey: So excited that we drank a bottle of gin and a case of beer in our communal motel room. Worst room I ever stayed in—I swear someone had smeared *shit* all over the walls before we showed up. Upon arrival the promoter told us we weren't playing; he already had two local bands opening. It's entirely possible he never even heard about us being "added" to the show. We were too drunk to care that much, and marched backstage to find the Replacements in a state of extreme disrepair.

There were bowls of spaghetti—Paul had tomato sauce halfway up his shirt sleeve. We had purchased a second bottle of gin which we offered to him but he waved it away, signifying that he was either trying to sober up, or maybe sticking to beer for the moment. About two minutes later we cracked up seeing him guzzling straight from the gin bottle, rather desperately.

The Replacements' set that night wasn't hideous; I vaguely remember some early numbers rendered somewhat intact. The four Fellows and our traveling pal/photographer/road crew, Marty Perez, had all managed to push front and center for the show.

After about an hour, as it became apparent that the band was reaching the point of complete incapability, Paul suddenly announced, "Ladies and gentlemen, the Young Fresh Fellows!" Instruments were abandoned, and we clambered onstage and claimed them. I was amazed at the volume and sheer monumental rock sound when I hit an A-chord through Paul's Marshall.

We staggered into some medley of our song "Big House" and Mott the Hoople's "Walkin' with a Mountain" and god knows what else. After about ten minutes we gave up, too. At that point I think the perplexed crowd readied itself for the Replacements' triumphant return to the stage. There wasn't a chance in hell that was going to happen.

High fidelity. Jim Peterson and Dave Ayers check out *The Voice*'s Pazz & Jop Poll at Garage D'or Records, 1987. © *Joan E. Bechtold*

Tommy Stinson: After seven years of trying to get to a certain point, you go over [to Europe] and it totally deflates your ego.

Paul Westerberg: You're sitting in a fucking hamster cage hotel room, and you're playing to a bunch of stupid skinheads. And you realize how much of an asshole you really are because you wanna ride in a big Cadillac and eat pot roast. And there's all these teeny cars, and this bullshit food. There were some good gigs in London, but no one had heard of us over there.

Tommy Stinson: We were like brothers, though, because we were locked in a van and we *had* to talk to each other because they couldn't speak English.[45]

Abbie Kane: I was working at Twin/Tone in 1987 as the office manager. The studios were on the first floor, and upstairs was the office, and in back of the office was a bunch of storage. And [receptionist] Roz, the face of Twin/Tone, sat at the front.

And I ran into Tommy, who was walking very swiftly towards the front door and carrying this huge big box of something, and I didn't know what it was, and I was right by the front door, and I said, "Oh, hey, Tommy! How ya doin'? Here, let me get the door for ya." And I open the door and held the door for him.

Tommy Stinson: It's true we threw the tapes in the [Mississippi River], but they weren't actually tapes of any worth.[46]

Abbie Kane: And I walked him out, and there was the van and there was the band, and I'm like, "Hey, guys. How ya doin'? What's going on?" And they hopped in the van. And then Paul [Stark] came running by and said, "Did Tommy just come by here and leave with something?" And I said, "Well, he had

a box of stuff with him." He ran back to the storage area to look, and then, I don't know, he probably called his attorney.

Paul Westerberg: I don't know what my legal rights are at this point. The contract was sold, the masters were sold, I don't even know who owns 'em anymore or what. Jeez, I never did understand that—you need to be a lawyer to understand it. Can you blame us for going in there with 10 cocktails in us, trying to steal the tapes and throw them away? We didn't know what to do. We didn't wanna get screwed. We wanted to help ourselves. We didn't get what we wanted. I think we ended up throwing out some outtakes and the acoustic version of "Can't Hardly Wait."[47]

Abbie Kane: We found out that they had thrown the tapes in the river shortly after, and the reaction in the office was shock. And I actually remember laughing. There was an underlying current of humor. And anger and disbelief.

Bill Tuomala: The Replacements played the Orpheum in Minneapolis in November of 1987. They wore jumpsuits and were blotto drunk and quit playing their songs halfway through more often than not. The band went from downright goofy to determined to play lights-out at the change of a hat. In those instants that they held it together, like during a cover of the Stones' "Gimme Shelter," it was mesmerizing. There were a lot of people there bent on hearing their early fast songs and seemed to relish provoking the band. I was in the balcony and a crowd of people up there continued chanting "Fuck School"—even after the band played it. To end the show, the band just walked offstage without acknowledging that they had just finished the show. Many people booed, and Westerberg told the crowd: "We're not playing any more so fuck you." More booing ensued. I had taken a date to the show and she was livid, proclaiming her hate for the band. I was in my early stages of love for the band and was taken in by the chaos of the whole thing. I had seen U2 earlier that month in an arena show, and that was so polished and careful compared to the spectacle I had just witnessed.

DJ: When are you playing in town?
Paul Westerberg: Maybe tomorrow night.
DJ: Where?
Westerberg: I don't know.

DJ: [Sarcastically] That's a good answer, my friend. The next song up is "I.O.U." What can you tell us about it?

Westerberg: God, he's got a great voice, don't he?

Tommy Stinson: It's a fake voice. Listen to him.

Westerberg: No, he's a fucking professional. Oops. I'm not supposed to swear, I guess.[48]

George Regis: They came to my bachelor party in New York City in '87, and when they arrived they had been doing a day of press, which they invariably would find taxing and tedious beyond belief. And they had been out to lunch two or three times during the day, and at each lunch, whatever record executive was picking up the tab for lunch, they would grab the carbon from the charge slips and rub it all over their faces. By the time they showed up at my bachelor party, they looked like refugees of *Lord of the Flies.*

This party was on the twenty-fifth floor of a hotel on Central Park South, and they rampaged in, tipped over the apple carts, and knocked over all the booze and grabbed sandwiches and started flinging them off the railing of this terrace that overlooks Central Park South. It was really something.

Slim Dunlap: I was kind of an independent contractor. I got to keep myself sane by saying, "You guys do that. That's not something I would do." But no band is really a band like that. All bands are phony, all bands are just four people trying to be an identity. Replacements became an identity, but it wasn't a reality. It still isn't. Luckily for them. But that's like, a legend. You don't put yourself in the same breath of a legend like that.

Paul Westerberg: "Seen Your Video" isn't necessarily "every video sucks, all video is absolutely taboo." It's *"Seen your video/Your phony rock 'n' roll,"* and it's pointed at videos that glorify how "cool" it is to be in a band. You know, the chicks at your feet, the chains, the leather, that kind of stuff. But we might do a video. It's a definite maybe.

But if you see our video, it's not going to be anything you've seen before. It's gonna be something that isn't at all like the spirit of the band. The "Bastards of Young" video was the *attitude* of the band, but the spirit of the band together is something that shouldn't be filmed. Almost like—it might be stupid, it probably is—like the Amish people, or whatever, who won't have their picture taken because it steals their soul. I almost feel like that, too. Because it steals something that the cameras should not take away from the band. I think that mys-

tery is far, far better than to splash it out in front of 'em, and show 'em exactly what the bands look like, and exactly what they do. I mean, that's the fun of seeing a band live. [Record companies] see video as selling more records and making more money, but to me it's crass and it's wrong for the Replacements.

We don't get down on our knees and say, "I want to be a star. I will look it, act it, dress it, be it. Make me one." We just say we don't want to *fail*, and we'd like to go at our own pace. So we'll probably end up being something really boring like fuckin' REO [Speedwagon], who were around for nine years before they made it. I can see that happening to us more than us ever being on the cover of *Newsweek*.[49]

DJ: How many songs did Paul write on the album?
Paul Westerberg: Paul wrote 'em all. Paul's a creep. He takes all the credit.
DJ: Does anyone else in the band write songs?
Westerberg: Tommy and Chris also write songs. They're just not as good as Paul.
Tommy Stinson: That's the truth.
DJ: Uh, huh. [laughter] Why do you write songs?
Westerberg: I do it to make Tommy and Chris look bad. [pause] No, I do it because I'm gay.
DJ: What can you tell us about the new single, "The Ledge"?
Westerberg: Well, it's in E minor, and—if you're following along at home—E minor, C major seventh, D suspended with a B seven turnaround.[50]

Slim Dunlap: They brought me along for the anti-thumbing-the-nose move that it was. My contributions were extremely minor in that band. I just filled that other spot enough so that it floated. It was never as good as it was before, but it wasn't that way because of me. As a working band, it gave you the representation of what they did, as good as I could do it.

People always ask me, "Why don't you say 'we' this or 'we' that?" It's because that never was my spot. I wasn't an original member of the Replacements; I didn't want to act like it, like, "Yeah, me back in the old days." It wasn't even like that. I came in in the gravy years. I get to live with the shame of that for eternity.

It's a tough chair. Anybody who's had it since me will tell you it's a tough chair, and it comes with some. . . . It's not everything it appears to be. Paul is a tough person to deal with. He's got a wonderful, twisted sense of humor that's fun from a distance. It was really hard to be around him when people would

just fall down laughing at his saying something about somebody or to someone, and sometimes it was really hard to not just say, "Hey. That isn't right. Stop bugging someone like that."

Because he's just a needler; in order to be a comedian, you have to make a thousand bad jokes in order for one to be successful. So you have to be the butt of a lot of bad failed Paul punch lines.

But he's a rarified person. He has that strange thing: originality. You just don't bump into that. You don't ever really get to be his confidante. People like that don't need a confidante. Paul is a collaborator; people would never believe that, but he absorbs a lot of things around him, and I got to see a lot of those things he absorbed. You kind of had to feed him music and keep him going, so I spent a lot of time just trying to find music that was similar to what . . . because it's really hard when you're making a record, and everyone else in the studio has no idea, "What the fuck is this? What kind of song is this?"

It's really hard to hear someone's vision, when they don't even know what it is. It makes you feel bad if your contributions let the air out of that one. It's easy to do when you're around someone like that. "No, I insist. Make it go this way. I'm telling you, this is the best way." And ten years later, listening to it, you go, "Oh, fuck. He was right."

But he wrote a lot of songs that I heard that were awfully good. I mean, maybe the best of 'em were used, but still, some of the alternates were so good. It's scary, because he doesn't remember them, and me and only a few other people heard those songs and then they sailed away into the netherworld. He always had these little cassettes. That's the great lost Paul album, if he had saved all those little cassettes he'd leave in his guitar case. And you'd listen to it, and it'd be just the coolest song, and you'd ask him about it later and he'd be all miffed you'd heard it.

Martin Devaney: A couple years back—2004 I think—my band and I played the annual Buttaball benefit at the Turf [Club in St. Paul]. It's a food shelf benefit where they get three bands to play sets by the more famous Minnesota bands. This particular year was Dylan, the Replacements, and Hüsker Dü. We were asked to do the Dylan set. It's a popular show and we went on [the University of Minnesota's] Radio K to plug it the Thursday before the show. Shortly after that, I get a call from Slim: "Hey Marty, you need another guitar player for tomorrow night?" What was I gonna say? So I asked him if he wanted to run through any tunes and he said no, he'd just jump up there with us. We had opened for Slim and his band a number of times, including the first

[Senator Paul] Wellstone World Music Day, and he had become a friend—always kind words and funny stories every time I saw him.

So that night he comes down with his guitar and hops right in with us, going through a dozen or so Dylan tunes, taking solos with Josh, my regular guitar player, and trading harmonica duties with me. One of the better times I've ever had on stage. One of the best parts of the evening was that the band that was doing the 'Mats was only doing "Bob-era" material to close out the night, but they seemed psyched Slim was there and I think wanted him to sit in with them. When we were done, the Hüsker Dü band took the stage, and after a song or two I asked Slim if he was gonna stick around for the rest of the night. He kinda smiled and said, "Nah, I've heard all these tunes enough," picked up his Rickenbacker and headed out the door.

CHAPTER 4

Someone Take the Wheel

Hey!
People they ask me
What I think about
Soul Asylum
Or Hüsker Dü
I say
I don't care
And I won't care
And you cannot possibly make me care
My world crumbled
Nearly stumbled
I own Stinson's guitar

We were at the old Uptown
It was the old Tuesday
When I thought I saw him standing there
It was Bobby Stinson
He looked so sad
And I could not understand it until
Someone whispered
Listen, mister
You got Stinson's guitar

Sold in Germany in 1962
Passed up by Paul McCartney
And slipped through the hands of
The wonderful old Curtiss A
Bob Stinson's guitar

It was three weeks later
Someone said
Check out the obituary column
Which I did and
It was Bobby Stinson
Man, he was gone
But his guitar would rock
on in my arms, yeah
And I wound out
When I found out
I own Stinson's guitar
Whoa!
I got Stinson's guitar

—The Legendary Jim Ruiz,
"Bobby Stinson's Guitar"

I'd usually sit around
And drink up all my dreams
Then ask for yours
I go to bed
But not to sleep
I'm just one of those things
Life can't keep

—Bob Stinson,
unrecorded Static Taxi verse

Greil Marcus: Bands break up because of artistic differences. Everybody knows that. And also, as Tolstoy said, all unhappy families are unhappy in their own way. With the Sex Pistols, I think it was a matter of one smart guy realizing he didn't want to spend any more time with cretins—and fighting with the other smart guy (McLaren). For the Rolling Stones, there's simply too much money to walk away from—which is why there are so many bands now that have been together 20 years or more and will never break up: Aerosmith, Fleetwood Mac, etc. This has nothing to do with fans' expectations. It has to do with fans' gullibility and their refusal to open themselves to anything new.

Peter Jesperson: I think [a band is] like a marriage, and it's more remarkable when people stay together. An artistic relationship is a difficult thing to hang on to because often the artistic distribution is not an even thing. That's one of the great things about what R.E.M. did—the sharing of the writing credits equally, even though you know and I know that those songs weren't all written by those four guys, or those three guys now.

Rock bands break up because usually there's one person that's carrying more of the load than the rest of them, and a bitterness develops. Look at Soul Asylum. I mean, that's a tough one: Dave Pirner is probably some kind of millionaire, right? I don't think anybody else is. It's gotta breed frustration, and in the rock 'n' roll world, there's not a lot of level-headed sober thinking that goes on on a regular basis.

Danny Murphy: The deals that go down early in your band career don't have any implications early on, but later, if you get successful, some of those things you agreed to or didn't agree to early on create kind of a class system that didn't exist in the early days of your band. That seems to be an incredibly common theme of breakups. The other reason is the singer or songwriter gets most of the attention: "Well I don't need to talk to the band, people listen to my band because I'm writing the songs." And that's a thing that managers are oftentimes persuasive with.

Bands also grow to fucking hate each other. Being in a band with someone for that long, you see all their worst tendencies. It just seems like if you're unstable to begin with, which most great rock bands are, any time there's a change, it's hard to deal with rationally if you don't deal with things rationally as a rule.

When we made *Grave Dancer's [Union]*, we kind of did demos for it, and Dave [Pirner] had this hearing problem, and we made it thinking that we were either going to have more success and we were going to be able to tour more com-

fortably or we were going to break up. That was the [crossroads] time for us. No one wanted to tour, we weren't getting along particularly great, the shows weren't that great or well-attended. We were in a rut. It was "Let's either make a great record, and a different record, or let's not do this anymore." It was a very concrete breaking-up point. And then when that record blew up, we went from selling 40,000 to three million records, then it was a scramble and "Now what do we do?" because we never even thought about that.

Chan Poling: When a band breaks up, most people on the outside are thinking, "Why would you throw away such a good thing?" People go, "The Replacements broke up?" "The Suburbs broke up?" "Why do R.E.M. and U2 stay together?" And my perspective is that R.E.M. and U2 were smart. They put aside their personal differences and the smaller things that came between them for the greater good.

There's all sorts of heavy stuff that goes on. Drug and alcohol abuse and personal health and mental health, and then, of course, you think your ideas are the greatest things to come along and everybody else's ideas should take a backseat to yours. There's all this ego and basic human stuff, and most rock bands start when they're teenagers. All of these bands we're talking about formed as boys' clubs or gangs, and you know how important music is when you're in high school. It identifies your tribe. You're in your own pirate ship, grinding the seas, and everybody else can go to hell.

Lori Barbero: By the end of Babes [in Toyland], I was sick of being with them—and they were my friends. You can only do it for so long before you can't stand each other's faces.

Paul Westerberg: Most of [my heroes] are dead. I've met Dylan and Van Morrison and Keith [Richards]. There's three right there. I don't have a lot of heroes. I never realized I had any. We listened to the Rolling Stones throughout the career of the band, even though we pretended they were the enemy. I mean, I couldn't give two shits about John Lydon now, but at the time I thought he was the greatest thing ever. Well, yes, I could give two shits about him. One and a half.

Slim Dunlap: You know, there are a lot of bands who make it to the point that the Replacements did, where they start to make a living. They think it's not a bad way to make a little money. "This is not a bad way to go. We'll do

whatever we need to do to continue this little gravy train we got going here." Very often, this thinking helps destroy what you've done. That was never a goal of the Replacements, to become an institution like the Rolling Stones. We were always a little on the edge.[2]

John Beggs: We shared a practice space with those guys, and they'd always drink all our beer. We'd hide it from them, all over the place, in every secret place we could find, and every time they'd Easter-egg 'em out. They'd always be all gone. The weird thing is, Bob would always play out in the hallway, with the door shut. The rest of the band would be in there, blasting away, and he'd be playing in the hallway with his cord under the door and his amp inside. I never did get an answer to that one.

Paul Westerberg: The songs are Replacements tunes. I write 'em but they're for the Replacements to play. We figure we're gonna ride this till some-body's had enough. Nobody's gonna get fired at this point. If somebody quits, it's over. Then I'll do what I want and they can do what they want, but at this point what I want is to keep the Replacements together. 'Cause I think we're a good band. I can be as egotistical as hell and say, "This is a great song! We should do this one!" and they'll bring me down to earth. They'll roll their eyes and say, "This is pretty cool, James Taylor." And then it hits me: Yeah, why should I subject them to this? It's not rock 'n' roll, it's not the Replacements. I used to say we'd stay together forever, but Bob leaving the band sort of shook me there. I figured we were supermen, we could always keep it together to the bitter end. Now we'll keep it together till it isn't fun anymore.

We've been together longer than the Faces! I remember when I saw them in 1975 the preview in the paper called them a "Veteran English Band." At the time I was mad 'cause I thought they were calling them old. Now, Christ, by the end of this tour we'll have been together eight years. So we'll stick togeth-er and then after that. . .[3]

Slim Dunlap: We opened for Keith Richards on his birthday [December 18, 1988, at the Meadowlands in New Jersey]. I guess he was a fan, but I never put too much stock in [playing in front of a hero]. After you've done it enough, just being an opening band, there's no illusions to it. Keith is one guy who you're gonna have your ass handed to you, any way you look at it. You can't go up there thinking you're gonna get a lucky knockout punch. It just ain't gonna happen.

That was the early arena-type environment for me. We never really were

geared up for that. We actually made complete fools of ourselves that night, because that was the dreaded snare-reverb return. The snare was returning to stage from echoing in the hall, and it was difficult to determine what was the snare beat and what was Chris's actual beat. It kind of fouled up any thinking that we'd done well for us.

I just remember extreme drunkenness that night. At those free [drinks] backstage gigs, we'd just go howdy, because we just didn't get that very often. The night before, we got introduced to some guy who was supposedly the promoter, and I remember Paul arguing with him about what time we'd start, and when you're the opening band you have no control over anything like that. It was a very odd scene.

I remember Keith coming into the dressing room with a Polaroid camera and taking pictures of himself with everyone. I know Paul walked away with one of those.

Jeaneen Gauthier: I've never met him, but I have this sort of sixth sense that tells me that Paul is probably someone who grew up hearing he was a piece of shit all his life. I was such a person. I grew up hearing that nonstop from my dad. When you hear all your life that you're a piece of shit, and then at some point some other people come along and tell you you're great, it's a total mindfuck. You don't believe them, because you gave up long ago on believing what anybody says about you. You think a good opinion about you couldn't possibly be the truth—instead, you wonder what the person wants from you now, what their agenda is. You've learned to be cynical and unmoved by other people's opinions about you. That's how you protected yourself in the past—how you kept the bad stuff that was said about you from sinking in. Unfortunately, it also keeps the good stuff from sinking in, too.

Paul Westerberg: Writing [*Don't Tell a Soul*], I wasn't feeling like the Replacements, the mighty rock band. I was just feeling like myself, and very casually just writing pop songs. And when I played them for the band, it was like Tommy would say, "Where are the rockers, man?" So we compromised: I went back and kicked out a couple more rockers, and he came around and kind of understood what was going on.[4]

Slim Dunlap: [Recording] comprises all of the lowlights. That was the hardest part of it, was making records. That was extremely difficult from my end. You could hide live; you could be playing and making enough noise to . . . but

you can't hide in the studio. And Paul is a complete natural, and he expected somebody to play what he could play. Which is what a lot of songwriters always want their guitarists to be. That was not a good challenge to have to do in a studio. Especially when you're handed songs that your part is going to be recorded *now*, and you didn't get a chance to listen to it and think about it, because he just wrote it minutes ago, or whatever.

Peter Jesperson: I went over to Paul and Lori [Bizer]'s house and he played me *Don't Tell a Soul*. He said, "Peter, this is supposed to be my dark pop album and they want me to write 'Bastards of Young' all over again." He played me "Rock 'n' Roll Ghost" and I remember thinking, "Wow. This is a song about all of us, a little bit." Sort of like, hopefully we don't all end up rock 'n' roll ghosts—because everybody had the potential to at the time. Bob especially.

Slim Dunlap: I had difficult times in the studio. I used to think that usually that would be the most fun, leisurely time in the cycle of a rock star, but that guy [Westerberg] was not about leisure. It was about pressure, unrelenting pressure.

So you get to enjoy the songs and over years the curse of it wears off. You can listen to it, where you couldn't ever before. You let yourself give into it. It's sometimes fun to hear things, and listen to it as if someone else is listening to it, and forget about the things that perturb you.

Robert Christgau: Westerberg's got his own artistic interests, and he probably doesn't miss [Bob] Stinson any more than the programmers who've positioned "I'll Be You" not just twixt Lou and Elvis in *Billboard*'s "modern rock" top five but at the top of the "album rock" heap—outdrawing .38 Special, Chris Rea, Julian Lennon! Nor has the demon airplay been appeased at the expense of guts ball. With new guy Slim Dunlap reaching bell-like through serious clamor, "I'll Be You" tastes like the Placemats of old, comparatively speaking.[5]

Slim Dunlap: I have a horrible mistake in "I'll Be You" that I hear all the time. Other people don't really hear the mistake, but I do. It's a little slip of the finger that I think they threw in there for a joke. Any mistake you would make, Paul's eyebrow would kind of lift. And he'd look over at Tommy. Because that's what they were looking for. They didn't want perfection. They wanted warts kind of thing, and it was hard to talk them out of it, "Please don't put that on your song; that's me dropping my guitar."

I remember sitting in the [Hubert H. Humphrey Metrodome in downtown Minneapolis] once during a Twins game, and they played ["I'll Be You"] over the speakers between innings. And it cut right on my mistake, and it echoed out over the stadium, and only I could have been the one sitting there thinking, "This sounds so bad."

Ken Ornberg: I got hired by Warner Bros. prior to *Don't Tell a Soul* coming out. Those first records were on Sire/Warner, and *Don't Tell a Soul* was Warner/Reprise. So then I went on the road with them and worked a couple of their tours. I try to get the radio stations to play the record as much as possible. My job isn't technically a sales job, but it really is.

I don't directly sell CDs, but I'm trying to make the job of the sales department, the marketing department, easier. If I've done my job, when they go into a record chain, they'll hear, "Yeah, we're hearing a good buzz about this record. We'll rack more copies of it, we'll put it on an end cap, or we'll let you put up a big display."

Tommy Stinson: When I listen to the radio I think, "We ought to be on here and this shit shouldn't be. Because face it, no one needs to hear Jethro Tull on the radio anymore. I don't want to dog AOR radio, because they're giving us support now and they never did in the past, but this is the fucking Eighties, and they're still playing the worst shit of the Seventies and calling that classic rock. Boy, if "Aqualung" is a classic, then fucking "I'll Be You" is *history*.[6]

Slim Dunlap: At the time of the Replacements, the real competition for heading toward the mainstream was R.E.M. At one time both bands were in similar positions, and were poised to make that leap. R.E.M. made that leap, and the Replacements didn't. Who knows why that is, but I think a lot of it is that R.E.M. was more willing to adapt to the marketplace. They'd write the songs, record them, and then hand them to the record company and say do what you want with them.[7]

Ken Ornberg: My title was the Midwest promotional manager for Warner/Reprise Records. My territory was the Upper Midwest. All the things that you hear on the radio are up to me. If a band's being interviewed, I'm the one who brought 'em there. If there's ticket giveaways or backstage passes or sound-check party—any sort of thing when a band's coming through town and subsequently when a new record's out, anything that I can get the radio

stations to do to play the record more and raise the profile of the record so that you hear it and you go buy it. That's what I do.

Howie Klein became president of Reprise, who Paul knew or knew of, and alternative [rock] radio wasn't a big deal. The Warner staff was working Van Halen records. There were no alternative stations, so a band like the Replacements didn't really get a lot of attention or priority. So when Reprise started, it was a boutique label to work all these bands. We worked records longer. It wasn't just "Put out one track [as a single], if it doesn't stick, move on."

It was an exciting time, working "I'll Be You." It's a romantic cliché to say "a band ahead of its time," but they really were. If that band would have come out with those records another generation later, I really think they'd talk about Paul the way they talk about Kurt Cobain. That band would have had half a dozen number-one records.

Getting "I'll Be You" to be the number-one rock track is really phenomenal if you look at what kind of stuff was around at the time. At the time, they were competing for chart position with Van Halen and Tom Petty and Rod Stewart and Traveling Wilburys and things like that. The mighty KQRS [the classic rock station in the Twin Cities] added it, and that meant it would be added in Chicago and Detroit and everywhere. And we got it all the way to number one [on airplay charts]. It was the most played record in that format at the time.

Slim Dunlap: You know, there's nothing wrong with being appreciative of the fact that they're playing us on the radio. To me, it's important that Paul's songs be on the radio. If it helps for me to go make a fool out of myself at a radio station, I'll do it. There's nothing wrong with this band, and Paul Westerberg, seeking a larger audience. Because he deserves it.[8]

Ken Ornberg: One night my wife, Julie, and I had Paul and Lori and another couple over for dinner, and on KDWB [the Top 40 station in the Twin Cities] that night they had one of those battles—some stations call it "Battle of the Bands" or "Pump It or Dump It." They generally play 'em at night, at nine o'clock or later, because that's when the most active audience listens. It's generally eighteen- to twenty-four-year-olds, which is the bulk of the record-buying public, and it's also right in the wheelhouse of Top 40 stations. So if you get a good reaction from that demographic, then the likelihood of you getting a record programmed on that station is infinitely better.

We had dinner that night, and gathered around the radio at nine o'clock. It was the cornerstone of the evening. Almost like you do for a movie of the week,

or a sporting event, we had dinner and scheduled everything to culminate at nine o'clock. I don't even think we voted, I just think we listened. It was like old-time radio: We gathered around the theater of the mind, and "I'll Be You" won. I remember everyone in the room being pretty elated, and I hoped it was a sign of big things to come. This meant that kids with their paper route money and babysitting money were going to go buy a Replacements record.

It was a legit thing. Those things have been fixed, but this one was real. It was a big step, not a gigantic leap, and it didn't guarantee that it was going to get played alongside Madonna and Prince. But I remember Paul being thrilled at the notion of being on Top 40 radio. He was a little childlike when it won. He liked to make mix tapes to bring with on the bus, and he always had a lot of cool bubblegum pop music, or corny bubblegum pop, on these tapes. He was a true music fan, and I think he was excited because now "I'll Be You" was crossing over to KDWB. A pop station. One of the top four or five Top 40 stations in the country.

Paul Westerberg: When "I'll Be You" dropped off the Top 40 I was going, "Damn." But now I go, "Great," because now it's not like "I'll Be You" is No. 1 and I'll have to play it for the rest of my life. Next year no one will even remember it so I can play whatever I want.[9]

David Menconi: One of my favorite Replacements shows ever was in Denver in 1989, touring for *Don't Tell a Soul* to a disappointingly small crowd at the Paramount Theatre. Part of the show is being broadcast to a nationwide radio audience. Before the on-air part, Westerberg coaches the crowd to boo on his signal. So the broadcast starts, they play a song—I believe it was "Talent Show"—and Westerberg gives the signal: "BOOOOOOOOO!" "Aw, c'mon," Westerberg pleads while giving the crowd a broad wink. "You might like us if you just gave us a chance." Alienating an invisible audience of millions for a had-to-be-there joke for a few hundred—what could be a better summation of the Replacements' career?

Michael Dregni: In 1989 when *Don't Tell a Soul* was released, the 'Mats came back to St. Paul on tour and played the Roy Wilkins Auditorium. We were all used to seeing them blow the doors off little bars, and now they're in this soulless echo chamber of a hall set up with folding chairs. Paul and Tommy didn't look any too happy about this either, but they came out rocking. At heart, they were still the same great band, even if they were now "rock

Tommy gets his make-up on. The Tom Petty tour, Gainesville, Florida, August 1989. *Author photo*

stars." I remember them launching into "Cruella De Ville," Paul standing on a chair for some reason as he sang, then fumbling up the song, quitting halfway through, and giggling at themselves. They seemed to want to prove they could never make it big.

Peter Jesperson: They did [the Who's] "I Can See for Miles" that tour. That was *awesome*.

Paul Westerberg: There aren't as many people who come to see us fuck up anymore. It's not like last time or the time before, when it seemed like eighty percent of the people came to see the circus. And if you fucking writers would stop writing about that stuff, *no one would* come to see it. [grins] Hint hint.[10]

Ryan Cameron: By *Don't Tell a Soul*, their energy level had changed. To some extent, they'd sort of given up a little bit. On one hand, they were willing to let [producer Matt Wallace] polish the shit out of the record, and it was certainly

The February 1989 issue of *Musician* with a 'Mats feature by Twin Cities journalist Steve Perry and cover photo by Steve Marsel. *Author collection*

an attempt to be radio-friendly. I think they lost their roots credibility to that, and that, along with booting out Bob, made people think, "Well, this isn't Minneapolis' little garage punk band anymore. This is a band that's trying to make it."

Paul Westerberg: In a nutshell, we've gotten better. We've lost a little bit of what we used to have, in terms of the old kamikaze spirit. But we can't do what we used to do, and we don't wanna. We don't want to be a joke, or a young rising band, forever. It's like, we're a good band, period. Not a great one, but a good one.[11]

Slim Dunlap: It was always a total honor and a pleasure to be around Paul, but he did make records very agonizingly. It wasn't like other bands. You'd be in a big studio and there'd be two or three other acts and they'd come and go after a few days with their completed records, and they'd be listening to it after a couple nights, and there we would be, in like week six. It was grueling, but he was dealing with a different level. He had to produce better fidelity recordings, and I kind of came at a bad time. I never had to worry about any of that crap.

I don't ever talk about it. I get my little memories of parts I threw in there, but that's kind of the unwritten rule when you work with someone like that. You don't get to lay claim later, because you had your chance there to declare ownership of it. And any collaboration deals with that, where there's an extremely gray line where a lot of people, their name is on that tune, but would that tune ever have come about if other people hadn't been standing there helping them do it? But over time, people don't care about that. So I don't ever bring that up: I don't ever discuss my part of writing any of those songs.

Paul Westerberg: [Opening for Tom Petty on an arena tour in the summer of 1989] knocked me down a notch on the ego ladder. We're a band with this raw attitude and spirit, and we can certainly be seen as a band that doesn't play very good. With Petty it got to the point where we just had this attitude: "Well, they don't like our music, let's just let them remember us." We started drinking at noon. We got under each other's skin a bit.[12]

Tommy Stinson: God, that was dreadful. We were worn down by the end. We had to play when it was still daylight, all our fans were stuck near the back because the record company had given away the best seats to (company reps) and Petty's fans didn't know who the hell we were.[13]

Slim Dunlap: The further you get, the more protected you are, and for us it just wasn't fun to play for 15,000 people. They're so far away. Plus, it was the Tom Petty audience that had a lot to do with it. That was not our crowd. When Paul Westerberg stands behind that microphone, there's danger. And when Tom Petty stands behind the mike, you're safe. Paul is one of the greatest "anger channellers" in the business, but in an artful way. That's not what Tom Petty does.[14]

Paul Westerberg: I was bummed when nobody realized [that Tommy Petty lifted the line "a rebel without a clue" from "I'll Be You" for Petty's "Into the Great Wide Open"]. Same thing with these interviews that gave me a hard time. It isn't the interview that ever affects me or the fact that somebody lifts from me. It's the fact that a band won't come forward and say we were an influence on them. Or someone won't defend us. Or someone won't say, "Yeah, I took the line from him." In any of those cases it would be fine, but it was the fact that it goes without reference or without anyone saying anything. That irritates me a little.[15]

Ryan Cameron: People were disappointed in *Don't Tell a Soul*. It's the only one of those first three [Warner Bros.] records that almost instantly went to the cut-out bins. Probably within six months, we had cut copies at the store [Let It Be Records in downtown Minneapolis].

Steve Perry: "Maybe I'm from the working class," Westerberg says, "but I've hardly worked a day in my life." He and Chris Mars then embark on an explanation of the theory of social classes according to the Replacements, which differs significantly from Karl Marx's version.

"The middle class is the best," says Westerberg. "They make the best rock 'n' roll. Elliot Murphy said that. I don't know the exact reason, but I think the lower class is so desperate to rise above where they are that they'll do anything, even to the point where it makes them look stupid. Like metal, for instance. They're all stupid, but they want to make it. The upper class of wealth and affluence will try to make art, 'cause they've already seen money and power, and they go, 'well, we're above that.'"

"They try to imitate art," says Mars, "where the lower class is doing anything they can to bust out. . ."

"And the middle class," continues Westerberg, "doesn't give a shit. 'Cause they're right in the middle. They've never been rich, they've never been poor. We

don't want to rule the world, but we don't want to be at the bottom of the ladder."

But maybe the Replacements protest too much. Westerberg, at least, certainly shares some of what he dismisses as the "lower-class" urge to make it, which is finally just the urge to win respect. At 28 he isn't content to be a "rebel without a clue," the perpetual outsider; trouble is, he isn't content to come all the way inside, either. Whatever the commercial fortunes of *Don't Tell a Soul*, that ambivalence isn't likely to go away. "I get in trouble," he says, "whenever I try to write like I'm the life of the party, which I do sometimes. My own personality isn't like that. The people who relate best to my songs are the ones who see themselves over in the corner. However much they'd like to, they can't quite get into the swing of things."[16]

Jon Pareles: The Replacements came to the Beacon Theater on Thursday night with a chip on their shoulders and something to prove. . . . But the band's volatile chemistry was a little off, tinctured by unexplained hostility. At one point, Tommy Stinson threw his bass at Chris Mars's drum kit, saying something like, "Stay awake"; Mr. Mars, who had been putting real muscle into the music throughout the set, responded by flinging a drumstick at the bassist. And

Stinson, Mars, Dunlap, and Westerberg, in a shot made for Sire but never used, circa 1989 in Santa Barbara, California. © *Robert Matheu*

Mr. Westerberg seemed disgruntled. Between songs, he said, "Is it my imagination, or are we flopping?" and, later, "Here's another one that we don't like."[17]

Jim Walsh: Replacements drummer Chris Mars has left the band, effective immediately, in what he describes as a "mutual" decision reached by him and former bandmates Paul Westerberg, Tommy Stinson, and Bob Dunlap.

Mars says he came to the decision after Westerberg apologized for—but refused to retract in print—some statements Westerberg made to the national press regarding Mars's drumming ability and his lack of rehearsal time away from the band. As a result, Mars "felt it was time to leave the nest." Westerberg declined comment for this story.

"It ran its course," Mars said. "Actually, I feel like a great weight has been lifted off of me. Things have been kind of weird in the past year—I don't know if you've been reading the press . . . I don't want to drag it through the mud or anything like that, but I just felt like it was time for me to go."

Asked if the Replacements could still be the Replacements without him, Mars, who co-founded the band with Westerberg, Stinson and Bob Stinson 11 years ago, responded: "I would say no. I wish 'em luck. I'm not bitter about it; I hope they can get someone to replace me, but I wouldn't consider it the Replacements, myself. Paul, of course, did a lot of the songwriting, but that last record (*All Shook Down*), I don't really consider that a Replacements record either. The Replacements had a certain sound, and after *Pleased to Meet Me*, I think we started getting away from that sound. We started getting a little bit more subdued. It didn't quite have that edge for me."

Last week, the Replacements began preparing for their first tour in over a year. The group is looking for a new drummer, and a couple names have already cropped up locally as possible contenders for the vacated drum throne. As for Mars, an accomplished painter, he says he's anxious to get on with his life.

"I feel good (about the move); sort of peaceful. You spend so much time and energy just thinking about the band . . . I feel like I'm just glad to be rid of that. Of course it was fun—all the attention we got and stuff—but it is nice to not have to think of yourself in terms of 'I'm one of the Replacements.' You know, it's funny. I always thought to myself, like when things'd get sort of ugly, 'what is it gonna feel like when it actually happens?' But when it finally did happen, I was waiting for this big thing to hit. I imagined this big huge empty hole, but instead there was this freedom. I just feel free. So it's a good thing."

"Actually," he concluded whimsically, "I was thinking that I could get together with that other Stinson brother. We could call ourselves 'the Replaced.'"[18]

Chris Mars: I'm surprised I stayed in it as long as I did. [laughs] Now that I look back. I mean, I think there was a [point] it would've been a nice time for all of us to kind of say, "We passed our peak, and let's call it a night here." But I think what we all did is, we kind of tried to maybe—especially after Bob left—I think we tried to sort of "flog a dead horse." That's sort of what it felt like. I think, with *Pleased to Meet Me* (Sire, 1987), we did a pretty good job of trying to capture the spirit of the band. But after that, we never could quite get back. And so I think after *Pleased to Meet Me*, right around there would have been a good time to hang it up. But we didn't know what was gonna happen at that time, too. And there's all kinds of elements that came into play. But obviously, in retrospect, it did go on a few years longer than it should've.[19]

Steve Foley: I started drumming in bands in 1979. My first band was the Overtones. I played with Things That Fall Down, the Suprees, Wheelo, Routine 11, and Curt[iss A] every Wednesday for ladies' night for a decade. I've been in so many bands, I'm probably forgetting some.

I was playing with Pete Lack and Jimmy Thompson in Wheelo at the time. I was with my brother Kevin and another guy, Paul Miller, on a Saturday morning, and we went to the Uptown [Bar] for brunch like every other swingin' dick in town. You'd go up there for a big old breakfast. But it was too packed, so we went over to the CC Club.

And we're sitting there—it was pretty empty—and Paul and Tommy walked in. They sat in a booth behind us, and my brother Kevin is like, "God, Steven, your ears are burnin'. They're talking about you. They keep looking over here."

So I got up and went to the bathroom, and I said, "Hey, guys. Love the new CD." And Paul's like, "Really? Wanna join the band?" I'm like, "What do you mean?" And he's like, "Well, Tommy's got his black book out and he's running back and forth to the phone, trying to find a drummer." I think he was calling Clem Burke and all these other guys. So I was like, "Fuck, yeah. Are you kidding?"

Paul said, "No. We've got a CD obviously that's just come out, and we're going on tour. We're gonna have to audition you."

So we finished the meal, got in my car, and I had just bought a copy of *All Shook Down*, and I just had it cranked before I went into the CC, so when they got into the car and turned on the ignition, I think it was "Bent Out of Shape" just blasted out of the stereo. Perfect. It was pretty good. They both looked at each other and went, "You're already in."

They called Slim, and Slim met us down there. And my brother tagged

223

Bill Sullivan, 1993. © *Daniel Corrigan*

along. To be honest with you, I was a big fan, so I think I nailed every song pretty good. I didn't know the older stuff that well. Tommy loved the sound of my snare—I always tuned it high. Afterwards, we're walking to the van, and Paul goes, "How do you know all those songs?"

I said, "I don't know. I just know 'em. Who doesn't know 'em?"

So we get to the van and he goes, "So? Tomorrow night? You wanna rehearse?" In other words, do you want to join the band? And I was like, "Fuck, yes," and then I couldn't sleep for two weeks.

Tommy Stinson: The band's a lot better with the new drummer, not only because he drinks less (than Mars), but because he can keep more than one beat.[20]

Peter Jesperson: 1) MAYFLY – Could be a bad move but I thought I better get this baby outta the way. It completely paralyzed me when I was fifteen and shows no sign of letting up. From his 2nd l.p., just called "TERRY REID", released Oct. 1969. Paul W. got him to do this in the studio when the 'Mats were working on "A.S.D." and said it was sort of tentative until he hit the ". . . to unwind. . ." part and apparently threw his head back and let 'er rip. Tommy swears there were two pair of eyes not entirely dry. Tommy actually called me from the studio (it was the first time we'd talked since I'd been relieved of my duties 'Mats-wise). I said "Tommy who?", and he said "I've gotten to meet a lot of people over the last few years but I just gotta say thanks for turning me on to Terry Reid. I just met him, he sang 'Mayfly' and he's gonna sing on our new album." I said that I'd better sit down and could he run that by me again. . .

2) SPEAK NOW OR FOREVER HOLD YOUR PEACE – best known by Cheap Trick, this is the original. One of those classic R&R songs.

3) STAY WITH ME BABY – some would say this is the one Terry Reid performance that eclipses all others. I have a vivid recollection of being in Austin, Texas at a huge club called Liberty Lunch in 1983. We were playing a tape of mine prior to the 'Mats going on. I was talking with some friends when this song started and out of the corner of my eye I noticed someone running full tilt across the room towards the sound board. I guess Paul had decided it wasn't quite loud enough.[21]

Tommy Stinson: [W]hile we were doin' *All Shook Down* there was a guy who Paul and Slim admired for a long time, Terry Reid, a singer from England. He came into our session to meet us and hang out because our guitar tech was his roommate and we were just blown away. He sat down in the waiting room of the studio and he sang us this song called "Mayfly" which is on one of his records that we always listened to. He sang it to us with just an acoustic guitar and it was so moving that we were all bawling at the end of the song. His voice was just so incredible.[22]

Chris Dafoe: The cover [of *All Shook Down*] may have read Replacements, but to most fans, it sounded a lot like the first Paul Westerberg solo record.

"In my mind I wanted it to be a solo record, but towards the end the band got involved," said Westerberg during a visit to Toronto last fall.

"I've been making my own demos for the last two or three records and I'd always liked the feel of them. But then the band would take the songs and add their personality to them and they would always change. I didn't want that to happen this time.

"I did it with the thought that I can't make an all-for-one-one-for-all record this time. I said I'm going to make this one this way, or we have to make the next move, which is for me leave the band. Did it cause a lot of tension? That's putting it mildly."[23]

Paul Westerberg: I stopped drinking this time in August [1990] and as far as I can tell I would like this to be the last time I stop. I have no desire to drink at all. There is no excuse to drink because you are on tour and you are on a bus.

225

Stinson, Dunlap, Westerberg, and Foley in a photo from a Warner Bros. shoot, 1990.
© *Daniel Corrigan*

You play music for a living and people want to come hear you play. What is the big pressure in that?[24]

Tommy Stinson: [Bob Dylan] was recording down the hall [from the *All Shook Down* sessions]. He flagged me into this lounge area and started asking me all these questions about the Minneapolis area. So we sat and talked about Minneapolis for about forty minutes, talking like the average Joe about nothing important or great. I don't know if he was a fan or not, but he brought his two kids, Jakob and Anna, to meet us and hang out.[25]

John Pacenti: [*All Shook Down*] has been praised by many music critics, including *Rolling Stone* magazine, which gave the LP four stars or "an excellent"

rating. The disc also netted the band a Grammy nomination in the Alternative Rock Performance category. They lost to Sinead O'Connor.[26]

Peter Jesperson: I never really went through a phase of "I can't listen to those guys anymore." I was shocked by what happened [getting fired], but I would run into those guys at the CC Club or whatever it was. It wasn't like we palled around, but slowly but surely, I would see Paul and visit him wherever he and Lori were living.

Paul Westerberg: I wasn't the best husband. We had a good thing, and I don't think I was really ready to be married. I thought I was, made a mistake and wasn't. But once that was over, oddly enough, I didn't want to go out on dates. I didn't want to go out and pretend I was nineteen again. And oddly enough, I ended up with a girl I had known for a long time, someone I knew seven or eight years ago.[27]

Danny Murphy: There were rumors about them quitting long before they actually did. Bill Sullivan talked about that when he left the band and started working for us [Soul Asylum]. He said that they were just hatin' life and the writing was on the wall. He said, "They've opened for Tom Petty. What else is left for them to do?"

Paul Westerberg: Without stopping long enough to really look at it clearly, it was the end of many things. My band. My marriage. My excessive lifestyle. They all came to an end, but I made [*All Shook Down*] before I dealt with any of it.[28]

Jay Walsh: *All Shook Down* seemed so downbeat and depressed and nostalgic and kind of whiny. I think Paul bought into the whole tortured artist deal at some point. Before, they'd kind of sneered at not "making it," whatever making it means. Then it just turned. Paul was crafting his songs, which was great. But there should always be room for a "Gary's Got a Boner."

Peter Jesperson: *All Shook Down* is one of my favorite records by them. This sounds like I'm begrudging the records they did after I was involved, but I really think the first four records are great from start to finish, and I think every record after that is spotty. I think *All Shook Down* is one of the pinnacles of Westerberg's writing. He was still reaching for it, and he was close. He still had

the ability to grab on to those sorts of things, but he just couldn't do it for a whole album.

Ken Ornberg: Mo and Lenny Waronker were the big shots at Warner Bros. at the time, and Paul wanted to record a solo record, but they didn't think a Paul Westerberg solo record would sell as much as a Replacements record. I remember asking Paul if [*All Shook Down*] was a solo record or a band record and he said—in classic Paul fashion—he answered without technically answering me. He said, "Everybody plays on the record, on at least one track."

Ryan Cameron: There was anticipation at the store before the release of all their records, but it was obvious to everyone when *All Shook Down* came out that the band was disintegrating. Warner Bros. held a listening party for it at the old Loring Café [in Minneapolis], and I just remember being underwhelmed by it, thinking, "Boy, oh boy, oh boy, this is not what I had been hoping for." Warner Bros. didn't push it very much, and I think they, like everyone, saw the writing on the wall: It's the sound of a band falling apart, much like watching [the Beatles' film] *Let It Be* is watching the Beatles fall apart.

Steve Foley: My debut was at the twentieth anniversary of First Avenue. I was pretty nervous, but I did OK, I think. We did four or five songs—"Talent Show," "Bastards of Young," "I'll Be You," and a couple others. It was an unannounced thing, but the cat got out of the bag when Paul and I showed up to see what amps we needed and stuff.

Jay Walsh: I remember seeing them in the main room at First Avenue right after Chris Mars left. The new drummer was Steve Foley, I think. Nice guy, but he played right on the beat. Their sound was totally different. Chris always played behind the beat, kind of like Charlie Watts. He had to, with all the craziness going on in front of him. Chris held it all together, that thin rope of sanity that was always there, never trying to compete with the guitars. That was the end for me, when Mars left. They petered out.

Lori Barbero: Seeing them in the beginning was like doing drugs for the first time. You just can't believe how good it is.

Steve Foley: We hit the road in early January [1991]. The first show was Bakersfield, California, and the next show was at the fucking Forum in L.A.,

and Paul was like, "Well, Steve. You better be good tonight, because there's about fifteen guys out there that want this gig from you." I'm like, "Great."

George Wendt [Norm from *Cheers*] was there, and three months later, we're in a lobby in Chicago and there he is again, and we all go, "Norm!" He's like, "Hey, guys. Can I get on the guest list again?" There was no shortage of laughter and fun.

We toured opening for Elvis Costello, and Elvis had his say whether we could do an encore or not. We got to hang out, and they were all nice to us, and his wife had a little thing for me because I had glasses just like him, but I was a way thinner version of him.

We toured Europe and flew into Amsterdam, and we're thinking, "Where's our bus? I don't see a bus. Is our bus late?" And the guy goes, "There's your bus right there." It was a Volkswagen minibus, and in the first hour we got in a major car accident. Our equipment rental truck cut this lady off and she did a 720 on the freeway, and we're like, "Oh my God, here we go, and we haven't even hit the Autobahn yet."

Danny Murphy: At some point, you have to have some record sales so you can do bus tours.

Steve Foley: One night in Europe we were so tired, and Paul goes, "OK, everybody do pushups." We got a third wind and we played like there was no tomorrow. We could barely walk, but we lit the place on fire.

Another time in Europe, the road manager comes downstairs [in the hotel] and goes, "Well, we're getting a new tour bus, and it's a little nicer and it's got bigger wheels." Paul goes, "Who gives a shit about the wheels? Who cares about the tour bus?" Then the guy goes, "Also, do you guys want to do *Saturday Night Live*?" And Paul's like, "No." I'm like, "Oh, shit. C'mon. Just say, 'yes.' Let's just do it."

Paul Westerberg: Everybody in the band has cried in the van on the way to the show. And Tommy did it the best once, when he was 15 or 16. He was looking out the window as we were passing some farm area, and he's going, "That's real; that's life—a fuckin' house, a home where you stay, where you live, where you wake up, where you work." Sometimes it's like what we're doing is like this funky, weird little dream thing. And that's the kind of stuff, if you let it get to you, it'll really get you down. That's where "Unsatisfied" came from. You just don't know what you're doing, or why you're doing it. You're not really working

229

a job for your life, you're just sort of going around *entertaining* people; entertaining strangers. I feel like I'm doing something that's sometimes fun and sometimes powerful, but never really *real.* Not thinking about that stuff is the key.[29]

Danny Murphy: As far as I know, the [Replacements'] last couple tours were bus tours, but most of the touring they did was in a fucking van, totally haphazardly. That's something you can do in your twenties or even your late twenties, but then you want a little privacy and your own room and some fuckin' comfort.

Steve Foley: I knew it wasn't gonna last much more than a year. For me, it was November through July. One night Tommy and I were in one of our rooms, and he was like, "Steve, this isn't going to last forever. I've got some songs, and do you want to start a band [Bash & Pop] afterwards?" He never really said it was going to be over, and neither did Paul.

It was a frustrating band to be in. There were a lot of quiet times where you would just be walking on egg shells around Paul, the artist guy. Wasn't a lot of "Hey, how's it going today?" It was more like, "Oh, God. What kind of mood is he in today?"

Paul had his temper on stage, and I took the brunt of some of the stuff. I don't know if he and Chris would banter like that on stage, or if they were enemies, but one night in Texas, we had just done our first song of the set, and he said, "Goddamn it, is there a fuckin' drummer in the house?" I must have made a mistake or something. A couple times he kicked my cymbals over.

He would say stuff like, "Does Slim need a rocking chair tonight?" But then after the show, everything was cool and all part of the deal. But it could be a little nerve-wracking on stage. Yeah, I was tempted to tell him to fuck off a couple times, seriously, and sometimes I think that bad karma has kept him from making it bigger than he did.

I was just like, "Fuck you, buddy." But I thought about it and I let it go and figured that's kind of who he is and how they've been and part of the entertainment that the crowd wants. Even though being a new guy, it was like, "What the fuck have I gotten myself into?"

Paul Westerberg: Look, it's too early in the morning to construct an elaborate lie—the truth is, I was sick of the others. We'd toured for six months, and then it was straight back to writing songs. I just couldn't stand the thought of going back to writing songs, and I just couldn't stand the thought of going

back to the same old way of doing things. I decided to write how I felt, and not worry whether the songs were playable live.

It's such a cliché, but I lost my identity. And I was tired of being known as the leader of The Replacements, or one fourth of something. Because it's always basically been me calling the shots, and if that's the case, I finally wanted to have control over how it sounded. Democracy fell to pieces on this one! I don't see this record as Paul stepping out, and then it's back to the old Replacements groove. I think this is me trying to lead them into the one direction I think we should go. They don't look to the future, they do what they do, and sort of walk around thinking, "We're the Replacements and we're great." Whereas I think, "We've done this, let's do something else, don't you like other music? I like to work with other musicians."[30]

Steve Foley: I kind of felt sorry for Chris. I had read about Paul dissing Chris' drumming, and I always liked Chris. I saw him at a wedding in Delano [Minnesota], after we'd come back from touring the states, and Chris and his wife [Sally] came up to me because she wanted to meet me. She said, "Well, just do me a favor and play all [the] parts right." I didn't take it as an insult. I knew he was probably pissed off at that point. Or, maybe not. I just knew that something happened, and I was glad to fill his shoes, and glad it could be a Minneapolis guy to do it.

Ironically, I got married a couple months ago [in 2007] and we moved into a place [in South Minneapolis], and guess who lives right across the street? Chris Mars. First time I saw him, he and Sally were super-chatty, really nice, and we've both got BMW motorcycles. It's kind of cool.

Peter Jesperson: As I recall it, the last show was quite good for the most part. They played with some real spunk and fire. It was at Taste of Chicago [on July 4, 1991], [in front of] thousands of people. There were few indications it was their final gig. NRBQ were opening—along with a local Chicago band whose name escapes me—and I know the 'Mats felt weird about that 'cause they were big fans.

Steve Foley: I was in the dressing-room bathroom taking a shit before we went on, and Paul and Tommy and Slim were outside the bathroom door singing "For He's a Jolly Good Fellow." Their way of saying, "Good job on the tour, Steve." It was good humor.

Peter Jesperson: They kicked it off with "I Will Dare." Did a surprisingly good version of "Within Your Reach." The two moments that stand out most in my memory are "Talent Show"—when the band hit the breakdown in the middle, Paul stepped to the front of the stage and played the melody of "Send in the Clowns"—that gave me a lump in my throat the size of a baseball. And when they closed with "Hootenanny," it was pretty sad, not funny like it used to be.

Steve Foley: I took Paul's guitar, and Paul took the drumsticks, and some guy replaced him, and someone else took the guitar, and I was glad to get rid of it, because I don't know one chord. They played for fifteen minutes or something, and that was about it. We all filed off within a couple minutes of each other.

Peter Jesperson: Tommy sang most of it. After a couple of minutes Paul handed the drumsticks over to a roadie, I think, and left the stage. Then Slim and Steve handed their instruments to roadies and walked off, too. It ended with Tommy front and center, playing guitar and shouting things like "You were robbed!"

Jim DeRogatis: It seems to me that the alleged fire the band had for the first half of that set has been exaggerated by nostalgia. I had certainly seen the group be much, much better, even after Bob left, and I remember Westerberg being royally pissed off and trading harsh words with Tommy Stinson. The second half devolved into a lot of clatter and noise and everybody changing instruments, with long pauses before they'd finally pulled it together and hacked through a half-hearted, half-finished cover. In retrospect, I can say it was the perfect bookend to that first show I saw, the one with "Louie Louie," but at the time, I just felt sad, and I was glad to see the 'Mats call it a day when their hearts clearly weren't in it anymore.

Tommy Stinson: We ran our course. We just got to the point where we said, "OK, now let's do something else." Paul felt that way more so than the rest of us, but certainly I was right there. I was very understanding about what he wanted to do and I quickly jumped to my own thing. It wasn't like we went home and cried in our beer.[31]

Peter Jesperson: I guess, like the band, I was of the opinion they had run their course and just wasn't all that upset about it. I thought it was especially cool that they didn't make a big deal about it being their last show. That was

very "Replacements-esque" to me. I don't remember bumping into anyone I knew besides Maggie Macpherson and Chrissie Dunlap, who I had flown down with that morning.

Steve Foley: Tommy and Paul didn't think it was a very good show, but I did. I had a bunch of people from Minneapolis come down, and I was like, "Fuck, this is it." It didn't hit home for me because, I think, I was still drunk on the bus on the way home, playing *All Shook Down*. I put it in. Paul had flown home, and I think Tommy stayed there, so I think it was just me and Slim and Chrissie. The cooler was full of Heinekens and I was pretty hammered. I was going, "Fucking A, I played in this band," and romanticizing about how it's over and how great it was and all that B.S.

I didn't bring a camera or anything because, I'll admit it, I was doing my fair share of drinking and blow. I didn't really do that much before [joining the Replacements], but playing these incredible shows, and then your adrenaline is so high, and Paul and Tommy are so nonchalant and I'm like, "That was the greatest show I've ever done." And we're in a place where there's 2,000 people and there's people coming backstage. It's mind-blowing.

To be honest, I was in denial. It was a hard one to come down from. Everyone just loved the band. Every time the screen went up, people just went ape shit. Not to mention that it was my favorite songs ever, and here I am playing 'em, and there's free booze and free coke and the women and you've got your own five-star hotel room, and then it comes to a screeching halt and you're like, "Fuck, now what am I gonna do?" I was collecting unemployment, living in a small apartment on Aldrich (Avenue), and going, "Geez, what just happened?"

Jay Walsh: It's a sure thing, like death and taxes: Bands break up. There was no way that band was ever going to settle comfortably into middle age. Who'd want them to? God forbid they become something like the Stones, who should have stopped after *Some Girls*.

Tommy Stinson: There's radio stations all over the country saying, "It's *final*—the 'Mats are done." And it kind of irks me that people even would take it upon themselves to make a final statement for us. Me and Paul have never said we're done for good. We just didn't say anything, and with that, I still won't say anything. I'm not giving a written notice to Warner Bros. because I don't think it needs to be done. I think if there's any possibility in the future, why not just let it rest and see if it wants to rear its head?[32]

Slim Dunlap: A lot of the people who loved the Replacements at the beginning stuck with them until the end, and there were some that thought they lost something at some point. You can't win with everybody. I think to a lot of the younger musicians, the Replacements are a shining example of all you end up with in the end is your dignity. The time you are in the limelight is very important because you live with it the rest of your life.[33]

Ryan Cameron: A sideways reference might be Big Star. Here's a band that makes two critically acclaimed records that are great, and then you have Alex Chilton, who thinks he's a god, much in the way Paul Westerberg does, then they break up before their [acclaim] really starts. The only difference is that Big Star never had *any* acclaim. Those records [*#1 Record* and *Radio City*] didn't sell at all when they came out.

Slim Dunlap: All of the Replacements are proud of what they did and they have nothing to look back on in a bad way. I know some musicians that had a huge hit and when it comes on the radio and you're sitting there next to them you can just feel them bristle. That never happened to the Replacements. I think the saga of the Replacements is not over yet. I think in a weird way the band going under may have been the best thing for each person involved.[34]

Danny Murphy: The Replacements' legacy was sort of like proving a point the whole time, and that can be toxic after a while.

Slim Dunlap: The record company tried their damnedest but I really think the Replacements were different from other bands in that they weren't writing songs specifically to be hits. They were writing songs that said something to the right person, the words meant a lot to this person in particular. . . . If the Replacements had made that leap, I don't think we'd be discussing them in the same way we are now. There'd be a big success, a peak, and a burnout period, and it'd be done. The whole time before I joined and then afterwards, I never saw this as a possibility for the band. In a weird way that music is too literate, too intelligent to make it big.[35]

Curtiss A: [Bob Stinson] used to talk to me about Slim, and he used to talk to Slim about Slim. Bob didn't have anything against him, unless maybe he got drunk or something and said something. But in real life, he knew that he'd fucked up and made everybody mad at him. He was a very individual-

type guy, but not necessarily someone I would want to hang around with every day.

Bob Stinson: I met Alan White and Steve Howe—he called security on me even though I was on the guest list for their last show. That was like a dream, next to meeting Paul McCartney. I'll meet Lennon when I'm dead, so I'm not worried about that. It's alive when it really matters.[36]

Jay Walsh: It seemed like [Bob] just loved to play. I saw him at Oarfolk a few times. Once, he told me he'd just written this new song called "Every Sock Needs a Shoe." He told me that Paul wrote all the guitar parts for all the 'Mats' songs, but there was so much pure Bob in all his leads. He also said Paul was a better guitar player than he was. They were both great. I know one thing— Paul could never play as fast as Bob, and Bob's rhythm guitar just drove the whole band. His leads were really melodic and wild but he knew what he was doing and where he wanted to go and then after a lead, he'd raise his pinkie. God, could he wail. He just took over on stage. His guitar was so loud and fast and intense. He was titanic and subtle and a real screwball—the loosest cannon on a deck that was full of them.

Wally Marx: I was getting loaded with a parent of one of my daughter's friends the other night. We both graduated in '86 [from the University of Minnesota] and quickly found out that we had a lot in common. Out of nowhere he asks me, "Did you see that 'Mats show at Coffman [Union on the campus of the university] in '84?" I nearly fell to the floor. At the same time, we both started blurting memories: They opened with "Color Me Impressed"; Paul had a gray guitar that said "4 Sale" on it; the green lights that shot up from behind Chris to the ceiling during "Go"; the skinhead in the white sweatshirt that was head-butting people; how "slam-dancing" was supposedly banned at the time by the U of M; and, the best memory of all, the second encore, when they all switched instruments and played "If I Only Had a Brain." Wow. Mayhem.

Bob was God. He saturated that place with riffage. He had this way of playing that was well beyond playing a scale around the chords. He used chords in his solos and he got these overtones that were like bells and organs and voices. That way Bob held the guitar, he used to squeeze it up and to his body when he was pulling notes out. And that's what he did—pulled it, like he was sticking his fingers in a near-empty box of Junior Mints and pulling that last

235

piece of candy out with the very tip of his finger. Pulling notes out like that. Bob was a player where it truly was *all in the fingers.* As if the moment one of his fingers touched a string a current was gapped and electricity began to flow.

Most of the time, you couldn't see his fingers, but you almost never watched his fingers anyway, because his face was what you were drawn to. That little grin, the eyes, the facial expressions that kind of seemed involuntary and self-conscious at the same time. Bob sang that night at Coffman, taking the lead on "Yeah, Yeah, Yeah, Yeah, Yeah." I remember him wearing a tutu that night. My friend said it was a trench coat. Another guy I know swears it was a towel-and-duct-tape loincloth. Whatever. Bob, Bob, Bob. We hardly knew ye.

Ryan Cameron: Bob would come into [Let It Be Records] drunk, looking to borrow money or selling CDs. I had run-ins with him where I just had no idea what he was on. He was one of those people who, if you handed him a hand- ful of pills, he would take them and not even bother to ask what they were. Wouldn't occur to him to think about it. At the time, my roommate was in a band with his wife, Carleen, and I heard all sorts of Bob stories, and they were all kind of the same.

Mary B. Johnson: I set my sights on Bob when REMs and the Replacements played Regina [High School in 1981]. He first noticed me that night, and we became boyfriend-girlfriend off and on for years—or as much of a girlfriend as someone can be to Bob. The night the Replacements opened for the Ramones at First Avenue, Bob and I slept together and I got pregnant. I didn't tell Bob—I think Tommy finally did. I obviously didn't have it, because I can barely take care of myself, much less a baby.

Basically, I'd call him up and he'd put me on the guest list and we'd go home, and the next time they'd play, I'd call him up and he'd put me on the guest list and we'd go home. We hung out a few times down on Nicollet Island, drinking beer, and he told me about his dad and about when he spent time in [the teen correctional facility in] Red Wing [Minnesota], and how he was abused by his dad, or Tommy's dad, one of the two, I can't remember which one.

He wasn't doing heroin at the time. Smoking pot was all. For all I know, from Bob's words, Tommy turned him onto heroin. He could be hurt real easy. One night—Bob and I weren't sleeping together at the time—I was mad at him, and me and Katie [O'Brien] went to pick up Paul and Tommy after practice to go out, and he was crushed that he wasn't invited.

I like to think I was the love of his life, but Carleen and Joey are the love of his life. He respected Carleen. She's probably the only one he listened to. I broke up with him in 1983 once, and I devastated him. And I didn't think I could.

Carleen Stinson: Paul came over with a bottle of champagne [during the five-night stand for *Tim* at the 7th St. Entry in 1986] and he said to Bob, and I'll never forget this, he said, "Either take a drink, motherfucker, or get off my stage." It was the first time I'd seen Bob cry. He came home that night in tears, he didn't know what to do. He'd been completely dry for the 30-day program and the three weeks following. But after that night, Bob felt that no one liked him unless he was drunk.[37]

Daniel Corrigan: I hung with him for that *SPIN* story, and I think that drugs and alcohol had taken a huge toll on his head. He was out of the band at that point, and that obviously had been the biggest thing in his life. And it was over.

Bob Stinson: People are afraid of who I really am: a nice guy, very open, very honest, silly sometimes, willing to take a big risk for nothing. That's pretty important because a lot of people misjudge me. I've been having a lot of problems with people who kinda get close and think they know you and then discard you. It's not right; I've never done it to anyone I know of, but I've had it done to me. One's in, one's out, one's half way there. People get misconceptions by reading too many fucking papers. I mean, if you want to know somebody—and this is important to me—ask them, don't believe what you read or what other people say. A lot of people have done that to me, they've called me completely insane to almost a saint. I'm in there somewhere in between, I don't know where but, I mean, I'm vulnerable like anybody else, so treat me like I'm human.[38]

Daniel Corrigan: Bob had this classic move where he'd walk in the room, hock up a huge loogie and spit up on the ceiling. And then, surprise for whoever happened to walk under it. I saw him do that three or four times, personally.

Bob Stinson: People just believe what they hear too much. I mean, look what happened to John Lennon. He more than any other, more than any of the other fellas could've ruined the (the Beatles') reputation with that one sentence. When in fact, he was just misquoted when he said, "We're bigger than

Message from Bob, 1994. *Mary B. Johnson photo*

God" (*sic*). . . . And everybody accused him of being into acid and all that. That was bullshit, he was into heroin. If you want to know somebody, ask them, and I do that to anybody. I wouldn't say "what's this girl like?" or "what's this fella like here?" "Does he got a big knob?" or "Does she have nice tits?" I'd just go up and ask her, ah, well, as long as I don't get hit, anyway.[39]

Curtiss A: One time, around my second divorce, I saw these girls I liked and they were going to St. Cloud [about an hour northwest of Minneapolis]. And he jumped in the car, and he was like the fifth wheel. So from six at night 'til six the next morning, there wasn't hardly a time when he wasn't right there jabbering at me about this kind of stuff. It could have been a movie in itself. On the way home, we flipped the car, it went down into a ditch and rolled over and back on its wheels again. We were all laughing. We both could have died that night.

Bob Stinson: Half the people in this town have written me off, saying "there he goes again, he's way over his head; he's on the edge, stay away," because they don't know me. There's only three people in this town I'd spill my guts to. People don't think I'm responsible. Sorry, pals, but rock 'n' roll people aren't responsible anyway. I guess I've been thrown to the masses again, so it's like I'm being judged.

It kinda sucks. I don't like it.[40]

Bob Stinson, 1994. *Mary B. Johnson photo*

Peter Jesperson: We were in San Francisco once, and everybody had split up and gone to stay with different people, and Tommy had stayed with a girl who worked at the Rough Trade record shop in San Francisco, and when we picked him up, she had given him a bunch of magazines to put in the van for us to read.

There was an *NME* that had Little Richard on the cover, and Bob and I wrestled over it, and he got it first. After he read it, he said, "Hey, I didn't know Little Richard was born in a gay camp." And I was like, "What is he talking about?" And I read the piece and it said, "Little Richard and his music sprang from gay camp." But in Bob's mind, there was a camp of all gay people, and that's where Little Richard came from. But I don't think he was kidding. And again, here, I don't mean to say, "Isn't Bob dumb?" It was just like, "Wow."

Danny Murphy: I remember being on a Midwest swing with those guys pretty early on, right before [Soul Asylum's] *Made to Be Broken* came out. We'd just played Chicago, and we were heading East to Cleveland or somewhere, and we'd lost an hour, and that whole concept was so alien to Bob: "Well, where did it go? Where did they put the hour?"

Peter Jesperson: He always had those crazy things he'd say. We'd be having some problems, and he'd say, "Don't worry about it, it's only Tuesday." He'd say that all the time, and it was never Tuesday.

Replacements' 'lunatic guitarist,' Bob Stinson, dies

■ Unconventional musician struggled with drug abuse

JIM WALSH STAFF WRITER

Bob Stinson, who gained national notoriety as the madman guitarist for the seminal Minneapolis-based rock 'n' roll band, the Replacements, was found dead Saturday in his Uptown apartment.

Stinson's body was found about 7 p.m. by a friend. A syringe was found next to the couch in the apartment. The cause of death has not yet been determined, Hennepin County officials said Sunday.

Stinson's struggle with drug and alcohol abuse led to his ouster from the Replacements in 1986 as well as estrangement from his wife, Carleen, and his 6-year-old son, Joey.

Stinson, 35, was diagnosed as suffering from a manic-depressive disorder last year and was taking medication to combat intense mood swings, his mother, Anita Stinson Kurth, said.

"He had been going through a real hard time these last couple weeks with his depression," she said. "He was down about it. But he did say that he was taking steps to get with a psychiatrist on that. Other than that, he was Bob."

Despite his recent battles with depression, Stinson Kurth said she was convinced her son's death was not a suicide. "I think it was accidental; I really believe that," she said. "I don't think it was intentional."

News of Stinson's death yesterday elic-

STINSON CONTINUED ON **5A** ▶

Danny Murphy: I gave him a ride from Oarfolk once, and I had this little Honda Civic with a stick shift. He said, "What are you doing?" I said, "Shifting." He said, "They still make cars like that?" I don't know if he was putting me on, or if he'd just never noticed.

Mary B. Johnson: I made Bob court me for a year, and he did. When Kurt Cobain died, that's when I said [to myself], "If you want this guy, Mar, now is the time. If you want Bob to know how you feel, tell him." So I went to the Uptown [Bar] and left him a note with his mom, and he called me a couple days later, and right after my birthday, May of '94, we started dating exclusively.

Things turned bad that fall, before that. I don't know if he was doing heroin, or it was the bipolar, but he was lost. He was out of it. It was like seeing him drunk at one o'clock in the morning twenty-four hours a day. He was lying, he was out of control, I can't even describe it. One hundred and seventy-five miles an hour in a thirty-five-mile zone. I wouldn't say he got mean ... I wouldn't get him beer, but he'd find some chick who would.

The people who he was living with on 38th and Cedar—Ed and Lori. Ed was this groupie guy, big fan of the Replacements and thrilled to have Bob Stinson living in his basement. Lori was bipolar, too, and their kids were super ADD, and Bob became delusional. He thought Lori was in love with him and wanted to have an affair with him. It was bad. I was over there daily. He was living in the basement, and we'd go out. I wasn't making a whole lot of money, but I was supporting both of our drinking habits, and I'd buy him food. I don't know where he got his drug money, 'cause I didn't give it to him.

We drank together every day from May '94 to December '94. He'd drink anything I bought him. He'd drink whatever anybody would buy him. When Bob died, I felt extreme guilt. Because we fought that night, the last night I saw him, January 8 [1995]. My mom had bought me this necklace, and he liked it, and I took it off and gave it to him—and as he got out of the car I said, "Give this to the cunt you like." And he said, "I'll talk to you tomorrow," but he never did. I dropped him off at his mom's house, and I was a basket case for the next six weeks. I wanted to tell him I wanted to be with him.

John Beggs: I'm pretty sure I was the last one to see Bob alive. He came into [Garage D'or Records on Nicollet Avenue in South Minneapolis] and just wanted to drink a beer that night, and instead of closing up, I stuck around and said he could. I'm glad I did. I'm just glad I was nice to him.

Replacements' ex-guitarist found dead

By Jon Bream
Staff writer

Bob Stinson, 35, founding guitarist for the influential Minneapolis rock band the Replacements, was found dead in his Lake St. apartment Saturday night in south Minneapolis. No cause of death was available.

Stinson, his younger brother Tommy, Paul Westerberg and Chris Mars formed the Replacements in 1980. The group became a national sensation on the rock underground, known for their freewheeling and often inebriated performances.

Bob Stinson was widely regarded as the band's spirit, the chaotic force who took the band over the edge. He was kicked out of the band in 1986 because he couldn't curb his out-of-control lifestyle.

> "Bob was a sad person in life. Bob just needed a little peace and never found it."
>
> **Slim Dunlap, who replaced Stinson in the Replacements**

After his departure, the Replacements achieved greater renown on Warner Bros. Records and performed on TV's "Saturday Night Live." Among their better-known songs were "Bastards of Young" and "Achin' To Be." The Replacements' punkish spirit was considered an inspiration to the 1990s grunge scene that spawned Nirvana and other hit-making groups.

The Replacements disbanded in 1991. After his stint with the band, Stinson played with the Bleeding Hearts and other local rock bands.

"Bob was a sad person in life," said veteran Minneapolis guitarist Slim Dunlap, who replaced Stinson in the Replacements. "Bob just needed a little peace and never found it."

Dunlap said that he saw Stinson about two weeks ago and that Stinson "wouldn't tell me what was going on," he said. "He's had a rough time the last year or so. He'd been

bumped out of every band he'd joined. He was one hell of a guitar player when he was on. But it's hard to get old as a guitar player. Bob was finding that out."

Dunlap said that Stinson was "incapable of anything vicious toward anyone else. He was a nice person, which doesn't jibe with his wild man reputation."

Steve Groseth, Stinson's neighbor, said that the guitarist moved into an apartment above a Lake St. business about a week ago and that he was found by a friend Saturday night.

Stinson is survived by his mother, brother, sister and a son. Funeral services are pending.

Staff writer Robert Franklin contributed to this report.

Peter Jesperson: Everyone tried to say something to him many, many times at various points. It's ironic to me that, of our clique of people—the four guys in the band and me, Sullivan, and Carton—Bob was actually the one who quit drinking a couple of times. It was just one of those things where, every time you saw him you wondered if it would be the last time. And when it did happen, he had a new girlfriend. She was pretty freaky. I don't know if this was her real name, but it was Anna Nimity.

I remember them coming into the Twin/Tone building, 2217 (Nicollet Avenue), the [former] funeral home. He came into my office with her and he wanted to introduce her to me, and I was on the phone. And he came to the phone and stood there—this is February '95—and he stood there and poked his head in with that goofy grin and I was happy to see Bob walk in the room any time, but I put my hand up, like, "Just one second, I'm just gonna finish this phone call." And while I was finishing the phone call, I glanced out of the corner of my eye, and I saw him say to her, "He was the fifth, you know."

I completely lost track of what conversation I was having, and I thought, "He will never know how much that meant to me." That was the last time I ever saw him.

Mary B. Johnson: I feel exclusive and honored and blessed and significant to have known him, and to have seen those guys in the Entry when there was only seven other people in the crowd.

Russell Hall: A few hours ago, Bob's girlfriend phoned me from Minneapolis. In a soft, wispy voice, she asked if I was sitting down, and of course, I knew what her next words would be. Bob was dead, apparently of an overdose.[41]

Jim Walsh: Bob Stinson, who gained national notoriety as the madman guitarist for the seminal Minneapolis-based rock 'n' roll band, the Replacements, was found dead Saturday in his Uptown (Minneapolis) apartment.

Stinson's body was found about 7 p.m. by a friend. A syringe was found next to the couch in the apartment. The cause of death has not yet been determined, Hennepin County officials said Sunday.

Stinson's struggle with drug and alcohol abuse led to his ouster from the Replacements in 1986 as well as estrangement from his wife, Carleen, and his 6-year-old son, Joey.

Stinson, 35, was diagnosed as suffering from a manic-depressive disorder

last year and was taking medication to combat intense mood swings, his mother, Anita Stinson Kurth, said.

"He had been going through a real hard time these last couple weeks with his depression," she said. "He was down about it. But he did say that he was taking steps to get with a psychiatrist on that. Other than that, he was Bob."

Despite his recent battles with depression, Stinson Kurth said she was convinced her son's death was not a suicide. "I think it was accidental; I really believe that," she said. "I don't think it was intentional."

News of Stinson's death yesterday elicited shock and sadness—but not surprise—from his friends, family and former bandmates.

"We all knew that it was coming, but that didn't soften the blow one bit," said singer/songwriter Paul Westerberg, who joined Stinson, his brother Tommy Stinson and drummer Chris Mars in 1979 in the first incarnation of the Replacements. "We knew that Bob led the lifestyle he did. But it hurt as much as if he'd been hit by a truck."

Westerberg got word of Stinson's death late Saturday, when Tommy Stinson called him from his home in Los Angeles.

"Tommy was shook up," Westerberg said on Sunday. "I was stronger on the phone, and then when I got off the horn, that's when the tears started to flow. Tommy sounded a little more together this morning; I have a feeling as soon as I see him, it'll be all over again."

With the Replacements, Bob Stinson made six recordings: *Sorry Ma, Forgot to Take Out the Trash* (1981); *The Replacements Stink* EP (1982), *Hootenanny* (1983); *Let It Be* (1984), which was named one of the best 100 records of all time by *Rolling Stone* magazine; *The S— Hits the Fans* cassette tape (1985); and *Tim* (1985).

Over the years, Stinson developed a reputation as a lightning-wristed, wholly unconventional lead guitar player, inspired by his six-string heroes Steve Howe, Johnny Winter and Prince. "It certainly was one of the most unintellectual musicalities that I've ever experienced," said Peter Jesperson, former manager of the Replacements, who remembered Stinson as a "gentle giant."

"I mean, what he played just came from somewhere else. It was instinctual, more than most people that I've ever experienced. He just played a weird amalgamation of things that he admired, filtered through the weird Bob Stinson brain."

As a performer, Stinson took to playing gigs in skirts, make-up and the buff. As one observer once wrote, Stinson was, for many, "the lunatic guitarist for the only American band that ever mattered."

But that reputation became a burden, and toward the end of his time with

the Replacements, the band persuaded Stinson to seek treatment for his drug and alcohol problem.

"We paid for him to go into treatment, and he got out and scored some drugs that day," Westerberg said. "It was obvious he didn't want to quit, or wouldn't. But we were no angels at the time, either. I think the spectacle sort of took over the band, and we forgot about playing music."

When Stinson left, the Replacements filled the lead guitar slot with Bob "Slim" Dunlap. The group disbanded in 1990.

Stinson went on to play with various local outfits, including Sonny Vincent, Static Taxi, Dog 994, and, most recently, the Bleeding Hearts. The last year of his life was relatively inactive musically. But his legacy will always be as founder of the Replacements.

"I started that band, and I ended that band when I left," he said in an interview with the *Pioneer Press* last year. "In the Replacements, we all knew our positions.

"When the Replacements broke up, everybody went out and tried to be a lead singer and a frontman. I'm a guitar player. I don't have the ego . . . to do that. I'd rather be a guitar player lost in a band. I have a gas playing the guitar."

That much was evident at Lee's Liquor Bar a few months ago, when Stinson got up on stage and joined the local country-swing band Trailer Trash for an impromptu version of Lefty Frissell's "Lil' Ol' Wine Drinker Me."

Stinson became a regular at the Trailer Trash shows because he was drawn to one thing: the music.

"He'd come for the escapism of the scene," says Nate Dungan, leader of Trailer Trash. "When the music was right and the big mirror ball was spinnin' around, that little room would kind of take you away from the big city. And I think that's why he was there, though I couldn't really figure it, because Bob is as punk as they come. He was the true spirit of punk rock."

"He was one in a million; I haven't met his equal yet," added Westerberg with a laugh, after recounting some of Stinson's more inspired antics. "He didn't have much education, but he would say things sometimes that were utterly poetic. He wasn't dumb. You would think he was at times, and then he'd come up with something that was just brilliant."

Stinson is survived by his son, Joey of Minneapolis, his mother, Anita Stinson Kurth of Minneapolis; his father, Neil Stinson of Mound; his brother, Tommy of Los Angeles; and two sisters, Lonnie of Monticello and Lisa of Big Lake.

Visitation is Tuesday at McDivitt Hauge funeral home. Funeral services are Wednesday.[42]

Jay Walsh: He might have drank himself to death anyway if he'd never been in a band.

Jim Walsh: Ex-Replacements guitarist Bob Stinson, 35, died of natural causes, the Hennepin County medical examiner's office told the Stinson family Tuesday. All but one of a battery of toxicology tests on Stinson's body have been completed, but the county won't release the death certificate for another two weeks.

"We've told the family it was natural causes," said Dr. Lindsey Thomas, assistant Hennepin County medical examiner. "There is such a thing as total body failure. In general, all the organs—especially the liver—take a beating when they've been subject to years of excessive drug and alcohol abuse."

Reports of a syringe found next to Stinson's body Feb. 18 had led to speculation of a drug overdose.

"The M.E. said that there was a trace of heroin in his blood, but no way would it have been enough to kill him," said Anita Stinson Kurth, Stinson's mother.

Another theory was that Stinson was depressed and that his death was a suicide. According to autopsy findings, though, that wasn't the case.

Stinson's family met the news Tuesday with relief.

"It was just his time to die," said Carleen Stinson, the musician's former wife and mother of his 6-year-old son, Joey. "This helps, especially with the news channels running stories about "bad heroin," and using Bobby as an example."

"It eases a lot of the pain," Kurth said. "For the last week, I haven't wanted to do anything or go anywhere, because there were a million people with a million questions. This makes it much easier."

"It's not like it changes anything, but it gives me some peace," said Stinson's younger brother and former bandmate, Tommy Stinson. "Now we know that he wasn't trying to bail from his predicament. In the back of my mind, I was feeling guilty that I didn't do more, even though we all did for years."[43]

Ryan Cameron: It's sort of the same thing as when Charlie Parker died. The doctor thought he was in his sixties, and he was in his forties or something. Same thing with Bob. He just ruined his body.

Russell Hall: Last week, Bob asked me—whom he barely knew—to send him $200 "for rent," he said. I told him I would send the money. "Promise?" "Yeah." "Oh, I love you."

Before writing the check, I decided to phone a friend in Minneapolis, someone I trusted, who knew and loved Bob. "What should I do?" I asked. "Don't

send it," he said. "You don't know what he might buy. Remember the story of how Neil Young sent [Crazy Horse guitarist] Danny Whitten cash, and Whitten OD'd the next day? You don't want to have to live with that."

I never sent the money.[44]

Mary B. Johnson: I was in shock. I was in a coma for the whole next year, until the Fourth of July, and this is going to sound really weird, but the thing that finally put me at ease was one night it was really hot and I went to Lee's. I got really hammered and came home, and I dreamt about Bob that night. In my dream, I said, "Bob, why did you leave me?" And he said, "Mary, because we weren't getting along." And I woke up and I felt some peace. It was him—sure as I'm sitting here talking to you, he was sitting talking with me.

Charles Aaron: Nobody could fuck up a guitar solo more beatifically than Bob Stinson, and for that alone I always wanted to buy the big, cross dressing lug a beer. But by the time I did, just over two years ago, he demanded nothing less then a six pack, a cheeseburger deluxe platter, a ride to the hardware store to buy a gizmo for a blown speaker, a $20 loan, and well, you got the picture. Like most people who were transfixed by Bob's spirit, privy to his absurdly sharp sense of humor, and implicated in his sad demise, I coughed up the do re mi and exhaled a heavy sigh. You know, the whole "you can't help people who don't help themselves" routine. Besides, I wanted to get a decent interview from the guy. Which is a deathly lame cop out, I know. And Bob, who gave of himself like his soul was throwing a year round clearance sale, probably deserved better. Then again, the guy had a huge ego and couldn't wait to see his name in a magazine again. We all have our selfish motivations.[45]

G. R. Anderson, Jr.: About the time I met Bob, he had unfortunately turned into a running joke. In the early 1990s, with a new influx of bands around town, Bob came to symbolize the ultimate loser—a guy who managed to get kicked out of the Replacements, after all. These younger bands all worshiped that band, of course, but the way people viewed Bob was with a sense of irony and condescension, as if acknowledging anything other than his failure might be too difficult. The truth? What did that matter? Too painful.

This always bothered me, because I found Bob to be a rather vulnerable, even naïve, soul. I met him one night when I was driving home down Lyndale Avenue in South Minneapolis, and noticed him walking down the sidewalk, pretty aimlessly. I pulled up, rolled down the window, and asked him if he

needed a ride. At that point, I'd say the only thing that compelled me to do so was that I was simply star-struck, still, after all these years. This was probably sometime in 1993.

When Bob got in the car, it became apparent that he didn't have anywhere to go. This was embarrassing to him, I think. I was living in a house on Pleasant Avenue that had a huge screened-in porch and a couch—a crappy old piece of office furniture left to weather the elements outside. I told Bob he could crash there for the night, and he did. The next morning, he was up with the sun.

I didn't see him again for a few weeks, maybe longer, but once in a while he'd show up at my place, or he'd see me out in a bar, and he'd end up on the porch. I'm not sure he even really knew my name, and I can't quite explain how we ended up together, but that's sort of how it was with him, I think. He was sort of a happy wanderer.

We'd have some pretty good times together, one night drinking bottles of Blatz and listening to the stereo. His taste in music was very wide-ranging and surprising. I remember sitting up one night and listening to the purest of pop—*Odessey and Oracle* by the Zombies—and him absolutely loving it. He spoke with great knowledge and enthusiasm of '60s pap, like the Monkees and the Turtles. He talked in clipped bursts that sort of cut off from excitement. People said he was pretty rude and downright mean. He was sort of bellicose, but I didn't really take it that way. It was just his way of communicating.

That night, I remember being surprised to learn that he knew songs by my band [Rex Daisy]. We didn't even have a record out, but he knew our songs, obviously from seeing us live. I don't recall ever seeing him at one of our shows. Trip Shakespeare was pretty big then, and he loved them too. Not exactly the stuff of punk-rock guitar legends. I also remember that we ate bread-and-butter pickles out of the jar that night. I think he had half a pack of Oscar Meyer hot dogs, but maybe I made that up.

Everybody thought he was using, and I suppose some people knew whether it was true. I didn't want that shit in my house, so I told him when he stayed with me—which happened no more than five times, max—no drugs. One morning I found a spoon and a pack of matches in the bathroom. I didn't see him again after that.

Then in February of 1995, there was a classic Minnesota snowstorm. I had just returned from L.A. a couple days before with the bass player in my band. We'd been working on our record out there. The lead singer had stayed behind to do some vocals and was supposed to fly into town that day, but every flight was delayed for hours. We were supposed to play a gig that night at the Fine

247

Line, for "Minnesota Music Does Minnesota Music" or something. The idea was that a slew of local bands would play songs by other Minnesota artists. We were supposed to play three songs, and I'm sure we claimed one Replacements song for our set, but I don't remember which one.

Anyway, the bass player and I did the most respectable thing musicians could do in the face of waiting for a flight delay on a snow day: We went drinking. We hit the CC Club, right around noon, and started in on the Bloody Marys. Not long after, Bob came through the front door. He didn't look good. I remember noticing that he was sweating on such a cold, windy day. He immediately took his place on the corner of the bar, and the bartender and the handful of regulars took to razzing him. He got somebody to buy him his first drink. Then another. Then another.

He remembered me and Steve, the bass player. We got to talking. He was pretty belligerent, though. I thought he always looked at people askance, out of skepticism maybe. He talked about being in some kind of treatment—I couldn't discern if it was rehab or a nut house or a hospital stay. He talked about his ex-wife or old flame, and—memory gets a little fuzzy here—I think he said he had hepatitis.

We started talking music and playing songs on the fabled CC jukebox. An idea struck: Would Bob sit in with us later that night? Bob thought it was a put-on, that we'd just parade the village idiot up on stage, like some other bands had done with him. He was acutely aware of that. We were serious and sincere, though, and I think he sensed that. We settled on "Surfin' Bird"— Steve's suggestion—an idea that Bob loved. He was miming chord structures, and argued with Steve over what key the song was in. Bob was right, as I recall. He said he wanted to play a solo like Link Wray.

The day dragged on, and plenty of booze was consumed. This will probably get me in trouble, but Bob spent some time in the men's room, and when he came out, he was pretty much a wreck. I think he shot up in there, but I don't know for sure.

This was before cell phones, but somehow we figured out when Mike, the lead singer, was finally going to arrive at the airport. We told Bob that we were going to be tight for time, but that we'd go to the airport and then pick him up. He told us where he lived, right above Koppi Electric, across the street from the Bryant Lake Bowl. He told us to be there at nine o'clock, and told us not to be late. This struck me as a plea more than an order—he didn't quite believe that we'd come through.

The airport was a mess, of course. I was very concerned that we'd be late to pick up Bob, and we were, by about fifteen minutes. He had given me the apartment

number, and I buzzed the call box, but got nothing. The door to the building was open, so I went in and walked upstairs. I knocked on Bob's door—no answer. I waited and tried again. Same thing. It was eerily quiet, and a chill came over me. I don't think there was a single soul in the building. I got spooked, and left.

We went and played the gig, barely on time. We didn't play "Surfin' Bird," but we played "Can't Hardly Wait." The following Sunday, I was listening to Jesperson's radio show, and he announced that Bob had died. The phone rang immediately, and it was Steve on the other end. He asked me if I'd heard. I think I cried over the phone.

It was an odd feeling, given that Bob was a pretty tough guy to love. But it was there if you wanted it. I'd certainly never considered him a friend, but Steve and I went to the wake. The whole thing hit me hard, creeped the hell out of me, and to this day I don't really talk about it much. Certainly Bob's troubles weren't my responsibility, but I felt accountable somehow anyway. In a way, I think we all were.

Still, I carry a particular kind of regret I still can't make sense of. By the accounts that were going around, the time of death was sometime around 9 p.m., right about the time I came knocking on Bob's door.

Charles Aaron: Once, when we were endlessly traipsing around the snowy streets of Minneapolis, one of Bob's favorite pastimes, he tried to explain why he had such a striking impact on people—family, friends, fans, or otherwise. Sniffling and sipping an icy beer, he finally said, "The one that's the furthest out is the one that everybody lets their heart trust, completely. Completely," he emphasized, his voice going quiet and trailing off. Then he stared at me hard with an odd combination of pride and bewilderment. That trust, real or imagined, was something that Bob Stinson felt painfully, deeply. And he never figured out how to live with it.[46]

Paul Westerberg: Anita wanted Replacements songs played at the wake. When I walked up to the casket, "Johnny's Gonna Die" was playing.[47]

Kii Arens: I was working at Twin/Tone doing album covers at the time and the whole staff went to the funeral. As I remember it everyone was telling stories of Bob and it was really sad and joyous at the same time. When [Jim Walsh] stepped up to the mike to do the eulogy the mike began to seriously feedback. Without a second of thought he simply looked up to the heavens and said, "OK, Bob, we know you're here." Perfect.

The Replacements

Author's note: *The following is the text of the eulogy I delivered on February 22, 1995, at Bob Stinson's funeral at the McDivitt-Hauge funeral home in Minneapolis. It was originally reprinted in* The Squealer *fanzine, with permission of the Stinson family.*

Words fail me, as they have failed most of us over the past few days. Yesterday, Carleen asked me if I had known Bob very well. I couldn't rightfully say that I did—in the traditional sense of the term. For that reason, I was a little reticent when Anita asked me to deliver this eulogy. But like everyone here, and another multitude who aren't, I knew Bob's spirit very well.

And it is a spirit, as I have discovered, that is next to impossible to hold in a room, pin down on a piece of paper, or capture with a couple of stories. At first, I didn't have my own words, so I stole someone else's. This is from *On The Road* by Jack Kerouac:

> "The only people for me are the mad ones, the ones who are mad to live, mad to talk, mad to be saved, desirous of everything at the same time, the ones who never yawn or say a commonplace thing, but burn, burn, burn, burn like fabulous yellow roman candles exploding like spiders across the stars, and in the middle you see the blue center light pop, and everybody goes, 'Awwwww.'"

That was Bob. That is Bob. And you know what I mean, because we all have our Bob stories. They're etched in our faces, planted in our hearts, like seeds we never thought would bloom into anything much more than memory. Of course, now we know better. This week, all the seeds have blossomed into vines, and tangled permanently around our hearts. This week, we learned a lot about Bob, a lot about ourselves, and just how much we will miss this fabulous yellow roman candle.

Bob stories. Over the past few days, I've had the privilege of hearing quite a few told and retold. It was like a wonderful game of dominoes that elicited as many tears as laughs: Everybody recounting tales about Bob's wit, his loving gentleness, his sense of humor, his appetite for life. And, as a matter of fact, there have been an inordinate amount of stories about just his appetite.

Anita remembers when Bob was five years old. The family had moved from Minnesota to San Diego, and Bob and [his sister] Lonnie made a practice of taking the 25 cents Anita would give them for the church basket, and buying cherry pies. Clearly, it was a pattern that would play itself out in adulthood, for when Dog's Breath, and later the Replacements, started up, Anita remembers

feeding the entire band, and often a slew of their friends, after practice in the basement. Bob would always eat his fair share.

With the Replacements, his penchant for eating fast food in the van earned him the nickname of Bob "To Go" Stinson. As the rest of the guys would sit in the restaurant, Bob would go in, get his food, come back, and sit alone in the van until he was ready to eat. Two hours would pass sometimes before he'd dig in. Peter [Jesperson] always figured it was because he liked to eat his food at room temperature.

One of my earliest food memories of Bob is 15 years ago, when the 'Mats were making *Sorry Ma* over at Blackberry Way. Steve Fjelstad and Peter were in the control room, the band had just finished a take, and they were getting ready to do another. Suddenly, Bob was nowhere to be found. Then, just as suddenly, he was back. Before anyone could say, "Where's Bob?," he had snuck out of the studio, raced to Burger King—which was a good two blocks away—and returned. He set up his Whopper, fries, and Coke on his amp and was ready to go.

One of the last times I saw him, we sat at a bar and I bought Bob and Mike Leonard some drinks. Bob caressed the menu, rolled his eyes with that coy look he'd give you, but he never asked, because that wasn't his style. He just looked at me out of the corner of those mischievous winking eyes until I melted, caved in, and bought him a cheeseburger and fries.

Bob stories. It seems like we've been telling them most of our lives, and I have a very good feeling that it is a tradition that will not end after today. Carleen remembers his love for skipping stones, fishing, walking around the lakes and by the railroad tracks, and as a father who loved Joey with the fierce, all-encompassing passion of a papa bear. Tommy remembers him as a great brother, the two of them running around the house as kids, flicking the sides of each other's heads with their fingers until it felt like their ears were going to fall off.

Chris remembers the day Bob physically grabbed then 12-year-old Tommy, who was running around with his friends, by the shoulders, and dragged him into a Dog's Breath practice. Like any good big brother, he talked the other guys into letting the kid play with the bigger kids. Paul remembers Bob's special genius, his ability to rail against the stuffed shirts, the status quo—with aplomb. Paul calls it "creative insanity."

My memory is of him walking, always walking—down Hennepin, around the lakes, down Lyndale, clutching that omnipresent brown bag of his. I swear I saw him last night around midnight on 22nd and Hennepin—I even did a double-take—and I wouldn't be surprised if it was him. Last night. That's

when it hit me: the streets of this town are going to be a lot quieter, and a hell of a lot less fun, without our Spanky roaming them. Patrolling them.

Bob stories. The ones that probably stick in most of our heads are the ones that have to do with his guitar. It all started on Christmas in 1969, when Anita bought Bob his first guitar, an acoustic one. He took to it right away. By then, the family had moved from San Diego to West Palm Beach, Florida, where Bob played softball, joined Cub Scouts, and continued a love for the water that had started in California. Anita remembers the time he took a summer job mowing lawns, and, after a rainfall, tore up a customer's lawn on a riding mower. Clearly, landscaping was not his forte.

Around the same time, he learned how to play guitar, and he made some very good friends through it. When Bob's grandfather died in 1973, Anita moved the family back to Minnesota. Bob was 15 at the time, and the move was rough on him. He found solace, and learned to express what he couldn't verbalize, through his music.

For the first couple years after moving to Minneapolis, Bob was unhappy—until he found friends, again with his music. First time Chris ever saw him, Bob was bumming around the neighborhood on a girl's bike. He had long hair, like his hero, Steve Howe, and was sitting on the curb smoking a cigarette, sneaking a listen to Chris playing guitar and drums up in his bedroom. They eventually hooked up, formed Dog's Breath, and later the Replacements. The rest, as Anita says, "was destiny."

Throughout his life, the guitar was Bob's main mode of expression. And even though he will be remembered most as founder of the Replacements, the fact is, he got just as much joy playing in Static Taxi, as the collage attests, the Bleeding Hearts, and the numerous other bands he played with over the past few years. He brought the same no-holds-barred approach to all of it. He did not play for fame or wealth. He played simply because, as he once said, "I have a gas playing the guitar."

That was abundantly clear, just from watching or listening to him. He became an inspiration to hundreds of thousands of guitarists out there, but there never has been and never will be another guitar player like this one. More than any guitar player I have ever seen or heard, Bob had an uncanny ability to actually fuse his personality with his guitar, and express himself through it. His leads made you actually crawl inside him—they were funny, intense, sad, and joyful, all at once.

Chris talks about when the 'Mats would do "Rock Around The Clock" at 100 miles an hour, and about how much he loved it when the lead came, and

Chris Mars etching that appeared on the program for Bob Stinson's funeral service.
Author collection, appears courtesy of the artist and Tommy Stinson

Bob would, unfailingly, nail it to the floor. There are countless other such moments you could name: the otherworldly magic of "Go" and "Johnny's Gonna Die," the manic force of "Dose of Thunder," the goofy insanity of "Tommy Gets His Tonsils Out," the barely controlled chaos of "Customer," and on and on and on.

Along with his playing, of course, there was Bob's special panache he brought to the stage. I remember that magnificent face, scrunched up like he had a secret. I remember his falsetto on "Yeah, Yeah, Yeah, Yeah, Yeah" and "Little G.T.O." I remember him ripping off a lead he'd be particularly proud of, flicking his wrist like "Waiter, my check," then patting himself on the back, all in one motion.

And, of course, there was the wardrobe. The gorgeous, and always tasteful, dresses. The Hefty garbage bags. The overalls. The Prince "1999" T-shirt. The little jean jacket. The genie get-up that prompted Chris to start calling him "Sim Alabim." One night at Duffy's, my big brother and I rolled a garbage can up on stage. It came to rest perfectly, next to Paul. Bob pulled it back by the drum riser and climbed in it as the band spun out into "Rattlesnake" or something.

Halfway through, the thing tipped over in slow motion, and Bob and the entire contents—beer bottles, food wrappers—everything—spilled out all over the stage. I remember being worried about Bob for a second, but he kept playing, never missed a beat, and popped up, indestructible as ever. And when he did, we all saw that he'd lost his skirt and that he was buck naked underneath.

To this day, I have never laughed harder or had a single moment so fill me with the pure wonder and liberating power of rock 'n' roll.

That power was evident offstage as well. Paul talks about the last time he saw Bob. They were both walking on the same block, at different ends of the street, and they met in the middle. They hadn't seen each other in a while, but they talked about guitars, music, and Tommy—like no time at all had passed.

Others have said the same thing. Bob was one of those guys you had an ongoing conversation with. It always seemed like you picked up where you left off with him, even though you weren't quite sure if he remembered you, or if you mattered to him. But then he'd amaze you with some remembrance, or a lost nugget that he wanted to tell you that he'd filed away in that wonderful spin-art mind of his.

Slim remembers Bob as a teacher, the most uncompetitive, giving musician he's ever met. Lori Barbero remembers the last time she saw Bob. He was tugging on her shirt at the Uptown, urgently, peskily, until she finally turned

around and gave him a hug. He didn't want anything else. That was all. That's all he wanted to give, and to get. A hug. In some of their last encounters with Bob, Peter and Jim Boquist had similar experiences: After a typically all-over-the-map Bob conversation, he surprised them both with a hasty, out-of-the-blue "Love ya, man."

Yesterday, Anita got a letter from one of Bob's many fans. "I'm not sure guys like Bob know what they mean to people who love their music," he wrote. "For me, Bob's guitar playing always made me feel like I should keep moving in life, no matter how much the odds seemed stacked against me. I grew up with Bob as one of my heroes. . . . He will always be one of my heroes, somebody I'll tell my kids about someday."

I think that pretty much sums it up for all of us. Late Monday night, as I was gathering my thoughts to write this, my little brother called me up on the phone, and he was sobbing. He articulated some things that I had been feeling: that Bob's death was more than the passing of a tremendous musician, a wonderful father, son, brother, friend, husband, grandson, or uncle. He said that a little bit of all of us had died with him.

I suppose that's what people say whenever someone dies, but everyone here knows exactly how true it is. The weird thing of it is my little brother had never even seen Bob play. Still, he felt it. He felt the connection. He felt the spirit. He felt the loss.

And at the end of the day, that may have been Bob's greatest contribution: Through his guitar, through his magnanimous good nature, he made people feel like they were his closest friend. Better yet, he made us feel like we were in on that secret little joke that hid behind his omnipresent grin.

There are people in this room that I haven't seen, or seen together, for a very long time. Leave it to Bob to get us all together for one more swingin' party. He would've thought the suits and ties and pomp and circumstance were silly, he would have wondered where the beer was, and he would have been embarrassed by all the attention and the tears. And what his passing means I can't begin to explain, but as Robert Frost said: "In three words I can sum up everything I've learned about life: It goes on."

And Bob goes on. On the phone the other night, through his tears, my little brother told me that his band played "Sixteen Blue" at the Cabooze last week, and that when he went to Slim's gig Saturday night at the 400 Bar, Slim played one of his newer songs, "Big Star Big," and sang, "I wanna be a big star . . . like Bob Stinson." At this, my little brother and I were both getting pretty choked up, so we started to say goodbye. As we were about to hang up, I heard

myself say something that I haven't said to him in a very long time:

"Love ya, man."

In the past few days, you've probably said something like that to someone you haven't said that to in a very long time. Rock 'n' roll doesn't always lend itself to such blatant sentimentality, but this week we have all been provided with a chance to get a little closer to each other, and a lot of unspoken feelings have been spoken. We have been reminded that people are precious, that the bonds that we have made through this slippery thing called Rock Music are not dismissible, or intangible, or imaginary, or Other. They are real. For that, for all of that and so much more, we have Bob to thank.

So thank you, Bob. Thank you for bringing us, all of us, together—not just for a day, today, but for yesterday, all the yesterdays, and tomorrow. Thank you for touching us, for linking us, for helping us to recognize all the phony bullshit, all the stuff that doesn't matter, that the world throws our way. Thank you for cutting through the crap, always. Thank you for making us feel like we were part of something, like it was us against the world, and you were the third-base coach, wildly waving us all in. Jumping up and down. In a tutu.

Most of all, thank you for allowing us to glimpse, ever so briefly, your irrepressible, childlike spirit. Thank you for allowing us, forcing us, to acknowledge the very natural connection between hopelessness and happiness. Thank you for your glorious gift. Thank you, you fabulous yellow roman candle, for lighting our fuse. May it never burn out.

Bob Stinson, January 1993. © *Daniel Corrigan*

EPiLOGUE
Waiting to Be Forgotten

"All over but the shouting
Just a waste of time"

—The Replacements, "Never Mind"

Chris Mars: I was on YouTube a few months back [in 2007] and stumbled upon some early-'80s, punk-phase 'Mats footage from the Entry. It was so unexpected that for the first time it was as if I could objectively see what our appeal was from an audience standpoint. There this band was as if I were watching ghosts through some hazed and distant memory. With this newly acquired objectivity, through decades of distance, what struck me most was Paul's distinct voice and delivery, along with Bob's insane guitar style and stage presence. Whoever those other two guys were, they glued it all together well enough. It occurred to me that our strength was as a damned good little punk band. In my mind, that could quite possibly have been our peak.

Glen Morrow: To this day I still say the Replacements are my all-time favorite band. Westerberg wrote so many songs that struck that universal/personal chord. Their live performances never seemed rote. They always put on shows that were one-of-a-kind and completely heartfelt and in the moment. You always wanted to come back for more. They are the only band I ever found

Kinda like an artist. The Westerberg crayon-rendered self-portrait that accompanied the author's June 28, 2002, feature in the *St. Paul Pioneer Press. Author collection*

myself wandering off around the country to take in shows purely as a fan. The Replacements were my Grateful Dead.

Paul Westerberg: Whatever happened to all the punk bands? All the bands that we opened for and played with: Black Flag, Minutemen, Youth Brigade, Seven Seconds, Hüsker Dü, Effigies, all the fucking hardcore bands. There isn't a damn one of them left. We fucking outlasted the whole stinking lot of posers, and all the time they gave us shit for having plaid shirts and hair. There were some good ones, I can't lump 'em all together. . . . But I gotta say that R.E.M. is the only band that we've ever opened for that has stayed bigger than us. [1]

Peter Buck: Of course they should be in the Rock and Roll Hall of Fame. If we [R.E.M.] are, they [should be]. I don't need that to tell me I'm good at what I do, and neither do they, but it does say that they were here, and they've influenced a ton of bands—most of which were not very good, but more successful.

Bob Stinson: It's like reading a definition in a book, and having five people trying to rewrite it: It's going to come out five different ways, instead of one. [2]

Paul Westerberg: I hear his guitar everywhere now—Dinosaur Jr., wherever. Whether they know it or not, Bob was doing that in 1980. [3]

Peter Jesperson: No. I don't think they should [reform]. I just don't think any essence of what made the Replacements great could ever be present again.

Slim Dunlap: It's a fun dream, but dreams get crushed so horribly in the harsh light of reality. A few bands have pulled it off, but . . . I think if your band left with something still musically in the gas tank, but I don't know if we did. I think Paul can take anybody and turn them into the Replacements. The Replacements were living proof of that. And he's done that quite successfully two or three times now—taken three doofs and turned them into the Replacements.

Paul Westerberg: The Replacements album that they really want is—we should get back together and record a blank record, with a cover, and make them pay for it. They would hate it and hate us, but I guarantee you it would be exactly what the real fans would want. It was all about "What are they gonna do next?" As soon as the audience dictates it, it's gone. [4]

Slim Dunlap: But what would a comeback be for? Is it just for old times' sake, one more time to have fun? There's nothing wrong with that. But to have to come back and compete . . you'd be taking on bands in that genre that are pretty well entrenched. I think you'd look bad if you came back as a bunch of fat old guys. It's kind of scary, the Stooges coming back. And people had an anticipation of how cool that would be, but it turns out it isn't.

Paul Westerberg: It's a big old world, and anybody who wants to take those three fucking chords to the top is welcome if they can do it. We couldn't do it. I'm not going to say, "Oh man, we could have, we could have, if we'd just waited." Bullshit! We could not. We tried; we failed. But we didn't really fail. I think we spawned all these other bands and stuff. Of all these popular groups, let's see how many of them last 11 years. I think that will tell the tale.[5]

Steve Foley: Compared to all these other bands who've made it . . . I mean, these bands are a joke compared to the Replacements. I'm just glad to have been part of it. Some days I walk down the street and go, "God, I was in that fuckin' band?" Unbelievable. It is. It will always be a treasure in my mind.

Bob Stinson: [The Bleeding Hearts] is more like a BAND, as opposed to four idiots on stage trying to one-up each other, which is what the Replacements were.[6]

Slim Dunlap: Of course, I'm not adverse to ever considering anything like [a comeback]. But I would never instigate it. I don't really think it's a good idea. Whenever revivalist-type bands occur, it's because there's nothing else cooking. If something else was cooking, you wouldn't care or need it. I think we might be in a time like that. Someone like Paul Westerberg, he never really has lost it. He's still capable of it, and it's a rare thing that isn't in a lot of young people right now. They don't have enough to sustain it. Yet, that sounds like such an old fogey talking.

Paul Westerberg: You can imagine if the 'Mats ever did get back together, it would be a very 'Mats type thing and we would probably play in someone's living room and not let anyone see it.[7]

Michael Hill: If you juxtapose the Replacements and the Pixies, having lived through the Pixies, I think the Pixies were a cult band that got more and

more popular in a larger scheme of things after they stopped playing. And when they came back, it wasn't as if they had done all that much that all of us have these cherished memories of. It's almost as if they stopped before people figured it out. So to come back, it was almost like, now you're kind of ready for them.

Paul Westerberg: If our music wasn't as ferocious as the next wave that would come up, we felt alienated from them, too. So we were an alternative to the alternative as well as an alternative to the mainstream. We never found our niche. Maybe we were just a little too afraid, looking over our shoulders, thinking, "Is it *cool* to have a big record?" And our managers encouraged our high jinks more than they encouraged us to straighten up and fly right. We were a real band of the '80s. We lasted literally from the dawn of 1980 to the dawn of 1990.[8]

Michael Hill: My fear is that if they came back, people would want that drunken, shambolic thing that does nothing to bolster the legacy of records that are really remarkable. So if they came back, I just think fucking Ticketmaster would be jacking up the prices and it would just be a way to make money. But I work with a lot of young bands, and someone will tell them I worked with the Replacements back in the day, and they're [impressed]. The

Tommy and Bob post-Replacements, circa 1992. © *Daniel Corrigan*

Replacements hold an enormous weight. It's a fantastic calling card, and it really meant something. I just wish they could have reaped a little bit more of the rewards of what it all meant.

Paul Westerberg: I don't even know if it was the music. It was the fact that the four of us could make a noise—whether it was music or not. We could hold a stage and make a noise as good as the Stooges or Gene Vincent or the Dolls made a noise. We were a classic little rock 'n' roll band and no one will take that away.[9]

Terry Walsh: In the spring of 1997, Slim Dunlap asked me to join his band for a two-week tour to the East Coast and back, opening for Son Volt. Slim's bassist, Johnny Hazlett, couldn't make it, so I was drafted. The stories began to roll off his tongue even before we hit the Wisconsin border.

"The Goo Goo Dolls were opening for the Replacements, and they were all excited about it, so when they played, they jumped up and down and ran around the stage like they were out of their minds," Slim said with a grin and a soft voice that helped the listener understand that he or she should be paying close attention, because there's a point to the story—there is always a point to his stories.

"They walked off like they were the kings of rock and roll, and we were going to have to try to top them. So when we got out there, we decided to stay absolutely still, like a bunch of statues on stage. The crowd loved it.

"Once there was this young fan who wanted to give a tape of his songs to Paul, and he did, and he was all excited because now Paul had his tape, and he'd surely listen to it and love it and ask the kid to join the band. So we're on the bus, getting ready to go, and Paul yells out the window, 'Hey kid, come here.' So the kid comes scurrying up to the bus window, and Paul sticks his hand out and says, 'Hold this.'

"He hands the kid one end of a broken piece of recording tape, then yells to the driver to take off. The bus pulled away and the kid watches his tape spooling out of the window as we pick up speed."

Slim Dunlap: All the people that tried to shake Paul's hand and he'd snub them and shit, that's their memory of the band. I think as time fades, people tend to forget about those things. It was a hard band to love in its day. You had to really be dedicated. [laughs] It was a hard band to be in![10]

Paul Westerberg: The positive side is that I've always felt like I'm ahead of my time and I've got ideas. I remember telling somebody ten years ago, maybe longer—I said "One day, punk rock is gonna sell beer." [laughs] And they go "Get out of here!" I'm goin' "Mark my fuckin' words. It's gonna happen." And when it happened, it's like part of me wants to smile and the other part is "Why can't I ever parlay this into some sort of fortune?"[11]

Luke Zimmerman: My brother, Seth, was a big fan from back in the day, and while I'm too young to have a firsthand account, I really think that Westerberg is probably, along with maybe like Jim Croce, one of the wittiest writers around. I still think of listening to my brother's *Sorry Ma, Forgot to Take Out the Trash* and thinking of the brilliance of the line "You're in love and I'm in trouble." Then, "If bein' afraid is a crime, we hang side by side." "Well a person can work up a mean, mean thirst/after a hard day of nothin' much at all." "All you're ever losin' is a little mascara." "Here comes Dick, he's wearin' a skirt." Just brilliant.

Kris Kodrich: You wouldn't know it by the group's performance here. Four guys pounding away on guitars and drums, essentially not making any musical sense, just doesn't cut it. I've seen better bands in garages.

The four members that make up the Replacements looked like they obviously were having a great time on stage in the Concordia Ballroom. They wore party hats and began throwing drinks on each other.

At one point they asked the crowd what they wanted to hear. The crowd, of course, yelled out all sorts of things—at the same time. It made for a loud, steady drone.

Lead singer Paul Westerberg perhaps summed up the occasion best when he announced: "Are we gonna have a lot of fun at your expense."

At several points in the show, the excited crowd nearly toppled the lighting system. Beer cans—full ones—flew through the air about every 30 seconds.

I don't think too many members of the audience carried American Express cards.

The band played a mixture of music, often playing only the introductions to songs. They also played such classics as "I've Got You Babe" by Sonny and Cher and "I'll Be There" by the Jackson Five.

One of the band members also graciously took a few hits from a pipe offered by a couple of men from the audience.

Seeing as how it was Valentine's Day, the four band members also offered

to set up a kissing booth but only for men.

The Replacements were brought to La Crosse [Wisconsin] by a local band, the Slow Pedestrians, which opened the show.

When the members of the Replacements took the stage, they pretended they were the "Slow Children" and proceeded to sing off key and played a bad drum solo.

By the end of the evening, much of the audience had left the ballroom.

Most of the few that remained were busy in conversations or inebriated thoughts. Nobody noticed when the Replacements stopped playing. Nobody cared.[12]

Andrea Myers: In this town, if you are a part of the music scene, it seems you are in one of two major camps: the people who lived through the heyday of the 1980s, which fostered the 'Mats, Hüsker Dü, and the grandmaster of all Minnesotan guitar gods, Prince; and then there are the people like me, who are plenty involved in today's vibrant scene, but are constantly living under the shadow of the past, the chip on every burgeoning band's shoulder, the legacy of what came before.

I don't know if the Replacements were the greatest rock 'n' roll band to come out of Minneapolis. I have heard people make that claim with a straight face, so I have to believe it is at least possible. What I do know, however, is that the mark the Replacements made on Minneapolis is serrated and deep, like a battle scar left over from all-night jam sessions, binge-drinking benders, and full-body, punk rock freakouts. *You should have been here*, the walls of old venues like the 7th St. Entry seem to whisper to its younger patrons. *You should have seen it.*

The very first time I interviewed a band for a newspaper article, I sat down with a group of guys from South Minneapolis who were getting ready to release their first album. The five of us took over a corner booth in a dark, dingy rock 'n' roll bar called the CC Club, pounding down pints of beer and working through a set of questions about musical influence and inspiration.

"What makes your band unique?" I asked the lead singer, only half expecting to get a straight answer.

"We are trying to be the next Replacements," he replied, and his bandmates laughed nervously. I laughed too, thinking it was quite funny at the time, but now that I look back at the rawness of their ambition and their uncertainty as a group, the weight of the expectations set by their forerunners was palpable. The musical bar is set high in Minneapolis, especially for rock 'n' roll bands,

and the more I learn about it, the more I think that might all be the Replacements' fault.

Paul Westerberg: It's so hard for me to analyze what we were 'cause we had no idea what we were when we were doing it. To look back, it's like it was someone else who did it. No, I think that all that shit was overshadowed by the drinking and everything that we did. The fact remains that we were a good little rock and roll band. And if we weren't good, we wouldn't have gone as far as we did. All the drinking, and all the breaking, and all the destruction and all the crap that went along with us got all the attention. But the fact, I think, is we were a great little garage band—and that's what I want to be remembered for. That's, to me, the essence and what I'm most proud of.[13]

Tommy Stinson: We're over. Forget about it. Get a life.[14]

Bob Stinson: Replacements, shmeplacements.[15]

267

THE PLAYERS

Curtiss A (a.k.a. Curt Almsted)**:** Singer, songwriter and Minneapolis rock legend. His tribute to John Lennon every December is one of the most anticipated staples of the Twin Cities club calendar.

Charles Aaron: New York writer and editor.

Steve Albini: Former rock critic, the singer for Big Black, and a record producer whose credits include Nirvana and the Stooges.

G. R. Anderson, Jr.: Minneapolis journalist and musician, most notably as drummer for power-pop rockers Rex Daisy.

Kii Arens: Minneapolis artist and musician, now based in Los Angeles.

Jessica Armbruster: Writer for the Minneapolis alternative weekly *City Pages*.

Billie Joe Armstrong: Singer/guitarist for Green Day, some of whose first shows took place at Speedboat Gallery in St. Paul. Armstrong's love for the 'Mats extends to the fact that when Slim Dunlap was doing his Saturday-night specials at the Turf Club in the late '90s and early '00s, he would regularly stop by when he was in town to visit relatives.

Gina Arnold: Bay Area rock critic and author.

Dave Ayers: Stillwater, Minnesota, native, writer, and former rock critic turned manager and publisher.

Lori Barbero: Minneapolis musician, most notably as the drummer for Babes in Toyland, and the heart and soul of the Minneapolis rock scene.

John Beggs: Minneapolis musician and owner of the independent record store Roadrunner Records.

Emily Boigenzahn: Chrissie and Slim Dunlap's daughter.

Kevin Bowe: Minneapolis musician, songwriter, and producer who regularly performs as a solo artist and with his band, The Okemah Prophets, and with Paul Westerberg & His Only Friends.

David Brauer: Minneapolis writer, journalist, editor, and neighborhood activist.

Jon Bream: Veteran pop music critic for the Minneapolis-based *Star Tribune*.

Amy Buchanan: Singer, writer, burlesque dancer, and leader/emcee of Le Cirque de Rogue cabaret in Minneapolis.

Peter Buck: Guitarist for R.E.M., bassist for the Minus Five, and, as this author wrote in an early-'80s letter to one of the glossies in response to a Buck-penned piece about the importance of independent music: "Peter Buck is God."

Ryan Cameron: Former owner of the Minneapolis independent record store Let It Be, which continues to thrive online at www.letitberecords.com.

Keri Carlson: Twin Cities–based writer and journalist.

David Carr: Minneapolis native, writer, journalist, and editor who writes a business and media column for *The New York Times*.

Rosanne Cash: Writer, poet, goddess, and Grammy-winning singer/song-writer.

Alex Chilton: The former leader of '60s pop rockers The Box Tops and '70s cult figures Big Star.

Robert Christgau: The Dean of American Rock Critics.

Jodi Chromey: Minneapolis writer and founder of www.iwilldare.com.

Mike Cisek: Minneapolis musician, most notably as guitarist for early-'80s punks the Neglecters.

Daniel Corrigan: The dean of Minneapolis music photography, whose work has chronicled virtually every character, scene, and sub-scene the area has coughed up. See www.danielcorrigan.com.

Jeff Culhane: Minneapolis musician.

Chris Dafoe: Canadian writer, author, and editor.

Phil Davis: East Coast–based writer.

Jim DeRogatis: The pop music critic for the *Chicago Sun-Times* and co-host of Public Radio's *Sound Opinions*.

Cecelia Deuhs: St. Paul native and independent music retail veteran.

Martin Devaney: St. Paul–based singer/songwriter and founder of the independent roots-rock label Eclectone Records.

Chris Dorn: Minneapolis songwriter and musician, most notably as leader of psychedelic pop-rockers The Beatifics.

Michael Dregni: St. Paul–based author, editor, and publisher, and head of Voyageur Press.

Chrissie Dunlap: Wife of Bob "Slim" Dunlap, and the former band booker at First Avenue.

Delia Dunlap: Chrissie and Slim Dunlap's daughter.

Tommy Erdelyi: New York producer and musician. The Ramones' first drummer.

Matt Fink: Minneapolis musician, most notably as keyboardist ("Dr. Fink") for Prince and the Revolution.

Craig Finn: Twin Cities native and leader of indie-rock sensations Lifter Puller and The Hold Steady.

Steve Fjelstad: Minneapolis musician and recording engineer who was at the helm of many of the most important records to come out of the Twin Cities in the early '80s.

Bill Flanagan: Veteran music journalist whose books include the U2 biog-

raphy *At the End of the World* and the music-industry novel *A&R*. Also a contributing commentator to CBS News.

Rick Fuller: Minneapolis musician and one-half (with Phil Harder) of Harder/Fuller Films, which has produced videos for many of the most renowned independent rock artists of the past twenty years (www.harderfuller-films.com). Also co-directed, with Westerberg, the 2003 Westerberg documentary *Come Feel Me Tremble*.

Jeaneen Gauthier: St. Paul native, visual artist, singer/songwriter, bon vivant, and leader of the indie-rock outfit Jan (www.jeaneengauthier.com).

Burl Gilyard: Minneapolis writer, editor, and journalist.

Jon Ginoli: East Coast–based writer.

Brian Gomez: East Coast–based writer.

Casey Greig: Minneapolis actor and playwright.

Blake Gumprecht: Kansas native, writer, college professor, and former Twin/Tone Records publicist.

Michael Hafitz: East Coast–based writer.

Russell Hall: West Coast writer.

Grant Hart: The mayor of St. Paul (www.granthart.com).

Bea Hasselman: Minneapolis-based educator, musician, and founder of the Metropolitan Boys Choir.

Ralph Heibutzki: Michigan musician and writer.

Joe Henry: Los Angeles–based songwriter, musician, and producer.

Michael Hill: Writer, critic, and record-label talent scout.

Mike Hoeger: East Coast–based writer.

Bill Holdship: Michigan native, writer, and critic.

Don Holzschuh: Former lead singer of Minneapolis art-punks The Warheads, and a painter whose neighborhood vistas have drawn comparisons to Red Grooms and Norman Picasso.

Linda Hultquist: Minneapolis reader, listener, and thinker.

Darren Jackson: Minneapolis songwriter and musician, most notably with The Hopefuls and Kid Dakota.

Peter Jesperson: Co-founder (with Paul Stark) of Twin/Tone Records, former manager of the Replacements, and a vice-president at New West Records in Los Angeles.

Grant Johnson: Minneapolis musician and songwriter (www.myspace.com/babygrantjohnson).

Mary B. Johnson: Minneapolis native and music fanatic.

Rusty Jones: Minneapolis musician and songwriter, most notably with NNB,

Safety Last, the Front Porch Swingin' Liquor Pigs, and the Rockin' Pinecones.

Paul Kaiser: Longtime Minneapolis music fan.

Abbie Kane: Longtime Minneapolis music fan.

Terry Katzman: Minneapolis native, a soundman and former rock critic, the co-founder of independent labels Reflex Records and Garage D'or Records, and former manager of independent record stores Oarfolkjokeopus and Garage D'or.

Steve Kent: Minneapolis musician.

Kris Kodrich: Formerly a Wisconsin newspaperman, now a journalism professor at Colorado State.

Peter Kohlsaat: Cartoonist, artist, dentist, and longtime Minneapolis music fan.

J. Kordosh: Bay Area writer.

P. D. Larson: Minneapolis writer and critic, and author of the first-ever Replacements feature article, "Pop Go the Replacements" (*Sweet Potato*, February 18, 1981).

Eric Lindbom: Minneapolis native and Los Angeles–based writer, critic, and screenwriter.

Laurie Lindeen: Former leader of the Minneapolis punk trio ZuZu's Petals, a writing teacher, author of the memoir *Petal Pusher: A Rock and Roll Cinderella Story* (www.laurielindeen.com), the wife of Paul Westerberg, and the mother of Johnny Westerberg.

Kathei Logue: East Coast–based writer.

Robert Longo: New York visual artist.

Mary Lucia: The most popular rock DJ in the Twin Cities, as heard on Minnesota Public Radio's left-of-the-dial godsend The Current (89.3), and the sister of Paul Westerberg.

Casey MacPherson: Singer in several Minneapolis bands, including the X Boys, and a longtime behind-the-scenes worker in the local music scene.

Greil Marcus: Veteran music writer, critic, and author.

Jim Mars: Minneapolis native and the older brother of Chris Mars.

Kevin Martinson: Minneapolis musician, most notably as the guitarist for pop-punks REMs and Laughing Stock.

Wally Marx: Minneapolis musician, most notably as guitarist with the Delilahs and X Ray Hip.

Scott McCaughey: Seattle-based musician whose credits include the Young Fresh Fellows, R.E.M., and the Minus Five.

Steve McClellan: Former manager of the First Avenue nightclub, and the

founder of the Minneapolis nonprofit DEMO (www.demomn.org).

Todd McGovern: Michigan native, writer, and music fanatic.

David Menconi: Pop-music critic for *The News & Observer* (North Carolina).

Glen Morrow: Founder of the independent label Bar/None Records.

Bob Mould: Co-founder, with Grant Hart and Greg Norton, of Hüsker Dü, and founder of Sugar. Now works as a solo artist and DJ (www.bobmould.com).

Danny Murphy: Guitarist and co-founder of Loud Fast Rules, Soul Asylum, and Golden Smog.

Andrea Myers: Minneapolis writer, editor, and co-founder of the online music mag www.reveillemag.com.

Jimi Nervous (a.k.a. Greg Linder): Minneapolis-based writer.

Rick Ness: Minneapolis musician, most notably as drummer for dark pop-punks REMs and Laughing Stock.

Tim O'Reagan: Lawrence, Kansas, native and Minneapolis musician, most notably as one-half (with Todd Newman) of the lush pop duo the Leatherwoods, the drummer for the Jayhawks, and an accomplished singer/solo artist.

Ken Ornberg: St. Paul–based founder of KABL radio, and radio rep for Universal Music Group.

Chris Osgood: Co-founder (with Dave Ahl and Steve Almaas) of Minneapolis punk pioneers the Suicide Commandos, and a skilled mentor to the entire Twin Cities music and arts community.

John Pacenti: Florida writer and reporter.

Julie Panebianco: New York–based rock critic, music industry insider, and movie music supervisor.

Jon Pareles: Pop-music critic for *The New York Times*.

Marc Perlman: Minneapolis musician and songwriter, most notably as bassist for the Neglecters, the Jayhawks, and Golden Smog.

Dennis Pernu: A senior editor at St. Paul–based Voyageur Press.

Steve Perry: Minneapolis writer and journalist and the former editor of *City Pages*.

Jim Peterson: Longtime music fan, former manager of Oarfolkjokeopus, and librarian.

Dave Pirner: Lead singer of Soul Asylum.

Laura Poehlman: Minneapolis music fan and writer.

Chan Poling: Minneapolis musician and teacher. Also co-founder of no-wave punk pioneers the Suburbs and jazz surrealists the New Standards.

Tony Pucci: St. Paul native and drummer for Twin Cities punks Man-Sized Action.

Jack Rabid: Veteran rock critic, editor, and publisher of *The Big Take-Over* (www.bigtakeover.com).

George Regis: Stillwater, Minnesota, native and New York–based entertainment lawyer.

Brianna Riplinger: Minneapolis writer and music fanatic.

Missy Roback: San Francisco–based writer, editor, singer, and songwriter.

Lou Santacroce: Songwriter, journalist, and the Replacements' first roadie.

Bill Schneck: Minneapolis musician, most notably as bassist for the Neglecters.

Roscoe Shoemaker: Husband, father, and music nut living in Tulsa, Oklahoma.

Doug Simmons: New York–based writer and critic, and the former editor of *The Village Voice*.

Lianne Smith: Minneapolis native and New York–based singer/songwriter.

RJ Smith: Los Angeles–based writer and critic.

Paul Stark: Co-founder (with Peter Jesperson) of Twin/Tone Records.

Anita Stinson: The mother of Bob and Tommy Stinson, and the most popular waitress/bartender at the Uptown Bar & Grill in Minneapolis.

Carleen Stinson: Former wife of Bob Stinson, mother of Joey Stinson.

Kurse Stockhaus (*née* Kathleen Lee)**:** Former grade-school classmate of Paul Westerberg and Paul Kaiser.

Jim Sullivan: Boston-based writer and journalist.

Terri Sutton: Minneapolis writer, critic, editor, and teacher.

Matthew Tomich: East Coast writer and music fanatic.

Eric Tretbar: Minneapolis native, writer, and filmmaker, and former drummer with mod-rock combos the Funseekers and the Spectors.

Bill Tuomala: Minneapolis writer, most notably as the creator of the 'zine *Exiled on Main Street* (www.readexiled.com).

Ana Voog: St. Paul–based musician, writer, and Internet sensation (to wit, www.anacam.com).

Jay Walljasper: Minneapolis writer and editor whose latest book is *The Great Neighborhood Book: A Do-It-Yourself Guide to Placemaking*.

Jay Walsh: Minneapolis writer and musician, most notably as guitarist for the Neglecters, and father to two-fourths of The Falls.

Kim Walsh: wife of Jay Walsh and mother to two-fourths of The Falls.

Molly Walsh: Lawyer, music freak, and aunt/manager to two-fourths of The Falls.

Terry Walsh: Minneapolis musician, songwriter, and leader of the Van Morrison tribute bands the Belfast Cowboys and St. Dominic's Trio, and uncle to two-fourths of Minneapolis rockabilly punks The Falls.

Michael Welch: Minneapolis writer and former music editor of *City Pages*.

Mary Lou Philipp Westerberg: The mother of Paul Westerberg and Mary Lucia, and mother-in-law to Laurie Lindeen.

Pat Whalen: Michigan native, writer, and critic.

Tracie Will (*née* Holzinger): Minneapolis native and former neighbor to the Westerbergs.

Dan Wilson: Grammy-winning singer/songwriter, leader of the pop-rock trio Semisonic, and a member of the late Minneapolis psych-pop-rockers Trip Shakespeare.

Lizz Winstead: Minneapolis native, writer, critic, comedian, and co-creator of Comedy Central's *The Daily Show*.

Willie Wisely: Minneapolis native and musician/songwriter living in Los Angeles (www.wiselymusic.com).

Tommy Womack: Nashville-based writer and songwriter.

Craig Wright: Los Angeles-by-way-of Minneapolis songwriter, most significantly as one-half of the acoustic duo the Tropicals and pop-rockers Kangaroo (with Peter Lawton). Also a playwright (credits include the *Pavilion* trilogy), screenwriter (*Six Feet Under*, *Lost*, and *Brothers and Sisters*), and the producer/writer of ABC's *Dirty Sexy Money*.

Brad Zellar: Minneapolis writer and an editor at *The Rake* magazine.

Martin Zellar: Singer/songwriter and leader of Austin, Minnesota, heroes the Gear Daddies.

Luke Zimmerman: Minneapolis singer/songwriter and recording artist.

ENDNOTES

With the exception of noted passages, all material was gathered during the course of interviews conducted in 2006 and 2007.

Preface

1. Mark Brown. From "Dylan Fights to Escape His Father's Mythic Shadow," *Rocky Mountain News* (November 20, 2000). Reprinted with permission.
2. Lynn Hirschberg. "Strange Love," *Vanity Fair* (September 1992).
3. Eric Lindbom. "Call Them Irresponsible," *City Pages* (October 16, 1985). Copyright © 1985, Village Voice Media. Used with permission.

Introduction
Gimme Noise

1. Quoted in the author's interview with Green Day leader Billie Joe Armstrong, "Singer Says 'Seinfeld' Tune Was Much Ado About . . . Nothing," *St. Paul Pioneer Press* (May 22, 1998).

Chapter One
Raised in the City

1. From Davis' review of *Sorry Ma, Forgot to Take Out the Trash* that appeared in *NY Rocker* (Summer 1981).
2. www.minneapolis.org/travelinfo/facts_trivia.asp. Minneapolis retained its number-two position in the 2006 study, conducted by Dr. John W. Miller, while St. Paul climbed from number nine to number five in 2006. The 2007 results had not yet been compiled when this book first went to press.
3. David M. Ewalt on www.Forbes.com (posted August 22, 2006).
4. Quoted from the Rick Fuller–produced Westerberg tour documentary *Come Feel Me Tremble* (2003).
5. Dylan writing in *Chronicles* (New York: Simon & Schuster, 2004).
6. Quoted by Mark Brunswick in "On Day 5, Mondale Takes off the Gloves," *Minneapolis Star Tribune* (November 5, 2002). Lange was campaigning for former vice-president Walter Mondale, 74, who had replaced Paul Wellstone on the ballot for the Minnesota U.S. senatorial race. Wellstone had died in a plane crash on October 25.
7. www.theskyway.com (posted September 22, 1995).
8. From the transcription, as printed in the St. Paul–based 'zine *The Squealer* (May 1995), of the interview Steve Birmingham and Kevin Kruger conducted "on the sunny afternoon of Easter Sunday, 1994, and a snowy Monday, 4-4-94

277

(at the former home of Eric Peterson and Patricia Leonard on Harriet and 25th Street in Minneapolis, USA)" with Bob Stinson for the local public-access cable program *The Dewey Berger Show*.

9. Quoted in the author's *City Pages* cover story "Let the Bad Times Roll" (October 15, 2003). Mr. Westerberg passed away November 9, 2003. Copyright © 2003, Village Voice Media. Used with permission.

10. Quoted by Chris Mundy. "Achin' to Be Misunderstood," *Rolling Stone* (June 24, 1993).

11. Quoted by Eric Lindbom. "A Word from Mrs. Stinson," a sidebar to the cover story "Call Them Irresponsible," *City Pages* (October 16, 1985). Copyright © 1985, Village Voice Media. Used with permission.

12. Quoted by Julie Panebianco in "Sorry Ma, Forgot to Take Out the Paul Westerberg," a Q&A that appeared in the Chicago-based 'zine *Matter* (January 1986).

13. Quoted in the author's "Local Promoter: When Mary Lucia Hosts Her Live Local-Music Radio Show 'Popular Creeps,' She Comes off Less Like a Radio Pro and More Like Your Wiseacre Neighborhood Barkeep Who Likes to Listen as Much as She Likes to Talk," *St. Paul Pioneer Press* (April 16, 2000).

14. Quoted by Dave Ayers in "The Replacements: Getting No Place?," a Q&A that appeared in *Matter* (December 1983).

15. *The Dewey Berger Show* via *The Squealer* (May 1995).

16. Panebianco. "Sorry Ma, Forgot to Take Out the Paul Westerberg," *Matter* (January 1986).

17. Quoted in the author's feature story "'The Best Concert I Ever Saw': Thirty Musicians and Tastemakers Name Their All-Time Favorite Live Music Experiences," *St. Paul Pioneer Press* (January 21, 1996).

18. "Achin' to Be Misunderstood," *Rolling Stone* (June 24, 1993).

19. Quoted by RJ Smith. "Going Down with the Replacements: Not a Bunch of Loads" (December 11, 1984). Copyright © 1984, Village Voice Media. Reprinted with permission of *The Village Voice*.

20. Quoted in the author's "Worlds Apart," *City Pages* (March 2, 2005). Copyright © 2005, Village Voice Media. Used with permission.

21. Quoted in the author's "Alone Again Eventually: In a Two-Part Interview on the Eve of His Second Solo Album, 'Eventually,' Former Replacements Leader Paul Westerberg Talks About His Art, His Family, Prince, and the Death of His Former Bandmate, Bob Stinson," *St. Paul Pioneer Press* (April 21, 1996).

22. From the now-defunct *Twin Cities Night Beat* (July 23, 1984).

23. From "We Three," *City Pages* (September 26, 1990). The article was a discussion the author moderated with three of the Twin Cities' most visible songwriters: Westerberg, Soul Asylum's Dave Pirner, and Martin Zeller of the Gear Daddies. Copyright © 1990, Village Voice Media. Used with permission.

24. Quoted by Marc Weingarten in "Left of the Dial," an article about the Minneapolis music scene that appeared in *Guitar World* (August 1995).

25. Unpublished comment from an interview the author conducted in 2003.

26. Quoted by Richard Lopez in "The Replacements," a Q&A that appeared in the San Francisco–based 'zine *Riding the Blinds* (March 1984).

27. Quoted by Ralph Heibutzki. "Brats in Babylon," *Goldmine* (October 29, 1993).

28. Ayers. "The Replacements: Getting No Place?," *Matter* (December 1983).

29. *The Dewey Berger Show* via *The Squealer* (May 1995).

30. Lopez. "The Replacements," *Riding the Blinds* (March 1984).

31. *Route 666: On the Road to Nirvana* (New York: St. Martin's Press, 1993).

32. "Rock's Rudder Works at the 'Oar'," *Minneapolis Star* (September 11, 1979).

33. Quoted by Dave Ayers. "Considering Stock Options," from the University of Minnesota's student newspaper, *The Minnesota Daily* (March 9, 1984).

34. "Sorry Ma, Forgot to Take Out the Paul Westerberg," *Matter* (January 1986).

35. Quoted during an interview with Jimi Nervous (Greg Linder) on the Twin Cities classic-rock giant, KQRS-FM (Summer 1981).

36. Lopez. "The Replacements," *Riding the Blinds* (March 1984).

37. Walsh. "Let the Bad Times Roll," *City Pages* (October 15, 2003). Copyright © 2003, Village Voice Media. Used with permission.

38. Westerberg interviewed in *BLUR* (September 3, 1982).

39. Interview with Nervous, KQRS-FM (Summer 1981).

40. "Replacement Part," *The Minnesota Daily* (June 30, 1982).

41. From "We're Over. Forget About It. Get a Life," the Kris Nicholson interview with Tommy Stinson for the 'zine *yeah, yeah, yeah* (No. 10, 1997).

42. Westerberg introducing the Ramones, for whom the Replacements opened at First Avenue on September 28, 1981.

43. The author had forgotten about this until Peter Jesperson sent it to him, along with other artifacts for inclusion in this book. It's from a press release Walsh wrote in 1981 for a band he played with called REMs.

44. Excerpted by Martin Keller in "Young Spuds in a Longhorn Daze," *City Pages* 20th Anniversary Issue (August 4, 1999). Nervous' original piece appeared in the September 10, 1981, issue of *CP*'s predecessor, *Sweet Potato*. Copyright

© 1999, Village Voice Media. Used with permission.

45. Quoted in *BLUR* (September 3, 1982).

46. *The Dewey Berger Show* via *The Squealer* (May 1995).

47. "The Replacements," *Option* (June 1983).

48. Quoted by Bill Flanagan. "The Replacements: Paul Westerberg's Band May Ascend to the Stars or Splatter All over the Road," *Musician* (September 1987).

49. Lopez. "The Replacements," *Riding the Blinds* (March 1984).

50. Review of *Stink*, *The Boston Phoenix* (August 1982).

51. "Letters to the Editor," *City Pages* (December 15, 1982). Copyright © 1982, Village Voice Media. Used with permission.

Chapter Two
When It Began

1. "The Replacements," *Musician* (September 1987).

2. Quoted by RJ Smith. "Going Down with the Replacements: Not a Bunch of Loads" (December 11, 1984). Copyright © 1984, Village Voice Media. Reprinted with permission of *The Village Voice*.

3. Quoted by Steve Perry in the cover story "The Replacements: The Last, Best Band of the 80s," *Musician* (February 1989).

4. "Replacements Go for Gold," *Boston Rock* (August 1982).

5. *The Dewey Berger Show* via *The Squealer* (May 1995). *See* Note 8, Chapter One.

6. www.goski.com (posted December 30, 2002).

7. "Seagulls and Surf in the Snow," *The Minnesota Daily* (March 31, 2005).

8. Quoted by Marc Weingarten in "Left of the Dial," an article about the Minneapolis music scene that appeared in *Guitar World* (August 1995).

9. Quoted by Richard Lopez in "The Replacements," a Q&A that appeared in the San Francisco–based 'zine *Riding the Blinds* (March 1984).

10. *The Dewey Berger Show* via *The Squealer* (May 1995).

11. Lopez. "The Replacements," *Riding the Blinds* (March 1984).

12. Christgau writing for *The Village Voice*'s prestigious annual music poll (February 28, 1984). Copyright © 1984, Village Voice Media. Reprinted with permission of *The Village Voice*.

13. "Native Sons Rise in the East," *The Minnesota Daily* (April 22, 1983).

14. Review of the Replacements' February 2, 1984, show at the Pop Shop in Cleveland, Ohio, *The Cleveland Scene* (February 9, 1984).

15. Review of *Hootenanny* in the Champaign, Illinois, 'zine *Psychedelic Boneyard* (Fall 1983).

16. Quoted by Len Righi. "With the Replacements, You Can Expect Almost

Anything," a preview of the band's February 11, 1984, show at City Gardens in Trenton, New Jersey, which appeared in *The* (Allentown, Pennsylvania) *Morning Call* (February 10, 1984).

17. Review of *Hootenanny*, "Cool For 'Mats," *The Minnesota Daily* (May 6, 1983).

18. "Going Down with the Replacements . . . " (December 11, 1984). Copyright © 1984, Village Voice Media. Reprinted with permission of *The Village Voice*.

19. Review of *Hootenanny*, "The Replacements: A Puzzlement," from the erstwhile Boston-area weekly *Cambridge Express* (January 21, 1984).

20. From a review that appeared under the heading "Critic's Choice," *The Boston Globe* (July 15, 1983).

21. "Letters to the Editor," *City Pages* (March 7, 1984). Copyright © 1984, Village Voice Media. Used with permission.

22. Walsh. "The Making of a Classic: The Replacements' *Let It Be*," *St. Paul Pioneer Press* (January 15, 2001).

23. *The Dewey Berger Show* via *The Squealer* (May 1995).

24. *Goldmine* (October 29, 1993).

25. From "The Replacements Were Heavy, Funny, and Better Musicians than You Think," which appeared as part of *City Pages'* "I Hate 1984" cover story (July 28, 2004). Copyright © 2004, Village Voice Media. Used with permission.

26. Walsh. "Pleased To Meet Him," *Minnesota Daily* (May 1, 1987).

27. *Matter* (January/February 1985).

Chapter Three
What's That Song?

1. Quoted in "We Three," *City Pages* (September 26, 1990). Copyright © 1990, Village Voice Media. Used with permission. *See* Note 23, Chapter One.

2. Exchange in Gilyard's "Kinda Like an Artist: The Replacements' Paul Westerberg: Bored with Being 'The Laziest Band in Show Business,'" a Q&A that appeared in *The Minnesota Daily* (February 3, 1989).

3. "Going Down with the Replacements: Not a Bunch of Loads" (December 11, 1984). Copyright © 1984, Village Voice Media. Reprinted with permission of *The Village Voice*.

4. Ibid.

5. Exchange in the author's article "We Three," *City Pages* (September 26, 1990). Copyright © 1990, Village Voice Media. Used with permission.

6. Quoted by Holdship in "Going Down with the Replacements . . . " (December 11, 1984). Copyright © 1984, Village Voice Media. Reprinted with permission of *The Village Voice*.

7. Holdship. "Drinking (And Lots More) . . . ," *CREEM* (September 1986). Copyright © 1986, *CREEM* Media, Inc. Used with permission.

8. *The Dewey Berger Show* via *The Squealer* (May 1995). *See* Note 8, Chapter One.

9. Holdship. "Drinking (And Lots More) . . . ," *CREEM* (September 1986). Copyright © 1986, *CREEM* Media, Inc. Used with permission.

10. Ibid.

11. Ibid.

12. From "Interview with Paul," which appeared in the highly entertaining yet relatively short-lived Twin Cities music tabloid *The Bob* (June 1990).

13. Quoted by Eric Lindbom. "Call Them Irresponsible," *City Pages* (October 16, 1985). Copyright © 1985, Village Voice Media. Used with permission.

14. Quoted by Julie Panebianco in "Sorry Ma, Forgot to Take Out the Paul Westerberg," a Q&A that appeared in *Matter* (January 1986).

15. Albini, writing in *Matter*'s record-review section, "New Matter" (January 1986), in which several critics grade and weigh in on several albums. Eric Lindom gives *Tim* a B+, Gerard Cosloy and *Matter* publisher and editor Elizabeth Phillip both issue an A, while Albini abstains. *See also* Note 27, Chapter Two.

16. "Post-Punk Rebels Thrive in Minneapolis" (October 27, 1985). Copyright © 1985, *The New York Times* Co. Reprinted with permission.

17. Lindbom. "Call Them Irresponsible," *City Pages* (October 16, 1985). Copyright © 1985, Village Voice Media. Used with permission.

18. Holdship. "Drinking (And Lots More) . . . ," *CREEM* (September 1986). Copyright © 1986, *CREEM* Media, Inc. Used with permission.

19. Bream reporting in the *Minneapolis Star Tribune* under the headline "Replacements on National TV, But Not Locally" (January 17, 1986).

20. From "Bob Stinson Interviews Himself," which appeared in *Cake*, like *The Bob*, another short-lived but excellent independent Minneapolis-based music tabloid (September–October 1992).

21. "Drinking (And Lots More) . . . ," *CREEM* (September 1986). Copyright © 1986, *CREEM* Media, Inc. Used with permission.

22. "Growing Up in Public," *SPIN* (June 1987).

23. Quoted in the author's *SPIN* piece, "Growing Up in Public" (June 1987).

24. Quoted by Marc Weingarten. "Left of the Dial," *Guitar World* (August 1995). *See* Note 24, Chapter One.

25. Quoted by Gina Arnold. *Route 666: On the Road to Nirvana* (New York: St. Martin's Press, 1993).

26. *The Dewey Berger Show* via *The Squealer* (May 1995).

27. Quoted by Bill Flanagan. "The Replacements," *Musician* (September 1987).

28. Ibid.

29. Ibid.

30. "A Word from Mrs. Stinson," sidebar to the cover story "Call Them Irresponsible," *City Pages* (October 16, 1985). Copyright © 1985, Village Voice Media. Used with permission.

31. Flanagan. "The Replacements," *Musician* (September 1987).

32. Holdship. "The Replacements: The Pleasure Is All Yours," *CREEM* (September 1987). Copyright © 1987, *CREEM* Media, Inc. Used with permission.

33. From the author's article on Jesperson, "Peter's Passion," *City Pages* (July 14, 1993). Copyright © 1993, Village Voice Media. Used with permission.

34. Walsh. "Growing Up in Public," *SPIN* (June 1987).

35. "Peter's Passion," *City Pages* (July 14, 1993). Copyright © 1993, Village Voice Media. Used with permission.

36. Quoted by Holdship for the article "On & Off the 'Mats with Paul Westerberg," *BAM* (July 30, 1993).

37. "Peter's Passion," *City Pages* (July 14, 1993). Copyright © 1993, Village Voice Media. Used with permission.

38. Unpublished quote from the author's interview with Westerberg for "Growing Up in Public," *SPIN* (June 1987).

39. Holdship. "The Replacements: The Pleasure Is All Yours," *CREEM* (September 1987). Copyright © 1987, *CREEM* Media, Inc. Used with permission.

40. Quoted by Jeff Scharlau. "Pleased to Meet Mr. Mars," *Cake* (July 1992).

41. "The Replacements," *Musician* (September 1987). Luther Dickinson is now the singer/guitarist for the blues-rock band North Mississippi All-Stars.

42. "This Band Speaks for Lowbrows and Underdogs" (July 19, 1987). Copyright © 1987, *The New York Times* Co. Reprinted with permission.

43. Holdship. "The Replacements: The Pleasure Is All Yours," *CREEM* (September 1987). Copyright © 1987, *CREEM* Media, Inc. Used with permission.

44. Holdship. "On & Off the 'Mats . . . ," *BAM* (July 30, 1993).

45. Holdship. "The Replacements: The Pleasure Is All Yours," *CREEM* (September 1987). Copyright © 1987, *CREEM* Media, Inc. Used with permission.

46. Kris Nicholson. "We're Over. Forget About It. Get a Life," *yeah, yeah, yeah* (No. 10, 1997).

47. Quoted by Mark Brown in "Paul Westerberg," a Q&A that originally appeared

on the now-defunct Microsoft arts and entertainment website, <u>sidewalk.com</u> (February 1999), and is now online at <u>members.aol.com/pwfiles/mbrown.htm.</u>

48. Excerpt from KROQ (Los Angeles) interview (July 7, 1987).

49. Walsh. "Growing Up in Public," *SPIN* (June 1987).

50. Excerpt from KROQ (Los Angeles) interview (July 7, 1987).

Chapter Four
Someone Take the Wheel

1. Quoted by Chris Mundy. "Achin' to Be Misunderstood," *Rolling Stone* (June 24, 1993).

2. Quoted by Scott Hudson in the Slim Dunlap Q&A "The Consummate Sideman," Sioux Falls, South Dakota, *Tempest* magazine (November 2–15, 1994).

3. Quoted by Bill Flanagan. "The Replacements," *Musician* (September 1987).

4. Quoted by Steve Pond. "The Growing Pains and Pleasures of the Replacements," *Rolling Stone* (June 1, 1989).

5. "You Never Can Tell" (April 11, 1989). Copyright © 1989, Village Voice Media. Reprinted with permission of *The Village Voice*. The accompanying photo caption read, "Johnny ain't dead yet."

6. Pond. "The Growing Pains and Pleasures . . . ," *Rolling Stone* (June 1, 1989).

7. Hudson. "The Consummate Sideman," *Tempest* (November 2–15, 1994).

8. Pond. "The Growing Pains and Pleasures . . . ," *Rolling Stone* (June 1, 1989).

9. Quoted by Patricia Bibby. "One Foot in the Door, the Other in the Gutter," Associated Press (September 9, 1989).

10. Pond. "The Growing Pains and Pleasures . . . ," *Rolling Stone* (June 1, 1989).

11. Ibid.

12. Quoted by Jim Sullivan. "Westerberg Is All Shook Down," *The Boston Globe* (November 9, 1990).

13. Quoted by Chris O'Connor. "Rock Band Gives up Falling down Drunk," *The Toronto Star* (June 13, 1991).

14. Hudson. "The Consummate Sideman," *Tempest* (November 2–15, 1994).

15. Quoted by Bill Holdship. "On & Off the 'Mats with Paul Westerberg," *BAM* (July 30, 1993).

16. From the cover story "The Replacements: The Last, Best Band of the 80s," *Musician* (February 1989).

17. "On a Wild Joyride with the Replacements" (April 4, 1989). Copyright © 1989, *The New York Times* Co. Reprinted with permission.

18. "Mars, Mats Split," *City Pages* (December 8, 1990). Copyright © 1990,

Village Voice Media. Used with permission.

19. Quoted by Steve Roeser. "If No One's on Your Canvas: Catching up with Chris Mars," *Goldmine* (January 31, 1997).

20. O'Connor. "Rock Band Gives up Falling down Drunk," *The Toronto Star* (June 13, 1991).

21. From a note to the author that accompanied a homemade cassette entitled "The Absolute Best of Terry Reid."

22. Quoted by Richard Lopez in "The Replacements," a Q&A that appeared in the San Francisco–based 'zine *Riding the Blinds* (March 1984).

23. "Replacements Shown the Door as Westerberg Assumes Control," *The Toronto Star* (February 15, 1991). Reprinted with permission. Torstar Syndication Services.

24. Quoted by John Pacenti. "Sober Band Touring behind Acclaimed LP," Associated Press (March 4, 1991).

25. Lopez. "The Replacements," *Riding the Blinds* (March 1984).

26. "Sober Band Touring behind Acclaimed LP," Associated Press (March 4, 1991).

27. Mundy. "Achin' to Be Misunderstood," *Rolling Stone* (June 24, 1993).

28. Ibid.

29. Quoted in my Q&A "Pleased to Meet Him," *The Minnesota Daily* (May 1, 1987).

30. Quoted by Simon Reynolds. "The Replacements: Leaders of the Lost Generation," *Melody Maker* (November 10, 1990).

31. Quoted in the author's "Bandwagonesque," *City Pages* (January 8, 1992). Copyright © 1992, Village Voice Media. Used with permission.

32. Ibid.

33. Hudson. "The Consummate Sideman," *Tempest* (November 2–15, 1994).

34. Ibid.

35. Ibid.

36. *The Dewey Berger Show* via *The Squealer* (May 1995). *See* Note 8, Chapter One.

37. Quoted by Charles Aaron. "Hold My Life," *SPIN* (May 1993).

38. From "Bob Stinson Interviews Himself," *Cake* (September–October, 1992).

39. Ibid.

40. Ibid.

41. "Bob Stinson, 1959–1995," *Creative Loafing*, the Southeast's largest alternative newsweekly (February 20, 1995).

42. "Replacements' 'Lunatic Guitarist,' Bob Stinson, Dies: Unconventional Musician Struggled with Drug Abuse," *St. Paul Pioneer Press* (February 20, 1995).

43. "Drug Overdose Ruled out in Local Musician's Death," *St. Paul Pioneer Press* (March 1, 1995).

44. "Bob Stinson, 1959–1995," *Creative Loafing*, the Southeast's largest alternative newsweekly (February 20, 1995).

45. "Topspin," *SPIN* (May 1995).

46. Ibid.

47. Comment made to the author (February 22, 1995).

Epilogue
Waiting to Be Forgotten

1. Quoted by Steve Pond. "The Growing Pains and Pleasures of the Replacements," *Rolling Stone* (June 1, 1989).

2. *The Dewey Berger Show* via *The Squealer* (May 1995). *See* Note 8, Chapter One.

3. Quoted by Chris Mundy. "Achin' to Be Misunderstood," *Rolling Stone* (June 24, 1993).

4. Quoted by Mark Brown. "Paul Westerberg" (February 1999), members.aol.com/pwfiles/mbrown.htm. *See* Note 47, Chapter Three.

5. Quoted by Bill Holdship. "On & Off the 'Mats with Paul Westerberg," *BAM* (July 30, 1993).

6. Quoted by the author in "Bob Stinson's an Ex-'Mat, But He's Nobody's Doormat," *St. Paul Pioneer Press* (September 19, 1993).

7. Holdship. "On & Off . . . ," *BAM* (July 30, 1993).

8. Quoted in "Paul Westerberg," a Q&A that appeared in *Rolling Stone* (August 25, 1994).

9. Holdship. "On & Off . . . ," *BAM* (July 30, 1993).

10. Quoted by Scott Hudson in the Slim Dunlap Q&A "The Consummate Sideman," Sioux Falls, South Dakota, *Tempest* magazine (November 2–15, 1994).

11. Brown. "Paul Westerberg" (February 1999), members.aol.com/pwfiles/mbrown.htm.

12. "Replacements No Substitute for Good Band," *The La Crosse Tribune* (February 16, 1985).

13. Holdship. "On & Off . . . ," *BAM* (July 30, 1993).

14. Quoted by Kris Nicholson. "We're Over. Forget About It. Get a Life," *yeah, yeah, yeah* (No. 10, 1997).

15. Walsh. "Bob Stinson's an Ex-'Mat, But . . . ," *St. Paul Pioneer Press* (September 19, 1993).

ACKNOWLEDGMENTS

To the good citizens of Minneapolis and St. Paul, many of whom have invited me into their lives and homes over the years, and whose chip-on-shoulder-with-a-dose-of-wonder attitude birthed both the Replacements and this book

To the Replacements, especially Paul, who has given me a handful of books over the years (most significantly to this project, Nick Tosches' *Where Dead Voices Gather*), and who insisted that this be an unauthorized account, so as not to blur the lines of our friendship and because "unauthorized sells more than authorized."

To Peter Jesperson, who, along with my brother Jay, has turned me on to more books, films, and music than anyone else, and whose encyclopedic mind and heart for all things good and true and musical continues to be an inspiration. Peter is one of the people who taught me how to listen to everything and everyone; Paul is one of the people who taught me how to listen to nobody but myself.

To my family: my mom and dad; my wife, Jean (who was there from the very beginning, and whose excitement for reading the tale of our youth was a constant motivator); our kids, Henry and Helen (*"Read this, kids; this is why your dad is the way he is"*); my brothers and bandmates and bastards of forever young, Jay and Terry; my sisters, Minnow, Peggy, and Molly, and the rest of the gang—smart asses and good souls whose Irish gift of gab (tangents, interruptions, intent listening) was a template for the storytelling device that the book hangs itself on.

To Bruce Orwall, my former colleague at the *St. Paul Pioneer Press*, now at the *Wall Street Journal*, who first bugged me to write a book about the Replacements, because "it needs to exist." To Geoff Kloske, senior editor at Simon & Schuster, who first suggested this be an oral history rather than a straight narrative. To 'Mats fans John Davidson, Scott MacCrae, Tim O'Toole, and Todd McGovern, who provided me with some valuable archival material, and, of course, to Daniel Corrigan and Joan E. Bechtold for providing the bulk of the marvelous photography included.

To my attorney and friend, Steve Smith, who provided great counsel and acted as an eager sounding board from the beginning.

To my editor, Dennis Pernu, who finally convinced me to write the book, and who sweated out several blown deadlines and tolerated a few sensitive-artist fits, and who lent me his copy of Legs McNeil's inspiring and instructive *Please Kill Me*. Dennis' enthusiasm for the Replacements' music, and his dedication to good storytelling and accuracy, inspired me every day. To Michael

Dregni and the good people at Voyageur Press, who know an important story when they hear one, for giving me the opportunity to write about what I love, the dream of any writer. To the dozens of sources who agreed to be interviewed—by phone, in person, or by email (the new "oral" history tradition)—and whose enthusiasm to see this urban legend put down in black and white once and for all gave me legs.

To the various writers, publications, and representatives of those publications who generously allowed material from their archives to be included in this book, especially: Emily J. Banks, co-publisher and editor-in-chief, *The Minnesota Daily*; Richard Boehmcke and Aimee Schecter, Wenner Media; Catherine Davis, managing editor, and Kyle Anderson, assistant editor, *SPIN*; Brian Earnest, editorial director, *Goldmine*; Bill Holdship; Scott Hudson of the late Sioux Falls *Tempest*; Jeff Kitts, editorial director, *Guitar World*; Chante LaGon, operations editor, *Creative Loafing*; Robert Matheu at *CREEM*; Ander Murane at *Rocky Mountain News*; Maggie Shnayerson at *The Village Voice*; Steven P. Suskin, Esq., Village Voice Media; and Chris Zobin at Lee Enterprise (*La Crosse Tribune*).

Also, for generously allowing the use of their lyrics, Slim Dunlap, Jamie Kitman of the Hornblow Group (for They Might Be Giants), Jim Ruiz and Anthony Musiala at Minty Fresh, and Tommy Womack.

This is the first book on the Replacements, but not the last. Thousands of stories exist, stories similar to the ones compiled here. Paul says he'll write his own book one day and include all the tales of "Bob taking a dump in the dumbwaiter of a hotel and sending it down, and shit." He and Tommy and several others declined to be interviewed for the book, saying they didn't want to talk about the past; some ignored my interview requests altogether; Chris offered a summary email paragraph that appears in the epilogue; Slim and Steve Foley were invaluable in their contributions and willingness to assist in any way necessary. In the end, though, I was left to tell the story mostly to and for myself, and I was grateful for it. "Write something you want to read," goes the old writer's adage, and this is something I wanted to read before I go to the swingin' party down the line.

Thanks for the memories. More to come.

289

SONG AND ALBUM Index

INDEX

The Replacements

7th St. Entry, Minneapolis, October 17, 1985. © *Joan E. Bechtold*